God and Philosophy

Edited by
Eric A. Karahalis

Academica Press

ISBN-13: 978-1478325628
ISBN-10: 1478325623

Academica Press
A Division of SophiaOmni Publishing

Visit our website at:
www.sophiaomni.org

CONTENTS

Introduction

As if the word "philosophy" is not daunting enough to the average college student, adding the word "religion" at the end makes it even more fearsome. What is philosophy of religion? To a modern reader the phrase 'Philosophy of Religion' might seem strange or even an apparent contradiction of terms. But let us try to simplify and classify to better understand the subject.

The word philosophy can be divided into two Greek terms: *Philia* which means love and *Sophia* which translates into wisdom. So philosophy at its core is a love of wisdom and truth. According to the Oxford dictionary, "philosophy is the use of reason and argument in seeking the truth and knowledge of reality, especially of the causes and nature of things and of the principles governing existence, the material universe, perception of physical phenomena, and human behavior." Philosophy of religion is an attempt to use reason and analysis to understand the root and foundation of religion, holding it up to the light of truth to see through its many layers and seek to reveal its core. One of the central questions in the philosophy of religion is the relationship between religion and reason. Is religion blind and irrational? Is religion a sophisticated form of superstition? Is religion a human construct for social control? Is religion a psychological or emotional need? Is religion a projection of humanity's highest ideals? Or is religion rooted in reality? Does religion lead us to truth – indeed, the deepest truths? Can reason lead to faith? All of these questions and more become the focal point and subject matter of philosophy of religion.

Religion is a much more difficult word to simply define. The word "Religion" is rooted in the Latin words *Re* – "again" *Ligare* - "to bind back," as well as the Latin *religio* "respect for what is sacred, reverence for the gods." In other words religion is being bound and committed in reverence and devotion to something, and in most cases that something is God or gods. In a world drunk with labels and polarizations religion is often classified by atheists (from Latin *A* "without" *theos* "God:" Atheism is the philosophical position that God does not exist.) as belonging to the realm of pure speculation and illusion – an irrational otherworldly childish belief in imaginary beings that makes humanity feel better about the hardships of life, as well as an abandonment of reason and submission to religious authority. It is such authorities that have terrorized the world with bitter hatred, pious rivalries, holy wars, inquisitions and in the present age jihads. Many people might point to the reality of global terrorism fueled by radical Islamic fundamentalism, as well as Christian fundamentalists who say that Jesus hates gays and a good Christian should bomb abortion clinics.[1] Any New Yorker can testify to the atrocities humans have unleashed on each other in the name of God and religion. So, we must ask ourselves: Is religion inherently bad? Does it tend toward violence and hatred? Has it only darkened the world we live in, or is there a great light of truth to religion illuminating the world? Is it purely irrational? Does God exist or is this merely a human hope and projection?

Whatever the truth of such criticisms, they seem to be a blatant oversimplification of the rich tradition that is religion. The core principle of most religions is the "Golden Rule:" treat people the way you want people to treat you. At the heart of all of the world's religions is love and reverence for God and humanity. It is this love of humanity that has reached out to others in charity – curing, educating, and inspiring people to live lives of great meaning and purpose. There is a very positive side of religion that is responsible for countless accomplishments fueled by a passion for God and humanity. These contributions can be found in art, music, morality, architecture, universities, hospitals, and missions to the poor and sick, poetry, mysticism, saints, and even the sciences. All of these disciplines have benefited from religious traditions. Religions have done more good in the world than they are often given credit for – not to mention the quest for truth and meaning, virtue and benevolence, goodness and love it fosters in most of its followers. Recognizing that there are always many sides to every story, let us, through the lens of philosophy begin our examination of the many facets of religion. We shall focus primarily the western Christian tradition.

The first mode of religious-mindedness is religious fundamentalism. In its purest form fundamentalism is understood to entail an absolute, unquestioning loyalty to certain basics or "fundamentals" of a given faith tradition. Religious fundamentalism today is understood as relying on pure faith and a literal reading of sacred scriptures. Simply, religious fundamentalism is grounded on faith, feeling, and irrationality and is often categorized as rejecting many modern scientific findings. This form of religion is extremely skeptical of philosophy and science and relies solely on devotion to God and scripture. This understanding was best vocalized by the ancient church father Tertullian of Carthage. Tertullian lived at a time when many early Christians sought to use and reconcile ancient philosophy to the Christian worldview. He felt that philosophy would only pull the mind further away from God into heresies and that the truest way to understand God was pure faith. Tertullian states, "for worldly wisdom culminates in philosophy with its rash interpretations of God's nature and purpose...it is philosophy that supplies heresies with their equipment.[2] From Tertullian's perspective it is impossible to understand God rationally and any attempt through the use of philosophy is vain and destined for failure or worse heresy. Submission and devotion to God in faith is all that is needed to follow the divine.

Fundamentalism is more than just a rejection of reason and an extremely literal reading of scripture, but also a psychological condition that possesses an unreasonable certainty in their particular viewpoint. A fundamentalist is absolutely certain that their subjective position is the only objective reality. Every other belief, position, or understanding is misguided and false. Fundamentalists focus solely on the basic principles of their faith often a form of legalistic religion emerges, where any lack of strict adherence to the practice deems the violator a sinner and someone in need of God's punishment rather than love and forgiveness. This form of religion is very unaccepting of those who do not share their view point. It is this form of extreme fundamentalism that is the cause of violence perpetrated in the name of God. From the standpoint of philosophy it is hard not to recognize that when someone possesses an extreme position on any given subject that they are likely to be dismissive of any contrary vantage point. That explains the zealous rejection of science from many fundamental religious extremists and the rejection of religion from many scientific fundamentalist extremists. Scientific fundamentalist extremism is a viewpoint presented by many modern scientists, like Richard Dawkins, who hold that all religions and religious mindedness is inherently bad and the root of most of the world's troubles and evils. This is a fundamentalism that states if something cannot be observed, examined, and studied through the senses and reason it cannot have any reality or claim to exists. Therefore any belief in God is inherently irrational and dangerous. This position is equally inhospitable to religion as extreme religious fundamentalism is intolerant to the sciences. It is true that extremes are the opposite poles and that the rest of the spectrum of religious variances fall somewhere in the middle.

The Mystic tradition is another form of religious-mindedness. Mysticism is a submission of reason and the will to pure faith. The mystic recognizes that reason cannot understand God and so only faith can bridge the infinite gap between God and Humanity. Unlike the fundamentalist who rejects reason as uncertain and attribute an irrational certainty to faith, the mystic recognizes the limits of reason and certainty and embrace faith as an indeterminate openness to God. The mystic often practices a detachment from earthly desires and concerns freeing oneself in action and meditative passivity to receive communion with the divine. The mystic experience transcends the world and reason in an ecstatic (outside oneself) experience of God. This mode of the religious traditions is where we find many saints and religious heroes who submitted their lives to God and lived abundant lives of charity, love, and wisdom, transforming the world by their actions and words. There is something inspiring in dedicating one's life to God categorized by great acts of love and kindness. Mother Theresa is one such example: She lived her life caring for those sick and dying in Calcutta, India. Mother Theresa did not possess a deep rational understanding of God however she was a living example of unwavering faith, absolute commitment and submission, as well as a woman of deep unconditional love. Considering examples like Mother Theresa it is plain to see that faith without a rational understanding is not inherently bad.Another mode of religion is known as apologetics. Apologetics is derived from the Greek word *apologetikos* which means defensible. Apologetics is an attempt to defend and ground the belief in God through the use of reason and philosophy. This form of religious mindedness marries the tradition of philosophy to the tradition of religion helping to explain rationally the doctrines, practices, and issues of the faith community.

This way of conceiving philosophy as a useful tool is apparent in the writings of the early church father Clement of Alexandria. He states, "Philosophy came into existence for the advantages reaped by us from knowledge... accordingly before the advent of the Lord, philosophy was necessary to the Greeks for righteousness...philosophy therefore was a preparation, paving the way for him who is perfected in Christ." Clement tells us that philosophy is a kindred and useful tool of religion and not to be considered detrimental or dangerous to the faithful.

St. Augustine, Bishop of Hippo, is one of the greatest and most prolific writers of late antiquity in the Christian apologetic tradition. He uses philosophy to examine the human condition, the nature of God, time, evil, love, the Trinity, government, and scripture. Augustine declares, "I believe in order that I may understand" (*Credo ut intelligam*).[3] This statement demonstrates that faith is not the absence of reason but rather the prerequisite and root of reason. Augustine in his text on Christian Teaching states, "Any statements by those who are called philosophers, especially the Platonists, which happen to be true and consistent with our faith should not cause alarm, but be claimed for our own use."[4] Augustine views philosophy as a great assistant and useful discipline in bringing humanity to truth and faith adds a new depth to the understanding. It is Augustine's seamless synthesis of Greek Neo-Platonic philosophy to Christianity that has drawn people into his teachings and religious understandings to this day. Augustine's influence can be traced through later mathematicians and scientists like Rene Descartes and Sigmund Freud.

The problem of evil also known as theodicy is one of the major stumbling blocks of the Christian apologetic tradition, and is one of Augustine's inspired philosophical subject matters. The problem of evil is centered on the question: If God is a good, all-powerful, and all - loving God why is there evil in the world? Evil's existence implicitly concludes that God may not be good, loving, omnipotent, or real at all – for how can absolute love and goodness allow evil to flourish. Augustine understands evil as the privation of good – Evil is merely the corruption of goodness – much like a cancer cell exists as a mutation or corruption of a healthy cell, so too evil cannot exist without the presence of healthy cells. According to Augustine, God did in fact create everything good however through free will mankind has corrupted its goodness and that is what has become evil. Despite Augustine's insightful explanation, the problem of evil is still a central issue for Christian apologetics and belief in God, highlighted in the writings of the Russian novelist Fyodor Dostoyevski.

St. Anselm, Archbishop of Canterbury, is also member of the Christian apologetic tradition. Like Augustine, he eloquently explains that the use of philosophy in religion is not to prove rationally that God exists as a pretext for faith but rather to believe in order to understand. Faith proceeds understanding. In Anselm's own Latin, "*Fides quaerens intellectum*" or faith seeking understanding.[5] Anselm is full of faith and seeks to reason an indisputable argument for the existence of God. Anselm is best known for his Ontological proof for the existence of God. Anselm's proof is an attempt to demonstrate that God must exist necessarily and rationally. The Ontological proof is so named because "*Ontos*" in Greek means "being" and it is an argument on God's being or existence. Anselm tries to formulate a purely rational and impenetrable argument in support of God's existence. Anselm's argument is often criticized for not going deep enough. It is merely a logical rational syllogism (mathematical like rational arguments) based on pure reason rather than an argument from experience and observation.

In philosophy there are two schools of thought regarding how humans come to knowledge and understanding: rationalism and empiricism. Rationalism is the philosophical position that all knowledge comes to humans through reason alone (*a priori* – Latin meaning knowledge is prior to experience). This understanding holds that all knowledge is hidden in the recesses of our minds waiting to be explored and discovered. Rationalism and its pure logic is the basis for the science of mathematics. Empiricism on the other hand the position that all knowledge comes to humans through the senses and experience (*a posteriori* – Latin meaning knowledge comes from the posterior outside world). Empiricists hold that if you wish to understand the world you must observe and look to nature and experience to enlighten our minds with knowledge. It is this position that grounds all of the natural sciences for how else can we come to understand our natural world without the five senses taking in data and then trying to understand the underlying similarities and patterns. The best arguments and proofs for truth particularly with respect for God's existence tend to be empirically based or at least an amalgamation of both rationalism and empiricism.

St. Thomas Aquinas is another church father who is responsible for the promulgation of Christian apologetics. Aquinas, like Augustine, was extremely prolific and married Greek philosophy to the Christian tradition. Aquinas integrates the teaching and writings of the ancient Greek philosopher Aristotle to Christianity. Aristotle is often credited as a founding father to the scientific community and method. The scientific method is the use of reason and observation to dissect, divide, classify and understand what is the essential characteristics and causes of all natural phenomena, i.e. humans, animals, plants, elements, soul, God, etc. Thomas, like Aristotle, is an empiricist who looks to nature and reason to discover the truth. He borrows some of Aristotle's own arguments and baptizes them to present a very natural and rational argument's in support of God's existence. Aquinas' proofs known as the "five ways" attempts to rationally prove from experience and nature that God must necessarily exist. Unlike Anselm who uses a purely rational argument to prove God's existence, Aquinas makes use of natural observation and grounded experience to rationally show that God logically must exist.

Aquinas' five ways are can be broken into two main types of arguments: the cosmological argument and the teleological argument. The cosmological argument is given to Thomas from Aristotle. The word "cosmological" comes from the Greek word *cosmos* which translates "world" or "universe." This argument draws on the existence of the world and universe to conclude that God must necessarily exist as the first cause of everything. From nothing- nothing comes or in Latin *ex nihilo nihil fit*. Therefore if there is a world something must be responsible for its existence and that something is God.[6]

The teleological argument is one of the strongest arguments from experience that seek to conclude the absolute reality of God's existence. Teleology is a word derived from the Greek word *telos*, "purpose" or "end." This proof is grounded on the observation that everything in nature possesses an inner purpose and is aimed at some objective end. All one needs to do is contemplate the miracle of human reproduction: how from a fertilized egg, to human infant, to an adult human being – nature possesses an ingrained order and rationale. Everything in the universe and nature follows an inherent, knowable, predictable, and rational path and where there is order and rationality there is an intelligent being. The seasons, tides, day and night, the weather, astrological events, life cycles, food cycles, mathematics, genetics and chemistry are only a short list of the apparent examples of the world's apparent order. A world of observable intelligible order cannot be the product of chaos or chance, but rather a divine intelligent being/creator God. This argument also known as the argument from design is one of Thomas' greatest contributions to both philosophy and religion.

It is important to reflect for a moment on our philosophical understanding of religion. We have described three kinds of religious mindedness: fundamentalism, mysticism, and apologetics. Fundamentalism is an irrational submission of faith coupled with a literal reading of the bible; a psychological condition that clings to faith as an unreasonable desire for certainty. Driven by doctrinal legalism this religious mode does tend toward violence, discrimination, separation, and intolerance of others. It is this form of religious mindedness that can easily be radicalized stepping beyond the religious core of love, to kill in the name of God for not following their fanatical religious doctrines.

Mysticism is a submission of reason and the will to God in pure faith. There are countless saints and mystics of all religious traditions, East to West, who understood God as ineffable, inexpressible, and beyond reason's grasp. This faithful leap has produced heroes of faith who are immortalized as genuine examples of God's living love. This innumerable number of faithful people who have transformed the world with virtue and charity illustrate the inherent goodness of religion.

Apologetics is where philosophy comes to the assistance of religion to help rationally ground the beliefs and worldview of the faith tradition. The happy marriage of reason and religion bears witness to the coherence and compatibility of philosophy and religion. This tradition allows for an acceptance of empirical science rather than a rejection due to scripture or doctrine.

One need only think of Monsignor Georges Henri Joseph Édouard Lemaître, a Belgian priest, astronomer and professor of physics at the Catholic University of Leuven. He was the first person to propose the theory of the expansion of the Universe. Lemaître proposed what became known as the Big Bang theory of the origin of the Universe, which he called his "hypothesis of the primeval atom." The fact that the first formulation of the "Big Bang" theory was presented by a Catholic priest and scientist, absolutely demonstrates the rational and scientific, concern for truth that is part of the Christian apologetic system. Augustine himself held the position that the bible is an authority in spiritual matters not scientific matters, and that if science discovers something contrary to the scriptures it is the job of religious reason to revisit the prior belief and in light of any proven scientific understanding. He also states that arguing against science from the grounds of a religious, spiritual, text is foolish and only undermines the justice efforts of the faithful who seek to reconcile science to religion and deepen their understanding of God and the universe.[7]

In the most recent past Pope John Paul II declared that the theory of evolution and the big bang theory are accepted as scientific truth according to the Catholic Church. The Catholic Church declares the biblical creation stories as religious myths highlighting God as the author of everything. Today the Catholic Church understands evolution and the big bang as scientific examples of God's creative providence.[8] The long history of Christian apologetics from Augustine to the present demonstrates a seamless synthesis and integration of religious thinking and scientific discovery.

Considering the relationship between religion and philosophy it becomes apparent that there is a genuine kinship between the two disciplines. Philosophy and religion are siblings of one common parent: the human spirit/will/mind seeking to understand itself in relation to the universe, world, and others. Throughout time humans have stood in awe and amazement to the world and universe. Awe is a state of mental bafflement – things that are beyond our ability to comprehend cause within us awe. An awe experience can be positive or negative (a beautiful sunset, child birth, or death) and leaves the observer in a state of confusion, anxiety, and insecurity. Without an understanding of the world and things around them, humans become overwhelmed with fear and anxiety. This state of fear and anxiety is not sustainable for the human psyche and demands an acceptable explanation and rationale for the things we encounter in existence. A deep anxiety of the mystery, the unknown and mortality fosters the innate human desire to understanding the world, our place in it, as well as, our meaning and purpose. If the answer to our quest for meaning takes a leap of faith towards God be it a rational or irrational faith we are on the path of religion. If however we examine this inner anxiety or trepid malaise from the vantage point of rationality – philosophically we discover our final mode of religious mindedness: religion as psychological projection.

The mode of religious mindedness known as a psychological projection is not religious mindset at all. It is this mode of philosophy of religion that denies the existence of God as an objective, rational, existing being. This branch of philosophy of religion looks to the emotional roots: anxiety, fear, the desire for certainty, order, and the need for meaning as the rational cause of theism and religious traditions. In other words God and religion are merely human constructions invented to help mankind overcome the anxieties and fears inherent in the world. Ludwig Feuerbach and Karl Marx are two such modern thinkers who understand religion as being rooted in the human psyche. Feuerbach explains that God is truly an outward projection of the inner ideals and truest desires of mankind. In this analysis God is not a supernatural being, not the source of existence, not to be worshipped, but rather humanity's greatest hopes and ideals elevated into the heavens, as an ever-present deity – reminding of us of our noblest and greatest possibilities.

Karl Marx accuses religion of being a fabrication to comfort mankind's pain and anxiety in the face of a meaningless, unfeeling, and heartless world. It is Marx's position that humanity creates illusions like God and heaven to assuage the hardships and heartaches of both life and death. It is in this line of arguing that many modern radical fundamental atheists like Richard Dawkins, and Christopher Hitchens find their rational justifications. Remembering that the fundamentalist has an unreasonable certainty in regards to their own partial beliefs, we find such thinkers intolerant of any God, gods,

or religious tradition viewing the whole history of religion as living ignorance and inherently evil.

Philosophy and its intrinsic impartiality will always examine both the
positive and negative roots, as well as, contributions to posterity. It is a
rash unscientific conclusion to deem all religious mindedness as irrational,
ungrounded, and malicious. As we have seen the greatest threat to religion
is not religious at all but the psychological desire for certainty, i.e. fundamentalism. Radical fundamentalism with its ungrounded certainty in itself
and vehement opposition to everything contrary is the true cause of worldly
human sufferings perpetrated in the name of God. Religious fundamentalism
is an extremism that may root itself in religious doctrines, yet it reaches well
beyond the boundaries of religion. The most violent and extreme factions of
religious fundamentalism can be seen as cloaking hatred and violence under
the banner of religion. And it is this psychological disposition that has too
often been the root cause of all the heinous acts carried out in the name of
God, from medieval Christian crusades to the modern day Islamic jihad.

Reflecting on philosophy of religion there is a rich human tradition of
applying reason to help clarify, understand, and uncover the core of religion.
It is the judgment of philosophy that religion is not inherently bad, (though
it may be used to this end), but rather a belief that has assisted humanity
in edifying the individual, community, and world. Standing always as the
highest human ideal to love, forgive, seek to reconcile, and understanding
others, religion has much truth to offer us in our insatiable quest for wisdom.
Therefore in the true spirit of philosophy (a love of wisdom) be excited and
encouraged to examine for oneself the rich history and writings concerning
the philosophy of religion.

NOTES

1. Richard Dawkins, *The God Delusion.* New York: Houghton Mifflin Harcout, 2006.

2. Tertullian. "Prescriptions Against the Heretics." *The Ante-Nicene Fathers.* Vol. 3.
Trans. Alexander Roberts and James Donaldson. Edinburgh: T & T Clark, 1889.

3. Augustine. *The Confessions.* Trans. Rex Warner. New York: New American Library,
1963.

4. St. Augustine on Christian Teaching. Trans R.P.H. Green. Oxford: Oxford University
Press, 1996.

5. Alvin Plantigna. *The Ontological Argument: From St. Anselm to Contemporary
Philosophers.* New York, Double Day, 1995.

6. Donald Burrill, *The Cosmological Arguments.* New York: Double Day, 1965

7. St. Augustine. *On the Literal Interpretation of Genesis.* Trans. John Hammond. New
York: Paulist Press, 1982.

8. Evolution, a doctrine that Pius XII only acknowledged as an unfortunate possibility,
John Paul accepts forty-six years later "as an effectively proven fact." (ROA, 82)

The Presocratics
W.T. Stace

THE IONICS

The earliest Greek philosophers belong to what in after times came to be called the Ionic school. The name was derived from the fact that the three chief representatives of this school, Thales, Anaximander, and Anaximenes, were all men of Ionia, that is to say, the coast of Asia Minor.

Thales

As the founder of the earliest school in history, Thales of Miletus is generally accounted the founder and father of all philosophy. He was born about 624 B.C. and died about 550 B.C. These dates are approximate, and it should be understood that the same thing is true of nearly all the dates of the early philosophers. Different scholars vary, sometimes as much as ten years, in the dates they give. We shall not enter into these questions at all, because they are of no importance. And throughout these lectures it should be understood that the dates given are approximate.

Thales, at any rate, was a contemporary of Solon and Croesus. He was famous in antiquity for his mathematical and astronomical learning, and also for his practical sagacity and wisdom. He is included in all the accounts of the Seven Sages. The story of the Seven Sages is unhistorical, but the fact that the lists of their names differ considerably as given by different writers, whereas the name of Thales appears in all, shows with what veneration he was anciently regarded. An eclipse of the sun occurred in 585 B.C., and Thales is alleged to have predicted it, which was a feat for the astronomy of those times. And he must have been a great engineer, for he caused a diversion of the river Halys, when Croesus and his army were unable to cross it. Nothing else is known of his life, though there were many apocryphal stories.

No writings by Thales were extant even in the time of Aristotle, and it is believed that he wrote nothing. His philosophy, if we can call it by that name, consisted, so far as we know, of two propositions. Firstly, that the principle of all things is water, that all comes from water, and to water all returns. And secondly, that the earth is a flat disc which floats upon water. The first, which is the chief proposition, means that water is the one primal kind of existence and that everything else in the universe is merely a modification of water. Two questions will naturally occur to us. Why did Thales choose water as the first principle? And by what process does water, in his opinion, come to be changed into other things; how was the universe formed out of water? We cannot answer either of these questions with certainty. Aristotle says that Thales "probably derived his opinion from observing that the nutriment of all things is moist, and that even actual heat is generated therefrom, and that animal life is sustained by water, ... and from the fact that the seeds of all things possess a moist nature, and that water is a first principle of all things that are humid." This is very likely the true explanation. But it will be noted that even Aristotle uses the word "probably," and so gives his statement merely as a conjecture. How, in the opinion of Thales, the universe arose out of water, is even more uncertain. Most likely he never asked himself the question, and gave no explanation. At any rate nothing is known on the point.

This being the sum and substance of the teaching of Thales, we may naturally ask why, on account of such a crude and undeveloped idea, he should be given the title of the father of philosophy. Why should philosophy be said to begin here in particular? Now, the significance of Thales is not that his water-philosophy has any value in itself, but that this was the first recorded attempt to explain the universe on naturalistic and scientific principles, without the aid of myths and anthropomorphic gods. Moreover, Thales propounded the problem, and determined the direction and character, of all pre-Socratic philosophy. The fundamental thought of that period was, that under the multiplicity of the world there must be a single ultimate principle. The problem of all philosophers from Thales to Anaxagoras was, what is the nature of that first principle from which all things have issued? Their systems are all attempts to answer this question, and may be classified according to their different replies. Thus Thales asserted that the ultimate reality is water, Anaximander indefinite matter, Anaximenes air, the Pythagoreans number, the Eleatics Being, Heracleitus fire, Empedocles the four elements, Democritus atoms, and so on. The first period is thus essentially cosmological in character, and it was Thales who determined the character. His importance is that he was the first to propound the question, not that he gave any rational reply to it.

[M]an is naturally a materialist, and that philosophy is the movement from sensuous to non-sensuous thought. As we should expect, then, philosophy begins in materialism. The first answer to the question, what the ultimate reality is, places the nature of that reality in a sensuous object, water. The other members of the Ionic school, Anaximander, and Anaximenes, are also materialists. And from their time onwards we can trace the gradual rise of thought, with occasional breaks and relapses, from this sensualism of the Ionics, through the semi-sensuous idealism of the Eleatics, to the highest point of pure non-sensuous thought, the idealism of Plato and Aristotle. It is important to keep in mind, then, that the history of philosophy is not a mere chaotic hotch-potch of opinions and theories, succeeding each other without connection or order. It is a logical and historical evolution, each step in which is determined by the last, and advances beyond the last towards a definite goal. The goal, of course, is visible to us, but was not visible to the early thinkers themselves.

Since man begins by looking outwards upon the external world and not inwards upon his own self, this fact too determines the character of the first period of Greek philosophy. It concerns itself solely with nature, with the external world, and only with man as a part of nature. It demands an explanation of nature. And this is the same as saying that it is cosmological. The problems of man, of life, of human destiny, of ethics, are treated by it scantily, or not at all. It is not till the time of the Sophists that the Greek spirit turns inwards upon itself and begins to consider these problems, and with the emergence of that point of view we have passed from the first to the second period of Greek philosophy.

Because the Ionic philosophers were all materialists they are also sometimes called Hylicists, from the Greek *hulé* which means matter.

Anaximander

The next philosopher of the Ionic school is Anaximander. He was an exceedingly original and audacious thinker. He was probably born about 611 B.C. and died about 547. He was an inhabitant of Miletus, and is said to have been a disciple of Thales. It will be seen, thus, that he was a younger contemporary of Thales. He was born at the time that Thales was flourishing, and was about a generation younger. He was the first Greek to write a philosophic treatise, which however has been unfortunately lost. He was eminent for his astronomical and geographical knowledge, and in this connection was the first to construct a map. Details of his life are not known.

Now Thales had made the ultimate principle of the universe, water. Anaximander agrees with Thales that the ultimate principle of things is material, but he does not name it water, does not in fact believe that it is any particular kind of matter. It is rather a formless, indefinite, and absolutely featureless matter in general. Matter, as we know it, is always some particular kind of matter. It must be iron, brass, water, air, or other such. The difference between the different kinds of matter is qualitative, that is to say, we know that air is air because it has the qualities of air and differs from iron because iron has the qualities of iron, and so on. The primeval matter of Anaximander is just matter not yet sundered into the different kinds of matter. It is therefore formless and characterless. And as it is thus indeterminate in quality, so it is illimitable in quantity. Anaximander believed that this matter stretches out to infinity through space. The reason he gave for this opinion was, that if there were a limited amount of matter it would long ago have been used up in the creation and destruction of the "innumerable worlds." Hence he called it "the boundless." In regard to these "innumerable worlds," the traditional opinion about Anaximander was that he believed these worlds to succeed each other in time, and that first a world was created, developed, and was destroyed, then another world arose, was developed and destroyed, and that this periodic revolution of worlds went on for ever. Professor Burnet, however, is of opinion that the "innumerable worlds" of Anaximander were not necessarily successive but rather simultaneously existing worlds. According to this view there may be any number of worlds existing at the same time. But, even so, it is still true that these worlds were not everlasting, but began, developed and decayed, giving place in due time to other worlds.

How, now, have these various worlds been formed out of the formless, indefinite, indeterminate matter of Anaximander? On this question Anaximander is vague and has nothing very definite to put forward. Indeterminate matter by a vaguely conceived process separates itself into "the hot" and "the cold." The cold is moist or damp. This cold and moist matter becomes the earth, in the centre of the universe. The hot matter collects into a sphere of fire surrounding the earth. The earth in the centre was originally fluid. The heat of the surrounding sphere caused the waters of the earth progressively to evaporate giving rise to the envelope of air which surrounds the earth. For the early Greeks regarded the air and vapour as the same thing. As this air or vapour expanded under the action of heat it burst the outside hot sphere of fire into a series of enormous "wheel-shaped husks," resembling cart wheels, which encircle the earth. You may naturally ask how it is that if these are composed of fire we do not see them continually glowing. Anaximander's answer was that these wheel-shaped husks are encrusted with thick, opaque vapour, which conceals the inner fire from our view. But there are apertures, or pipe-like holes in the vapour-crust, and through these the fire gleams, causing the appearance of the sun, stars, and moon. You will note that the moon was, on this theory, considered to be fiery, and not, as we now know it to be, a cold surface reflecting the sun's light. There were three of these "cart wheels"; the first was that of the sun, furthest away from the earth, nearer to us was that of the moon, and closest of all was that of the fixed stars. The "wheel-shaped husks" containing the heavenly bodies are revolved round the earth by means of currents of air. The earth in the centre was believed by Anaximander to be not spherical but cylindrical. Men live on the top end of this pillar or cylinder.

Anaximander also developed a striking theory about the origin and evolution of living beings. In the beginning the earth was fluid and in the gradual drying up by evaporation of this fluid, living beings were produced from the heat and moisture. In the first instance these beings were of a low order. They gradually evolved into successively higher and higher organisms by means of adaptation to their environment. Man was in the first instance a fish living in the water. The gradual drying up left parts of the earth high and dry, and marine animals migrated to the land, and their fins by adaptation became members fitted for movement on land. The resemblance of this primitive theory to modern theories of evolution is remarkable. It is easy to exaggerate its importance, but it is at any rate clear that Anaximander had, by a happy guess, hit upon the central idea of adaptation of species to their environment.

The teaching of Anaximander exhibits a marked advance beyond the position of Thales. Thales had taught that the first principle of things is water. The formless matter of Anaximander is, philosophically, an advance on this, showing the operation of thought and abstraction. Secondly, Anaximander had definitely attempted to apply this idea, and to derive from it the existent world. Thales had left the question how the primal water developed into a world, entirely unanswered.

THE ELEATICS

The Eleatics are so called because the seat of their school was at Elea, a town in South Italy, and Parmenides and Zeno, the two chief representatives of the school, were both citizens of Elea. So far we have been dealing with crude systems of thought in which only the germs of philosophic thinking can be dimly discerned. Now, however, with the Eleatics we step out definitely for the first time upon the platform of philosophy. Eleaticism is the first true philosophy. In it there emerges the first factor of the truth, however poor, meagre, and inadequate. For philosophy is not, as many persons suppose, simply a collection of freak speculations, which we may study in historical order, but at the end of which, God alone knows which we ought to believe. On the contrary, the history of philosophy presents a definite line of evolution. The truth unfolds itself gradually in time.

Xenophanes

The reputed founder of the Eleatic School was Xenophanes. It is, however, doubtful whether Xenophanes ever went to Elea. Moreover, he belongs more properly to the history of religion than to the history of philosophy. The real creator of the Eleatic School was Parmenides. But Parmenides seized upon certain germs of thought latent in Xenophanes and transmuted them into philosophic principles. We have, therefore, in the first instance, to say something of Xenophanes. He was born about the year 576 B.C., at Colophon in Ionia. His long life was spent in wandering up and down the cities of Hellas, as a poet and minstrel, singing songs at banquets and festivals. Whether, as sometimes stated; he finally settled at Elea is a matter of doubt, but we know definitely that at the advanced age of ninety-two he was still wandering about Greece. His philosophy, such as it is, is expressed in poems. He did not, however, write philosophical poems, but rather elegies and satires upon various subjects, only incidentally expressing his religious views therein. Fragments of these poems have come down to us.

Xenophanes is the originator of the quarrel between philosophy and religion. He attacked the popular religious notions of the Greeks with a view to founding a purer and nobler conception of Deity. Popular Greek religion consisted of a belief in a number of gods who were conceived very much as in the form of human beings. Xenophanes attacks this conception of God as possessing human form. It is absurd, he says, to suppose that the gods wander about from place to place, as represented in the Greek legends. It is absurd to suppose that the gods had a beginning. It is disgraceful to impute to them stories of fraud, adultery, theft and deceit. And Xenophanes inveighs against Homer and Hesiod for disseminating these degrading conceptions of the Deity. He argues, too, against the polytheistic notion of a plurality of gods. That which is divine can only be one. There can only be one best. Therefore, God is to be conceived as one. And this God is comparable to mortals neither in bodily form nor understanding. He is "all eye, all ear, all thought." It is he "who, without trouble, by his thought governs all things." But it would be a mistake to suppose that Xenophanes thought of this God as a being external to the world, governing it from the outside, as a general governs his soldiers. On the contrary, Xenophanes identified God with the world. The world is God, a sentient being, though without organs of sense. Looking out into the wide heavens, he said, "The One is God." [Aristotle, *Metaphysics*, Book I. chapter v] The thought of Xenophanes is therefore more properly described as pantheism than as monotheism. God is unchangeable, immutable, undivided, unmoved, passionless, undisturbed. Xenophanes appears, thus, rather as a religious reformer than as a philosopher. Nevertheless, inasmuch as he was the first to enunciate the proposition "All is one," he takes his place in philosophy. It was upon this thought that Parmenides built the foundations of the Eleatic philosophy.

Certain other opinions of Xenophanes have been preserved. He observed fossils, and found shells inland, and the forms of fish and sea-weed embedded in the rocks in the quarries of Syracuse and elsewhere. From these he concluded that the earth had risen out of the sea and would again partially sink into it. Then the human race would be destroyed. But the earth would again rise from the sea and the human race would again {43} be renewed. He believed that the sun and stars were burning masses of vapour. The sun, he thought, does not revolve round the earth. It goes on in a straight line, and disappears in the remote distance in the evening. It is not the same sun which rises the next morning. Every day a new sun is formed out of the vapours of the sea. This idea is connected with his general attitude towards the popular religion. His motive was to show that the sun and stars are not divine beings, but like other beings, ephemeral. Xenophanes also ridiculed the Pythagoreans, especially their doctrine of re-incarnation.

Parmenides

Parmenides was born about 514 B.C. at Elea. Not much is known of his life. He was in his early youth a Pythagorean, but recanted that philosophy and formulated a philosophy of his own. He was greatly revered in antiquity both for the depth of his intellect, and the sublimity and nobility of his character. Plato refers to him always with reverence. His philosophy is comprised in a philosophic didactic poem which is divided into two parts. The first part expounds his own philosophy and is called "the way of truth." The second part describes the false opinions current in his day and is called "the way of opinion."

The reflection of Parmenides takes its rise from observation of the transitoriness and changeableness of things. The world, as we know it, is a world of change and mutation. All things arise and pass away. Nothing is permanent, nothing stands. One moment it is, another moment it is not. It is as true to say of {44} anything, that it is not, as that it is. The truth of things cannot lie here, for no knowledge of that which is constantly changing is possible. Hence the thought of Parmenides becomes the effort to find the eternal amid the shifting, the abiding and everlasting amid the change and mutation of things. And there arises in this way the antithesis between Being and not-being. The absolutely real is Being. Not-being is the unreal. Not-being is not at all. And this not-being he identifies with becoming, with the world of shifting and changing things, the world which is known to us by the senses. The world of sense is unreal, illusory, a mere appearance. It is not-being. Only Being truly is. As Thales designated water the one reality, as the Pythagoreans named number, so now for Parmenides the sole reality, the first principle of things, is Being, wholly unmixed with not-being, wholly excludent of all becoming. The character of Being he describes, for the most part, in a series of negatives. There is in it no change, it is absolutely unbecome and imperishable. It has neither beginning nor end, neither arising nor passing away. If Being began, it must have arisen either from Being or from not-being. But for Being to arise out of Being, that is not a beginning, and for Being to arise out of not-being is impossible, since there is then no reason why it should arise later rather than sooner. Being cannot come out of not-being, nor something out of nothing. *Ex nihilo nihil fit*. This is the fundamental thought of Parmenides. Moreover, we cannot say of Being that it was, that it is, that it will be. There is for it no past, no present, and no future. It is rather eternally and timelessly present. It is undivided and indivisible. For anything to be divided it must be divided by something other than itself. But there is nothing other than Being; there is no not-being. Therefore there is nothing by which Being can be divided. Hence it is indivisible. It is unmoved and undisturbed, for motion and disturbance are forms of becoming, and all becoming is excluded from Being. It is absolutely self-identical. It does not arise from anything other than itself. It does not pass into anything other than itself. It has its whole being in itself. It does not depend upon anything else for its being and reality. It does not pass over into otherness; it remains, steadfast, and abiding in itself. Of positive character Being has nothing. Its sole character is simply its being. It cannot be said that it is this or that; it cannot be said that it has this or that quality, that it is here or there, then or now. It simply *is*. Its only quality is, so to speak, "isness."

But in Parmenides there emerges for the first time a distinction of fundamental importance in philosophy, the distinction between Sense and Reason. The world of falsity and appearance, of becoming, of not-being, this is, says Parmenides, the world which is presented to us by the senses. True and veritable Being is known to us only by reason, by thought. The senses therefore, are, for Parmenides, the sources of all illusion and error. Truth lies only in reason. This is exceedingly important, because this, *that truth lies in reason and not in the world of sense*, is the fundamental position of idealism.

The doctrine of Being, just described, occupies the first part of the poem of Parmenides. The second part is the way of false opinion. But whether Parmenides is here simply giving an account of the false philosophies {46} of his day, (and in doing this there does not seem much point,) or whether he was, with total inconsistency, attempting, in a cosmological theory of his own, to explain the origin of that world of appearance and illusion, whose very being he has, in the first part of the poem, denied--this does not seem to be clear. The theory here propounded, at any rate, is that the sense-world is composed of the two opposites, the hot and the cold, or light and darkness. The more hot there is, the more life, the more reality; the more cold, the more unreality and death.

What position, now, are we to assign to Parmenides in philosophy? How are we to characterize his system? Such writers as Hegel, Erdmann, and Schwegler, have always interpreted his philosophy in an idealistic sense. Professor Burnet, however, takes the opposite view. To quote his own words: "Parmenides is not, as some have said, the father of idealism. On the contrary, all materialism depends upon his view." Now if we cannot say whether Parmenides was a materialist or an idealist, we cannot be said to understand much about his philosophy. The question is therefore of cardinal importance. Let us see, in the first place, upon what grounds the materialistic interpretation of Parmenides is based. It is based upon a fact which I have so far not mentioned, leaving it for explanation at this moment. Parmenides said that Being, which is for him the ultimate reality, occupies space, is finite, and is spherical or globe-shaped. Now that which occupies space, and has shape, is matter. The ultimate reality of things, therefore, is conceived by Parmenides as material, and this, of course, is the cardinal thesis of materialism. This interpretation of Parmenides is further emphasized in the disagreement between himself and Melissus, as to whether Being is finite or infinite. Melissus was a younger adherent of the Eleatic School, whose chief interest lies in his views on this question. His philosophical position in general is the same as that of Parmenides. But on this point they differed. Parmenides asserted that Being is globe-shaped, and therefore finite. Now it was an essential part of the doctrine of Parmenides that empty space is non-existent. Empty space is an existent non-existence. This is self-contradictory, and for Parmenides, therefore, empty space is simply not-being. There are, for example, no interstices, or empty spaces between the particles of matter. Being is "the full," that is, full space with no mixture of empty space in it. Now Melissus agreed with Parmenides that there is no such thing as empty space; and he pointed out, that if Being is globe-shaped, it must be bounded on the outside by empty space. And as this is impossible, it cannot be true that Being is globe-shaped, or finite, but must, on the contrary, extend illimitably through space. This makes it quite clear that Parmenides, Melissus, and the Eleatics generally, did regard Being as, in some sense, material.

Now, however, let us turn to the other side of the picture. What ground is there for regarding Parmenides as an idealist? In the first place, we may say that his ultimate principle, Being, whatever he may have thought of it, is not in fact material, but is essentially an abstract thought, a concept. Being is not here, it is not there. It is not in any place or time. It is not to be found by the senses. It is to be found only in reason. We form the idea of Being by the process of abstraction. For example, we see this desk. Our entire knowledge of the desk consists in our knowledge of its qualities. It is square, brown, hard, odourless, etc. Now suppose we successively strip off these qualities in thought--its colour, its size, its shape. We shall ultimately be left with nothing at all except its mere being. We can no longer say of it that it is hard, square, etc. We can only say "it is." As Parmenides said, Being is not divisible, movable; it is not here nor there, then nor now. It simply "is." This is the Eleatic notion of Being, and it is a pure concept. It may be compared to such an idea as "whiteness." We cannot see "whiteness." We see white things, but not "whiteness" itself. What, then, is "whiteness"? It is a concept, that is to say, not a particular thing, but a general idea, which we form by abstraction, by considering the quality which all white things have in common, and neglecting the qualities in which they differ. Just so, if we consider the common character of all objects in the universe, and neglect their differences, we shall find that what they all have in common is simply "being." Being then is a general idea, or concept. It is a thought, and not a thing. Parmenides, therefore, actually placed the absolute reality of things in an idea, in a thought, though he may have conceived it in a material and sensuous way. Now the cardinal thesis of idealism is precisely this, that the absolute reality, of which the world is a manifestation, consists in thought, in concepts. Parmenides, on this view, was an idealist.

Moreover, Parmenides has clearly made the distinction between sense and reason. True Being is not known to the senses, but only to reason, and this distinction is an essential feature of all idealism. Materialism is precisely the view that reality is to be found in the world of sense. But the proposition of Parmenides is the exact opposite of this, namely, that reality is to be found only in reason. Again, there begins to appear for the first time in Parmenides the distinction between reality and appearance. Parmenides, of course, would not have used these terms, which have been adopted in modern times. But the thought which they express is unmistakably there. This outward world, the world of sense, he proclaims to be illusion and appearance. Reality is something which lies behind, and is invisible to the senses. Now the very essence of materialism is that this material world, this world of sense, is the real world. Idealism is the doctrine that the sense-world is an appearance. How then can Parmenides be called a materialist?

How are we to reconcile these two conflicting views of Parmenides? I think the truth is that these two contradictories lie side by side in Parmenides unreconciled, and still mutually contradicting each other. Parmenides himself did not see the contradiction. If we emphasize the one side, then Parmenides was a materialist. If we emphasize the other side, then he is to be interpreted as an idealist. In point of fact, in the history of Greek philosophy, both these sides of Parmenides were successively emphasized. He became the father both of materialism and of idealism. His immediate successors, Empedocles and Democritus, seized upon the materialistic aspect of his thought, and developed it. The essential thought of Parmenides was that Being cannot arise from not-being, and that Being neither arises nor passes away. If we apply this idea to matter we get what in modern times is called the doctrine of the "indestructibility of matter." Matter has no beginning and no end. The apparent arising and passing away of things is simply the aggregation and separation of particles of matter which, in themselves, are indestructible. This is precisely the position of Democritus. And his doctrine, therefore, is a materialistic rendering of the main thought of Parmenides that Being cannot arise from not-being or pass into not-being.

It was not till the time of Plato that the idealistic aspect of the Parmenidean doctrine was developed. It was the genius of Plato which seized upon the germs of idealism in Parmenides and developed them. Plato was deeply influenced by Parmenides. His main doctrine was that the reality of the world is to be found in thought, in concepts, in what is called "the Idea." And he identified the Idea with the Being of Parmenides.

But still, it may be asked, which is the true view of Parmenides? Which is the historical Parmenides? Was not Plato in interpreting him idealistically reading his own thought into Parmenides? Are not we, if we interpret him as an idealist, reading into him later ideas? In one sense this is perfectly true. It is clear from what Parmenides himself said that he regarded the ultimate reality of things as material. It would be a complete mistake to attribute to him a fully developed and consistent system of idealism. If you had told Parmenides that he was an idealist, he would not have understood you. The distinction between materialism and idealism was not then developed. If you had told him, moreover, that Being is a concept, he would not have understood you, because the theory of concepts was not developed until the time of Socrates and Plato. Now it is the function of historical criticism to insist upon this, to see that later thought is not attributed to Parmenides. But if this is the function of historical scholarship, it is equally the function of philosophic insight to seize upon the germs of a higher thought amid the confused thinking of Parmenides, to see what he was groping for, to see clearly what he saw only vaguely and dimly, to make explicit what in him was merely implicit, to exhibit the true inwardness of his teaching, to separate what is valuable and essential in it from what is worthless and accidental. And I say that in this sense the true and essential meaning of Parmenides is his idealism. I said in the first chapter that philosophy is the movement from sensuous to non-sensuous thought. I said that it is only with the utmost difficulty that this movement occurs. And I said that even the greatest philosophers have sometimes failed herein. In Parmenides we have the first example of this. He began by propounding the truth that Being is the essential reality, and Being, as we saw, is a concept. But Parmenides was a pioneer. He trod upon unbroken ground. He had not behind him, as we have, a long line of idealistic thinkers to guide him. So he could not maintain this first non-sensuous thought. He could not resist the temptation to frame for himself a mental image, a picture, of Being. Now all mental images and pictures are framed out of materials supplied to us by the senses. Hence it comes about that Parmenides pictured Being as a globe-shaped something occupying space. But this is not the truth of Parmenides. This is simply his failure to realise and understand his own principle, and to think his own thought. It is true that his immediate successors, Empedocles and Democritus, seized upon this, and built their philosophies upon it. But in doing so they were building upon the darkness of Parmenides, upon his dimness of vision, upon his inability to grapple with his own idea. It was Plato who built upon the light of Parmenides.

Heraclitus

Heracleitus was born about 535 B.C., and is believed to have lived to the age of sixty. This places his death at 475 B.C. He was thus subsequent to Xenophanes, contemporary with Parmenides, and older than Zeno. In historical order of time, therefore, he runs parallel to the Eleatics. Heracleitus was a man of Ephesus in Asia Minor. He was an aristocrat, descendant of a noble Ephesian family, and occupied in Ephesus the nominal position of basileus, or King. This, however, merely meant that he was the Chief Priest of the local branch of the Eleusinian mysteries, and this position he resigned in favour of his brother. He appears to have been a man of a somewhat aloof, solitary, and scornful nature. He looked down, not only upon the common herd, but even upon the great men of his own race. He mentions Xenophanes and Pythagoras in terms of obloquy. Homer, he thinks, should be taken out and whipped. Hesiod he considers to be the teacher of the common herd, one with them, "a man," he says, "who does not even know day and night." Upon the common herd of mortals he looks down with infinite scorn. Some of his sayings remind us not a little of Schopenhauer in their pungency and sharpness. "Asses prefer straw to gold." "Dogs bark at everyone they do not know." Many of his sayings, however, are memorable and trenchant epitomes of practical wisdom. "Man's character is his fate." "Physicians who cut, burn, stab and rack the sick, demand a fee for doing it, which they do not deserve to get." From his aloof and aristocratic standpoint he launched forth denunciations against the democracy of Ephesus.

Heracleitus embodied his philosophical thoughts in a prose treatise, which was well-known at the time of Socrates, but of which only fragments have come down to us. His style soon became proverbial for its difficulty and obscurity, and he gained the nickname of Heracleitus the "Dark," or the "Obscure." Socrates said of his work that what he understood of it was excellent, what not, he believed was equally so, but that the book required a tough swimmer. He has even been accused of intentional obscurity. But there does not seem to be any foundation for this charge. The fact is that if he takes no great trouble to explain his thoughts, neither does he take any trouble to conceal them. He does not write for fools. His attitude appears to be that if his readers understand him, well; if not, so much the worse for his readers. He wastes no time in elaborating and explaining his thought, but embodies it in short, terse, pithy, and pregnant sayings.

His philosophical principle is the direct antithesis of Eleaticism. The Eleatics had taught that only Being is, and Becoming is not at all. All change, all Becoming is mere illusion. For Heracleitus, on the contrary, only Becoming is, and Being, permanence, identity, these are nothing but illusion. All things sublunary are perpetually changing, passing over into new forms and new shapes. Nothing stands, nothing holds fast, nothing remains what it is. "Into the same river," he says, "we go down, and we do not go down; for into the same river no man can enter twice; ever it flows in and flows out." Not only does he deny all absolute permanence, but even a relative permanence of things is declared to be illusory. We all know that everything has its term, that all things arise and pass away, from the insects who live an hour to the "eternal" hills. Yet we commonly attribute to these things at least a relative permanence, a shorter or longer continuance in the same state. But even this Heracleitus will not allow. Nothing is ever the same, nothing remains identical from one consecutive moment to another. The appearance of relative permanence is an illusion, like that which makes us think that a wave passing over the surface of the water remains all the time the same identical wave. Here, as we know, the water of which the wave is composed changes from moment to moment, only the form remaining the same. Precisely so, for Heracleitus, the permanent appearance of things results from the inflow and outflow in them of equivalent quantities of substance. "All is flux." It is not, for example, the same sun which sets to-day and rises to-morrow. It is a new sun. For the fire of the sun burns itself out and is replenished from the vapours of the sea.

Not only do things change from moment to moment. Even in one and the same moment they are and are not the same. It is not merely that a thing first is, and then a moment afterwards, is not. It both is and is not at the same time. The at-onceness of "is" and "is not" is the meaning of Becoming. We shall understand this better if we contrast it with the Eleatic principle. The Eleatics described all things under two concepts, Being and not-being. Being has, for them, all truth, all reality. Not-being is wholly false and illusory. For Heracleitus both Being and not-being are equally real. The one is as true as the other. Both are true, for both are identical. Becoming is the identity of Being and not-being. For Becoming has only two forms, namely, the arising of things and their passing away, their beginning and their end, their origination and their decease. Perhaps you may think that this is not correct, that there are other forms of change besides origination and decease. A man is born. That is his origination. He dies. That is his decease. Between his birth and his death there are intermediate changes. He grows larger, grows older, grows wiser or more foolish, his hair turns grey. So also the leaf of a tree does not merely come into being and pass out of being. It changes in shape, form, colour. From light green it becomes dark green, and from dark green, yellow. But there is after all nothing in all this except origination and decease, not of the thing itself, but of its qualities. The change from green to yellow is the decease of green colour, the origination of yellow colour. Origination is the passage of not-being into Being. Decease is the passage of Being into not-being. Becoming, then, has in it only the two factors of Being and not-being, and it means the passing of one into the other. But this passage does not mean, for Heracleitus, that at one moment there is Being, and at the next moment not-being. It means that Being and not-being are in everything at one and the same time. Being is not-being. Being has not-being in it. Take as an example the problem of life and death. Ordinarily we think that death is due to external causes, such as accident or disease. We consider that while life lasts, it is what it is, and remains what it is, namely life, unmixed with death, and that it goes on being life until something comes from outside, as it were, in the shape of external causes, and puts an end to it. You may have read Metchnikoff's book "The Nature of Man." In the course of that book he develops this idea. Death, he says, is always due to external causes. Therefore, if we could remove the causes, we could conquer death. The causes of death are mostly disease and accident, for even old age is disease. There is no reason why science should not advance so far as to eliminate disease and accident from life. In that case life might be made immortal, or at any rate, indefinitely prolonged. Now this is founded upon a confusion of ideas. No doubt death is always due to external causes. Every event in the world is determined, and wholly determined, by causes. The law of causation admits of no exception whatever. Therefore it is perfectly true that in every case of death causes precede it.....To give the cause is not to give any reason for an event. Causation is never a principle of explanation of anything. It tells us that the phenomenon A is invariably and unconditionally followed by the phenomenon B, and we call A the cause of B. But this only means that whenever B happens, it happens in a certain regular order and succession of events. But it does not tell us why B happens at all. The reason of a thing is to be distinguished from its cause. The reason why a man dies is not to be found in the causes which bring about his death. The reason rather is that life has the germ of death already in it, that life is already death potentially, that Being has not-being in it. The causation of death is merely the mechanism, by the instrumentality of which, through one set of causes or another, the inevitable end is brought about.

Not only is Being, for Heracleitus, identical with not-being, but everything in the universe has in it its own opposite. Every existent thing is a "harmony of opposite tensions." A harmony contains necessarily two opposite principles which, in spite of their opposition, reveal an underlying unity. That it is by virtue of this principle that everything in the universe exists, is the teaching of Heracleitus. All things contain their own opposites within them. In the struggle and antagonism between hostile principles consists their life, their being, their very existence. At the heart of things is conflict. If there were no conflict in a thing, it would cease to exist. This idea is expressed by Heracleitus in a variety of ways. "Strife," he says, "is the father of all things." "The one, sundering from itself, coalesces with itself, like the harmony of the bow and the lyre." "God is day and night, summer and winter, war and peace, satiety and hunger." "Join together whole and unwhole, congruous and incongruous, accordant and discordant, then comes from one all and from all one." In this sense, too, he censures Homer for having prayed that strife might cease from among gods and men. If such a prayer were granted, the universe itself would pass away.

Side by side with this metaphysic, Heracleitus lays down a theory of physics. All things are composed of fire. "This world," he says, "neither one of the gods nor of the human race has made; but it is, it was, and ever shall be, an eternally living fire." All comes from fire, and to fire all returns. "All things are exchanged for fire and fire for all, as wares for gold and gold for wares." Thus there is only one ultimate kind of matter, fire, and all other forms of matter are merely modifications and variations of fire. It is clear for what reason Heracleitus enunciated this principle. It is an exact physical parallel to the metaphysical principle of Becoming. Fire is the most mutable of the elements. It does not remain the same from one moment to another. It is continually taking up matter in the form of fuel, and giving off equivalent matter in the form of smoke and vapour. The primal fire, according to Heracleitus, transmutes itself into air, air into water, and water into earth. This he calls "the downward path." To it corresponds "the upward path," the transmutation of earth into water, water to air, and air to fire. All transformation takes place in this regular order, and therefore, says Heracleitus, "the upward and the downward path are one."

Fire is further specially identified with life and reason. It is the rational element in things. The more fire there is, the more life, the more movement. The more dark and heavy materials there are, the more death, cold, and not-being. The soul, accordingly, is fire, and like all other fires it continually burns itself out and needs replenishment. This it obtains, through the senses and the breath, from the common life and reason of the world, that is, from the surrounding and all-pervading fire. In this we live and move and have our being. No man has a separate soul of his own. It is merely part of the one universal soul-fire. Hence if communication with this is cut off, man becomes irrational and finally dies. Sleep is the half-way house to death. In sleep the passages of the senses are stopped up, and the outer fire reaches us only through breath. Hence in sleep we become irrational and senseless, turning aside from the common life of the world, each to a private world of his own. Heracleitus taught also the doctrine of periodic world-cycles. The world forms itself out of fire, and by conflagration passes back to the primitive fire.

In his religious opinions Heracleitus was sceptical. But he does not, like Xenophanes, direct his attacks against the central ideas of religion, and the doctrine of the gods. He attacks mostly the outward observances and forms in which the religious spirit manifests itself. He inveighs against the worship of images, and urges the uselessness of blood sacrifice.

With the Eleatics he distinguishes between sense and reason, and places truth in rational cognition. The illusion of permanence he ascribes to the senses. It is by reason that we rise to the knowledge of the law of Becoming. In the comprehension of this law lies the duty of man, and the only road to happiness. Understanding this, man becomes resigned and contented. He sees that evil is the necessary counterpart of good, and pain the necessary counterpart of pleasure, and that both together are necessary to form the harmony of the world. Good and evil are principles on the struggle {80} between which the very existence of things depends. Evil, too, is necessary, has its place in the world. To see this is to put oneself above pitiful and futile struggles against the supreme law of the universe.

W.T. Stace. *A Critical History of Greek Philosophy.* New York: The MacMillan Company, 1920..

The Apology
Plato

Speech I: Main Defense Speech

How you have felt, O men of Athens, at hearing the speeches of my accusers, I cannot tell; but I know that their persuasive words almost made me forget who I was—such was the effect of them; and yet they have hardly spoken a word of truth. But many as their falsehoods were, there was one of them which quite amazed me;—I mean when they told you to be upon your guard, and not to let yourselves be deceived by the force of my eloquence. They ought to have been ashamed of saying this, because they were sure to be detected as soon as I opened my lips and displayed my deficiency; they certainly did appear to be most shameless in saying this, unless by the force of eloquence they mean the force of truth; for then I do indeed admit that I am eloquent. But in how different a way from theirs!

Well, as I was saying, they have hardly uttered a word, or not more than a word, of truth; but you shall hear from me the whole truth: not, however, delivered after their manner, in a set oration duly ornamented with words and phrases. No indeed! but I shall use the words and arguments which occur to me at the moment; for I am certain that this is right, and that at my time of life I ought not to be appearing before you, O men of Athens, in the character of a juvenile orator—let no one expect this of me.

And I must beg of you to grant me one favor, which is this—If you hear me using the same words in my defense which I have been in the habit of using, and which most of you may have heard in the agora, and at the tables of the money-changers, or anywhere else, I would ask you not to be surprised at this, and not to interrupt me. For I am more than seventy years of age, and this is the first time that I have ever appeared in a court of law, and I am quite a stranger to the ways of the place; and therefore I would have you regard me as if I were really a stranger, whom you would excuse if he spoke in his native tongue, and after the fashion of his country;—that I think is not an unfair request. Never mind the manner, which may or may not be good; but think only of the justice of my cause, and give heed to that: let the judge decide justly and the speaker speak truly....

Socrates' Wisdom

I dare say, Athenians, that someone among you will reply, "Why is this, Socrates, and what is the origin of these accusations of you: for there must have been something strange which you have been doing? All this great fame and talk about you would never have arisen if you had been like other men: tell us, then, why this is, as we should be sorry to judge hastily of you." Now I regard this as a fair challenge, and I will endeavor to explain to you the origin of this name of "wise," and of this evil fame. Please to attend then. And although some of you may think I am joking, I declare that I will tell you the entire truth. Men of Athens, this reputation of mine has come of a certain sort of wisdom which I possess.

If you ask me what kind of wisdom, I reply, such wisdom as is attainable by man, for to that extent I am inclined to believe that I am wise; whereas the persons of whom I was speaking have a superhuman wisdom, which I may fail to describe, because I have it not myself; and he who says that I have, speaks falsely, and is taking away my character. And here, O men of Athens, I must beg you not to interrupt me, even if I seem to say something extravagant. For the word which I will speak is not mine. I will refer you to a witness who is worthy of credit, and will tell you about my wisdom — whether I have any, and of what sort—and that witness shall be the god of Delphi. You must have known Chaerephon; he was early a friend of mine, and also a friend of yours, for he shared in the exile of the people, and returned with you. Well, Chaerephon, as you know, was very impetuous in all his doings, and he went to Delphi and boldly asked the oracle to tell him whether — as I was saying, I must beg you not to interrupt — he asked the oracle to tell him whether there was anyone wiser than I was, and the Pythian prophetess answered that there was no man wiser. Chaerephon is dead himself, but his brother, who is in court, will confirm the truth of this story.

Why do I mention this? Because I am going to explain to you why I have such an evil name. When I heard the answer, I said to myself, What can the god mean? and what is the interpretation of this riddle? for I know that I have no wisdom, small or great. What can he mean when he says that I am the wisest of men? And yet he is a god and cannot lie; that would be against his nature. After a long consideration, I at last thought of a method of trying the question. I reflected that if I could only find a man wiser than myself, then I might go to the god with a refutation in my hand. I should say to him, "Here is a man who is wiser than I am; but you said that I was the wisest." Accordingly I went to one who had the reputation of wisdom, and observed to him—his name I need not mention; he was a politician whom I selected for examination—and the result was as follows: When I began to talk with him, I could not help thinking that he was not really wise, although he was thought wise by many, and wiser still by himself; and I went and tried to explain to him that he thought himself wise, but was not really wise; and the consequence was that he hated me, and his enmity was shared by several who were present and heard me. So I left him, saying to myself, as I went away: Well, although I do not suppose that either of us knows anything really beautiful and good, I am better off than he is — for he knows nothing, and thinks that he knows. I neither know nor think that I know. In this latter particular, then, I seem to have slightly the advantage of him. Then I went to another, who had still higher philosophical pretensions, and my conclusion was exactly the same. I made another enemy of him, and of many others besides him.

After this I went to one man after another, being not unconscious of the enmity which I provoked, and I lamented and feared this: but necessity was laid upon me—the word of God, I thought, ought to be considered first. And I said to myself, Go I must to all who appear to know, and find out the meaning of the oracle. And I swear to you, Athenians, by the dog I swear! — for I must tell you the truth—the result of my mission was just this: I found that the men most in repute were all but the most foolish; and that some inferior men were really wiser and better. I will tell you the tale of my wanderings and of the "Herculean" labors, as I may call them, which I endured only to find at last the oracle irrefutable. When I left the politicians, I went to the poets; tragic, dithyrambic, and all sorts. And there, I said to myself, you will be detected; now you will find out that you are more ignorant than they are. Accordingly, I took them some of the most elaborate passages in their own writings, and asked what was the meaning of them—thinking that they would teach me something. Will you believe me? I am almost ashamed to speak of this, but still I must say that there is hardly a person present who would not have talked better about their poetry than they did themselves. That showed me in an instant that not by wisdom do poets write poetry, but by a sort of genius and inspiration; they are like diviners or soothsayers who also say many fine things, but do not understand the meaning of them. And the poets appeared to me to be much in the same case; and I further observed that upon the strength of their poetry they believed themselves to be the wisest of men in other things in which they were not wise. So I departed, conceiving myself to be superior to them for the same reason that I was superior to the politicians.

At last I went to the artisans, for I was conscious that I knew nothing at all, as I may say, and I was sure that they knew many fine things; and in this I was not mistaken, for they did know many things of which I was ignorant, and in this they certainly were wiser than I was. But I observed that even the good artisans fell into the same error as the poets; because they were good workmen they thought that they also knew all sorts of high matters, and this defect in them overshadowed their wisdom—therefore I asked myself on behalf of the oracle, whether I would like to be as I was, neither having their knowledge nor their ignorance, or like them in both; and I made answer to myself and the oracle that I was better off as I was.

The Results of Socrates' Investigations

This investigation has led to my having many enemies of the worst and most dangerous kind, and has given occasion also to many calumnies, and I am called wise, for my hearers always imagine that I myself possess the wisdom which I find wanting in others: but the truth is, O men of Athens, that God only is wise; and in this oracle he means to say that the wisdom of men is little or nothing; he is not speaking of Socrates, he is only using my name as an illustration, as if he said, He, O men, is the wisest, who, like Socrates, knows that his wisdom is in truth worth nothing. And so I go my way, obedient to the god, and make inquisition into the wisdom of anyone, whether citizen or stranger, who appears to be wise; and if he is not wise, then in vindication of the oracle I show him that he is not wise; and this occupation quite absorbs me, and I have no time to give either to any public matter of interest or to any concern of my own, but I am in utter poverty by reason of my devotion to the god.

There is another thing:—young men of the richer classes, who have not much to do, come about me of their own accord; they like to hear the pretenders examined, and they often imitate me, and examine others themselves; there are plenty of persons, as they soon enough discover, who think that they know something, but really know little or nothing: and then those who are examined by them instead of being angry with themselves are angry with me: This confounded Socrates, they say; this villainous misleader of youth!—and then if somebody asks them, Why, what evil does he practice or teach? they do not know, and cannot tell; but in order that they may not appear to be at a loss, they repeat the ready-made charges which are used against all philosophers about teaching things up in the clouds and under the earth, and having no gods, and making the worse appear the better cause; for they do not like to confess that their pretence of knowledge has been detected —which is the truth: and as they are numerous and ambitious and energetic, and are all in battle array and have persuasive tongues, they have filled your ears with their loud and inveterate calumnies. And this is the reason why my three accusers, Meletus and Anytus and Lycon, have set upon me; Meletus, who has a quarrel with me on behalf of the poets; Anytus, on behalf of the craftsmen; Lycon, on behalf of the rhetoricians: and as I said at the beginning, I cannot expect to get rid of this mass of calumny all in a moment. And this, O men of Athens, is the truth and the whole truth; I have concealed nothing, I have dissembled nothing. And yet I know that this plainness of speech makes them hate me, and what is their hatred but a proof that I am speaking the truth?—this is the occasion and reason of their slander of me, as you will find out either in this or in any future inquiry....

Socrates' Mission

I have said enough in answer to the charge of Meletus: any elaborate defense is unnecessary; but as I was saying before, I certainly have many enemies, and this is what will be my destruction if I am destroyed; of that I am certain; — not Meletus, nor yet Anytus, but the envy and detraction of the world, which has been the death of many good men, and will probably be the death of many more; there is no danger of my being the last of them.

Someone will say: And are you not ashamed, Socrates, of a course of life which is likely to bring you to an untimely end? To him I may fairly answer: There you are mistaken: a man who is good for anything ought not to calculate the chance of living or dying; he ought only to consider whether in doing anything he is doing right or wrong — acting the part of a good man or of a bad. Whereas, according to your view, the heroes who fell at Troy were not good for much, and the son of Thetis above all, who altogether despised danger in comparison with disgrace; and when his goddess mother said to him, in his eagerness to slay Hector, that if he avenged his companion Patroclus, and slew Hector, he would die himself — "Fate," as she said, "waits upon you next after Hector"; he, hearing this, utterly despised danger and death, and instead of fearing them, feared rather to live in dishonor, and not to avenge his friend. "Let me die next," he replies, "and be avenged of my enemy, rather than abide here by the beaked ships, a scorn and a burden of the earth." Had Achilles any thought of death and danger? For wherever a man's place is, whether the place which he has chosen or that in which he has been placed by a commander, there he ought to remain in the hour of danger; he should not think of death or of anything, but of disgrace. And this, O men of Athens, is a true saying.

Strange, indeed, would be my conduct, O men of Athens, if I who, when I was ordered by the generals whom you chose to command me at Potidaea and Amphipolis and Delium, remained where they placed me, like any other man, facing death; if, I say, now, when, as I conceive and imagine, God orders me to fulfill the philosopher's mission of searching into myself and other men, I were to desert my post through fear of death, or any other fear; that would indeed be strange, and I might justly be arraigned in court for denying the existence of the gods, if I disobeyed the oracle because I was afraid of death: then I should be fancying that I was wise when I was not wise.

For this fear of death is indeed the pretence of wisdom, and not real wisdom, being the appearance of knowing the unknown; since no one knows whether death, which they in their fear apprehend to be the greatest evil, may not be the greatest good. Is there not here conceit of knowledge, which is a disgraceful sort of ignorance? And this is the point in which, as I think, I am superior to men in general, and in which I might perhaps fancy myself wiser than other men, — that whereas I know but little of the world below, I do not suppose that I know: but I do know that injustice and disobedience to a better, whether God or man, is evil and dishonorable, and I will never fear or avoid a possible good rather than a certain evil.

And therefore if you let me go now, and reject the counsels of Anytus, who said that if I were not put to death I ought not to have been prosecuted, and that if I escape now, your sons will all be utterly ruined by listening to my words—if you say to me, Socrates, this time we will not mind Anytus, and will let you off, but upon one condition, that are to inquire and speculate in this way any more, and that if you are caught doing this again you shall die;—if this was the condition on which you let me go, I should reply: Men of Athens, I honor and love you; but I shall obey God rather than you, and while I have life and strength I shall never cease from the practice and teaching of philosophy, exhorting anyone whom I meet after my manner, and convincing him, saying: O my friend, why do you who are a citizen of the great and mighty and wise city of Athens, care so much about laying up the greatest amount of money and honor and reputation, and so little about wisdom and truth and the greatest improvement of the soul, which you never regard or heed at all? Are you not ashamed of this?

And if the person with whom I am arguing says: Yes, but I do care; I do not depart or let him go at once; I interrogate and examine and cross-examine him, and if I think that he has no virtue, but only says that he has, I reproach him with undervaluing the greater, and overvaluing the less. And this I should say to everyone whom I meet, young and old, citizen and alien, but especially to the citizens, inasmuch as they are my brethren. For this is the command of God, as I would have you know; and I believe that to this day no greater good has ever happened in the state than my service to the God. For I do nothing but go about persuading you all, old and young alike, not to take thought for your persons and your properties, but first and chiefly to care about the greatest improvement of the soul. I tell you that virtue is not given by money, but that from virtue come money and every other good of man, public as well as private. This is my teaching, and if this is the doctrine which corrupts the youth, my influence is ruinous indeed. But if anyone says that this is not my teaching, he is speaking an untruth. Wherefore, O men of Athens, I say to you, do as Anytus bids or not as Anytus bids, and either acquit me or not; but whatever you do, know that I shall never alter my ways, not even if I have to die many times.

Socrates as Athen's Gadfly

Men of Athens, do not interrupt, but hear me; there was an agreement between us that you should hear me out. And I think that what I am going to say will do you good: for I have something more to say, at which you may be inclined to cry out; but I beg that you will not do this. I would have you know that, if you kill such a one as I am, you will injure yourselves more than you will injure me. Meletus and Anytus will not injure me: they cannot; for it is not in the nature of things that a bad man should injure a better than himself. I do not deny that he may, perhaps, kill him, or drive him into exile, or deprive him of civil rights; and he may imagine, and others may imagine, that he is doing him a great injury: but in that I do not agree with him; for the evil of doing as Anytus is doing—of unjustly taking away another man's life—is greater far. And now, Athenians, I am not going to argue for my own sake, as you may think, but for yours, that you may not sin against the God, or lightly reject his boon by condemning me. For if you kill me you will not easily find another like me, who, if I may use such a ludicrous figure of speech, am a sort of gadfly, given to the state by the God; and the state is like a great and noble steed who is tardy in his motions owing to his very size, and requires to be stirred into life. I am that gadfly which God has given the state and all day long and in all places am always fastening upon you, arousing and persuading and reproaching you. And as you will not easily find another like me, I would advise you to spare me. I dare say that you may feel irritated at being suddenly awakened when you are caught napping; and you may think that if you were to strike me dead, as Anytus advises, which you easily might, then you would sleep on for the remainder of your lives, unless God in his care of you gives you another gadfly.

And that I am given to you by God is proved by this:—that if I had been like other men, I should not have neglected all my own concerns, or patiently seen the neglect of them during all these years, and have been doing yours, coming to you individually, like a father or elder brother, exhorting you to regard virtue; this I say, would not be like human nature. And had I gained anything, or if my exhortations had been paid, there would have been some sense in that: but now, as you will perceive, not even the impudence of my accusers dares to say that I have ever exacted or sought pay of anyone; they have no witness of that. And I have a witness of the truth of what I say; my poverty is a sufficient witness....

Concluding Comments

Well, Athenians, this and the like of this is nearly all the defense which I have to offer. Yet a word more. Perhaps there may be someone who is offended at me, when he calls to mind how he himself, on a similar or even a less serious occasion, had recourse to prayers and supplications with many tears, and how he produced his children in court, which was a moving spectacle, together with a posse of his relations and friends; whereas I, who am probably in danger of my life, will do none of these things. Perhaps this may come into his mind, and he may be set against me, and vote in anger because he is displeased at this. Now if there be such a person among you, which I am far from affirming, I may fairly reply to him: My friend, I am a man, and like other men, a creature of flesh and blood, and not of wood or stone, as Homer says; and I have a family, yes, and sons. O Athenians, three in number, one of whom is growing up, and the two others are still young; and yet I will not bring any of them hither in order to petition you for an acquittal. And why not? Not from any self-will or disregard of you. Whether I am or am not afraid of death is another question, of which I will not now speak. But my reason simply is that I feel such conduct to be discreditable to myself, and you, and the whole state. One who has reached my years, and who has a name for wisdom, whether deserved or not, ought not to debase himself. At any rate, the world has decided that Socrates is in some way superior to other men. And if those among you who are said to be superior in wisdom and courage, and any other virtue, demean themselves in this way, how shameful is their conduct! I have seen men of reputation, when they have been condemned, behaving in the strangest manner: they seemed to fancy that they were going to suffer something dreadful if they died, and that they could be immortal if you only allowed them to live; and I think that they were a dishonor to the state, and that any stranger coming in would say of them that the most eminent men of Athens, to whom the Athenians themselves give honor and command, are no better than women. And I say that these things ought not to be done by those of us who are of reputation; and if they are done, you ought not to permit them; you ought rather to show that you are more inclined to condemn, not the man who is quiet, but the man who gets up a doleful scene, and makes the city ridiculous.

But, setting aside the question of dishonor, there seems to be something wrong in petitioning a judge, and thus procuring an acquittal instead of informing and convincing him. For his duty is, not to make a present of justice, but to give judgment; and he has sworn that he will judge according to the laws, and not according to his own good pleasure; and neither he nor we should get into the habit of perjuring ourselves—there can be no piety in that. Do not then require me to do what I consider dishonorable and impious and wrong, especially now, when I am being tried for impiety on the indictment of Meletus. For if, O men of Athens, by force of persuasion and entreaty, I could overpower your oaths, then I should be teaching you to believe that there are no gods, and convict myself, in my own defense, of not believing in them. But that is not the case; for I do believe that there are gods, and in a far higher sense than that in which any of my accusers believe in them. And to you and to God I commit my cause, to be determined by you as is best for you and me.

The jury finds Socrates guilty.

Speech II: Proposal of the Counter Penalty

There are many reasons why I am not grieved, O men of Athens, at the vote of condemnation. I expected it, and am only surprised that the votes are so nearly equal; for I had thought that the majority against me would have been far larger; but now, had thirty votes gone over to the other side, I should have been acquitted. And I may say that I have escaped Meletus. And I may say more; for without the assistance of Anytus and Lycon, he would not have had a fifth part of the votes, as the law requires, in which case he would have incurred a fine of a thousand drachmae, as is evident.

And so he proposes death as the penalty. And what shall I propose on my part, O men of Athens? Clearly that which is my due. And what is that which I ought to pay or to receive? What shall be done to the man who has never had the wit to be idle during his whole life; but has been careless of what the many care about—wealth, and family interests, and military offices, and speaking in the assembly, and magistracies, and plots, and parties. Reflecting that I was really too honest a man to follow in this way and live, I did not go where I could do no good to you or to myself; but where I could do the greatest good privately to everyone of you, thither I went, and sought to persuade every man among you that he must look to himself, and seek virtue and wisdom before he looks to his private interests, and look to the state before he looks to the interests of the state; and that this should be the order which he observes in all his actions. What shall be done to such a one? Doubtless some good thing, O men of Athens, if he has his reward; and the good should be of a kind suitable to him. What would be a reward suitable to a poor man who is your benefactor, who desires leisure that he may instruct you? There can be no more fitting reward than [public meals for life] in the Prytaneum, O men of Athens, a reward which he deserves far more than the citizen who has won the prize at Olympia in the horse or chariot race, whether the chariots were drawn by two horses or by many. For I am in want, and he has enough; and he only gives you the appearance of happiness, and I give you the reality. And if I am to estimate the penalty justly, I say that maintenance in the Prytaneum is the just return.

Perhaps you may think that I am braving you in saying this, as in what I said before about the tears and prayers. But that is not the case. I speak rather because I am convinced that I never intentionally wronged anyone, although I cannot convince you of that—for we have had a short conversation only; but if there were a law at Athens, such as there is in other cities, that a capital cause should not be decided in one day, then I believe that I should have convinced you; but now the time is too short. I cannot in a moment refute great slanders; and, as I am convinced that I never wronged another, I will assuredly not wrong myself. I will not say of myself that I deserve any evil, or propose any penalty. Why should I? Because I am afraid of the penalty of death which Meletus proposes? When I do not know whether death is a good or an evil, why should I propose a penalty which would certainly be an evil? Shall I say imprisonment? And why should I live in prison, and be the slave of the magistrates of the year—of the Eleven? Or shall the penalty be a fine, and imprisonment until the fine is paid? There is the same objection. I should have to lie in prison, for money I have none, and I cannot pay. And if I say exile (and this may possibly be the penalty which you will affix), I must indeed be blinded by the love of life if I were to consider that when you, who are my own citizens, cannot endure my discourses and words, and have found them so grievous and odious that you would fain have done with them, others are likely to endure me. No, indeed, men of Athens, that is not very likely. And what a life should I lead, at my age, wandering from city to city, living in ever-changing exile, and always being driven out! For I am quite sure that into whatever place I go, as here so also there, the young men will come to me; and if I drive them away, their elders will drive me out at their desire: and if I let them come, their fathers and friends will drive me out for their sakes.

Someone will say: Yes, Socrates, but cannot you hold your tongue, and then you may go into a foreign city, and no one will interfere with you? Now I have great difficulty in making you understand my answer to this. For if I tell you that this would be a disobedience to a divine command, and therefore that I cannot hold my tongue, you will not believe that I am serious; and if I say again that the greatest good of man is daily to converse about virtue, and all that concerning which you hear me examining myself and others, and the unexamined life is not worth living—that you are still less likely to believe. And yet what I say is true, although a thing of which it is hard for me to persuade you. Moreover, I am not accustomed to think that I deserve any punishment. Had I money I might have proposed to give you what I had, and have been none the worse. But you see that I have none, and can only ask you to proportion the fine to my means. However, I think that I could afford a minae, and therefore I propose that penalty; Plato, Crito, Critobulus, and Apollodorus, my friends here, bid me say thirty minae, and they will be the sureties. Well then, say thirty minae, let that be the penalty; for that they will be ample security to you.

The jury condemns Socrates to death.

Speech III: Final Address

Not much time will be gained, O Athenians, in return for the evil name which you will get from the detractors of the city, who will say that you killed Socrates, a wise man; for they will call me wise even although I am not wise when they want to reproach you. If you had waited a little while, your desire would have been fulfilled in the course of nature. For I am far advanced in years, as you may perceive, and not far from death.

I am speaking now only to those of you who have condemned me to death. And I have another thing to say to them: You think that I was convicted through deficiency of words—I mean, that if I had thought fit to leave nothing undone, nothing unsaid, I might have gained an acquittal. Not so; the deficiency which led to my conviction was not of words—certainly not. But I had not the boldness or impudence or inclination to address you as you would have liked me to address you, weeping and wailing and lamenting, and saying and doing many things which you have been accustomed to hear from others, and which, as I say, are unworthy of me. But I thought that I ought not to do anything common or mean in the hour of danger: nor do I now repent of the manner of my defence, and I would rather die having spoken after my manner, than speak in your manner and live. For neither in war nor yet at law ought any man to use every way of escaping death. For often in battle there is no doubt that if a man will throw away his arms, and fall on his knees before his pursuers, he may escape death; and in other dangers there are other ways of escaping death, if a man is willing to say and do anything. The difficulty, my friends, is not in avoiding death, but in avoiding unrighteousness; for that runs faster than death. I am old and move slowly, and the slower runner has overtaken me, and my accusers are keen and quick, and the faster runner, who is unrighteousness, has overtaken them. And now I depart hence condemned by you to suffer the penalty of death, and they, too, go their ways condemned by the truth to suffer the penalty of villainy and wrong; and I must abide by my award — let them abide by theirs. I suppose that these things may be regarded as fated, — and I think that they are well.

Reflections on Death

And now, O men who have condemned me, I would fain prophesy to you; for I am about to die, and that is the hour in which men are gifted with prophetic power. And I prophesy to you who are my murderers, that immediately after my death punishment far heavier than you have inflicted on me will surely await you. Me you have killed because you wanted to escape the accuser, and not to give an account of your lives. But that will not be as you suppose: far otherwise. For I say that there will be more accusers of you than there are now; accusers whom hitherto I have restrained: and as they are younger they will be more severe with you, and you will be more offended at them. For if you think that by killing men you can avoid the accuser censuring your lives, you are mistaken; that is not a way of escape which is either possible or honorable; the easiest and noblest way is not to be crushing others, but to be improving yourselves. This is the prophecy which I utter before my departure, to the judges who have condemned me.

Friends, who would have acquitted me, I would like also to talk with you about this thing which has happened, while the magistrates are busy, and before I go to the place at which I must die. Stay then awhile, for we may as well talk with one another while there is time. You are my friends, and I should like to show you the meaning of this event which has happened to me. O my judges—for you I may truly call judges—I should like to tell you of a wonderful circumstance. Hitherto the familiar oracle within me has constantly been in the habit of opposing me even about trifles, if I was going to make a slip or error about anything; and now as you see there has come upon me that which may be thought, and is generally believed to be, the last and worst evil. But the oracle made no sign of opposition, either as I was leaving my house and going out in the morning, or when I was going up into this court, or while I was speaking, at anything which I was going to say; and yet I have often been stopped in the middle of a speech; but now in nothing I either said or did touching this matter has the oracle opposed me. What do I take to be the explanation of this? I will tell you. I regard this as a proof that what has happened to me is a good, and that those of us who think that death is an evil are in error. This is a great proof to me of what I am saying, for the customary sign would surely have opposed me had I been going to evil and not to good.

Let us reflect in another way, and we shall see that there is great reason to hope that death is a good, for one of two things:—either death is a state of nothingness and utter unconsciousness, or, as men say, there is a change and migration of the soul from this world to another. Now if you suppose that there is no consciousness, but a sleep like the sleep of him who is undisturbed even by the sight of dreams, death will be an unspeakable gain. For if a person were to select the night in which his sleep was undisturbed even by dreams, and were to compare with this the other days and nights of his life, and then were to tell us how many days and nights he had passed in the course of his life better and more pleasantly than this one, I think that any man, I will not say a private man, but even the great king, will not find many such days or nights, when compared with the others. Now if death is like this, I say that to die is gain; for eternity is then only a single night. But if death is the journey to another place, and there, as men say, all the dead are, what good, O my friends and judges, can be greater than this? If indeed when the pilgrim arrives in the world below, he is delivered from the professors of justice in this world, and finds the true judges who are said to give judgment there, Minos and Rhadamanthus and Aeacus and Triptolemus, and other sons of God who were righteous in their own life, that pilgrimage will be worth making. What would not a man give if he might converse with Orpheus and

Musaeus and Hesiod and Homer? Nay, if this be true, let me die again and again. I, too, shall have a wonderful interest in a place where I can converse with Palamedes, and Ajax the son of Telamon, and other heroes of old, who have suffered death through an unjust judgment; and there will be no small pleasure, as I think, in comparing my own sufferings with theirs. Above all, I shall be able to continue my search into true and false knowledge; as in this world, so also in that; I shall find out who is wise, and who pretends to be wise, and is not. What would not a man give, O judges, to be able to examine the leader of the great Trojan expedition; or Odysseus or Sisyphus, or numberless others, men and women too! What infinite delight would there be in conversing with them and asking them questions! For in that world they do not put a man to death for this; certainly not. For besides being happier in that world than in this, they will be immortal, if what is said is true.

Wherefore, O judges, be of good cheer about death, and know this for a fact—that no evil can happen to a good man, either in life or after death. He and his are not neglected by the gods; nor has my own approaching end happened by mere chance. But I see clearly that to die and be released was better for me; and therefore the oracle gave no sign. For which reason also, I am not angry with my accusers, or my condemners; they have done me no harm, although neither of them meant to do me any good; and for this I may gently blame them.   Still I have a favor to ask of them. When my sons are grown up, I would ask you, O my friends, to punish them; and I would have you trouble them, as I have troubled you, if they seem to care about riches, or anything, more than about virtue; or if they pretend to be something when they are really nothing,—then reprove them, as I have reproved you, for not caring about that for which they ought to care, and thinking that they are something when they are really nothing. And if you do this, I and my sons will have received justice at your hands.

The hour of departure has arrived, and we go our ways—I to die, and you to live. Which is better God only knows.

Plato. "Apology." *The Dialogues of Plato*. Vol. 2. Trans. by Benjamin Jowett. Oxford: Oxford University Press, 1892.

Phaedo

Plato

Prologue to the Dialogue

Echecrates. Were you yourself, Phaedo, in the prison with Socrates on the day when he drank the poison?

Phaedo. Yes, Echecrates, I was.

Ech. I wish that you would tell me about his death. What did he say in his last hours? We were informed that he died by taking poison, but no one knew anything more; for no Phliasian ever goes to Athens now, and a long time has elapsed since any Athenian found his way to Phlius, and therefore we had no clear account.

Phaed. Did you not hear of the proceedings at the trial?

Ech. Yes; someone told us about the trial, and we could not understand why, having been condemned, he was put to death, as appeared, not at the time, but long afterwards. What was the reason of this?

Phaed. An accident, Echecrates. The reason was that the stern of the ship which the Athenians send to Delos happened to have been crowned on the day before he was tried.

Ech. What is this ship?

Phaed. This is the ship in which, as the Athenians say, Theseus went to Crete when he took with him the fourteen youths, and was the saviour of them and of himself. And they were said to have vowed to Apollo at the time, that if they were saved they would make an annual pilgrimage to Delos. Now this custom still continues, and the whole period of the voyage to and from Delos, beginning when the priest of Apollo crowns the stern of the ship, is a holy season, during which the city is not allowed to be polluted by public executions; and often, when the vessel is detained by adverse winds, there may be a very considerable delay. As I was saying, the ship was crowned on the day before the trial, and this was the reason why Socrates lay in prison and was not put to death until long after he was condemned.

Ech. What was the manner of his death, Phaedo? What was said or done? And which of his friends had he with him? Or were they not allowed by the authorities to be present? And did he die alone?

Phaed. No; there were several of his friends with him.

Ech. If you have nothing to do, I wish that you would tell me what passed, as exactly as you can.

Phaed. I have nothing to do, and will try to gratify your wish. For to me, too, there is no greater pleasure than to have Socrates brought to my recollection, whether I speak myself or hear another speak of him.

Ech. You will have listeners who are of the same mind with you, and I hope that you will be as exact as you can.

Phaed. I remember the strange feeling which came over me at being with him. For I could hardly believe that I was present at the death of a friend, and therefore I did not pity him, Echecrates; his manner and his language were so noble and fearless in the hour of death that to me he appeared blessed. I thought that in going to the other world he could not be without a divine call, and that he would be happy, if any man ever was, when he arrived there, and therefore I did not pity him as might seem natural at such a time. But neither could I feel the pleasure which I usually felt in philosophical discourse (for philosophy was the theme of which we spoke). I was pleased, and I was also pained, because I knew that he was soon to die, and this strange mixture of feeling was shared by us all; we were laughing and weeping by turns, especially the excitable Apollodorus—you know the sort of man?

Ech. Yes.

Phaed. He was quite overcome; and I myself and all of us were greatly moved.

Ech. Who were present?

Phaed. Of native Athenians there were, besides Apollodorus, Critobulus and his father Crito, Hermogenes, Epigenes, Aeschines, and Antisthenes; likewise Ctesippus of the deme of Paeania, Menexenus, and some others; but Plato, if I am not mistaken, was ill.

Ech. Were there any strangers?

Phaed. Yes, there were; Simmias the Theban, and Cebes, and Phaedondes; Euclid and Terpison, who came from Megara.

Ech. And was Aristippus there, and Cleombrotus?

Phaed. No, they were said to be in Aegina.

Ech. Anyone else?

Phaed. I think that these were about all.

Ech. And what was the discourse of which you spoke?

Flashback: Socrates in Prison

I will begin at the beginning and try to repeat the entire conversation. You must understand that we had been previously in the habit of assembling early in the morning at the court in which the trial was held, and which is not far from the prison. There we remained talking with one another until the opening of the prison doors (for they were not opened very early), and then went in and generally passed the day with Socrates. On the last morning the meeting was earlier than usual; this was owing to our having heard on the previous evening that the sacred ship had arrived from Delos, and therefore we agreed to meet very early at the accustomed place. On our going to the prison, the jailer who answered the door, instead of admitting us, came out and bade us wait and he would call us. "For the Eleven," he said, "are now with Socrates; they are taking off his chains, and giving orders that he is to die to-day." He soon returned and said that we might come in.

On entering we found Socrates just released from chains, and Xanthippe, whom you know, sitting by him, and holding his child in her arms. When she saw us she uttered a cry and said, as women will: "O Socrates, this is the last time that either you will converse with your friends, or they with you." Socrates turned to Crito and said: "Crito, let someone take her home." Some of Crito's people accordingly led her away, crying out and beating herself. And when she was gone, Socrates, sitting up on the couch, began to bend and rub his leg, saying, as he rubbed: "How singular is the thing called pleasure, and how curiously related to pain, which might be thought to be the opposite of it; for they never come to a man together, and yet he who pursues either of them is generally compelled to take the other. They are two, and yet they grow together out of one head or stem; and I cannot help thinking that if Aesop had noticed them, he would have made a fable about God trying to reconcile their strife, and when he could not, he fastened their heads together; and this is the reason why when one comes the other follows, as I find in my own case pleasure comes following after the pain in my leg, which was caused by the chain."

Upon this Cebes said: I am very glad indeed, Socrates, that you mentioned the name of Aesop. For that reminds me of a question which has been asked by others, and was asked of me only the day before yesterday by Evenus the poet, and as he will be sure to ask again, you may as well tell me what I should say to him, if you would like him to have an answer. He wanted to know why you who never before wrote a line of poetry, now that you are in prison are putting Aesop into verse, and also composing that hymn in honor of Apollo.

Tell him, Cebes, he replied, that I had no idea of rivaling him or his poems; which is the truth, for I knew that I could not do that. But I wanted to see whether I could purge away a scruple which I felt about certain dreams. In the course of my life I have often had intimations in dreams "that I should make music." The same dream came to me sometimes in one form, and sometimes in another, but always saying the same or nearly the same words: Make and cultivate music, said the dream. And thus far I had imagined that this was only intended to exhort and encourage me in the study of philosophy, which has always been the pursuit of my life, and is the noblest and best of music. The dream was bidding me to do what I was already doing, in the same way that the competitor in a race is bidden by the spectators to run when he is already running. But I was not certain of this, as the dream might have meant music in the popular sense of the word, and being under sentence of death, and the festival giving me a respite, I thought that I should be safer if I satisfied the scruple, and, in obedience to the dream, composed a few verses before I departed. And first I made a hymn in honor of the god of the festival, and then considering that a poet, if he is really to be a poet or maker, should not only put words together but make stories, and as I have no invention, I took some fables of Esop, which I had ready at hand and knew, and turned them into verse.

Tell Evenus this, and bid him be of good cheer; that I would have him come after me if he be a wise man, and not tarry; and that to-day I am likely to be going, for the Athenians say that I must.

Death as a Good and The Prohibition against Suicide

Simmias said: What a message for such a man! having been a frequent companion of his, I should say that, as far as I know him, he will never take your advice unless he is obliged.

Why, said Socrates,—is not Evenus a philosopher?

I think that he is, said Simmias.

Then he, or any man who has the spirit of philosophy, will be willing to die, though he will not take his own life, for that is held not to be right.

Here he changed his position, and put his legs off the couch on to the ground, and during the rest of the conversation he remained sitting.

Why do you say, inquired Cebes, that a man ought not to take his own life, but that the philosopher will be ready to follow the dying?

Socrates replied: And have you, Cebes and Simmias, who are acquainted with Philolaus, never heard him speak of this?

I never understood him, Socrates.

My words, too, are only an echo; but I am very willing to say what I have heard: and indeed, as I am going to another place, I ought to be thinking and talking of the nature of the pilgrimage which I am about to make. What can I do better in the interval between this and the setting of the sun?

Then tell me, Socrates, why is suicide held not to be right? as I have certainly heard Philolaus affirm when he was staying with us at Thebes: and there are others who say the same, although none of them has ever made me understand him.

But do your best, replied Socrates, and the day may come when you will understand. I suppose that you wonder why, as most things which are evil may be accidentally good, this is to be the only exception (for may not death, too, be better than life in some cases?), and why, when a man is better dead, he is not permitted to be his own benefactor, but must wait for the hand of another.

By Jupiter! yes, indeed, said Cebes, laughing, and speaking in his native Doric.

I admit the appearance of inconsistency, replied Socrates, but there may not be any real inconsistency after all in this.

There is a doctrine uttered in secret that man is a prisoner who has no right to open the door of his prison and run away; this is a great mystery which I do not quite understand. Yet I, too, believe that the gods are our guardians, and that we are a possession of theirs. Do you not agree?

Yes, I agree to that, said Cebes.

And if one of your own possessions, an ox or an ass, for example took the liberty of putting himself out of the way when you had given no intimation of your wish that he should die, would you not be angry with him, and would you not punish him if you could?

Certainly, replied Cebes.

Then there may be reason in saying that a man should wait, and not take his own life until God summons him, as he is now summoning me.

Yes, Socrates, said Cebes, there is surely reason in that. And yet how can you reconcile this seemingly true belief that God is our guardian and we his possessions, with that willingness to die which we were attributing to the philosopher? That the wisest of men should be willing to leave this service in which they are ruled by the gods who are the best of rulers is not reasonable, for surely no wise man thinks that when set at liberty he can take better care of himself than the gods take of him. A fool may perhaps think this—he may argue that he had better run away from his master, not considering that his duty is to remain to the end, and not to run away from the good, and that there is no sense in his running away. But the wise man will want to be ever with him who is better than himself. Now this, Socrates, is the reverse of what was just now said; for upon this view the wise man should sorrow and the fool rejoice at passing out of life.

The earnestness of Cebes seemed to please Socrates. Here, said he, turning to us, is a man who is always inquiring, and is not to be convinced all in a moment, nor by every argument.

Socrates Attitude Towards His Own Death

And in this case, added Simmias, his objection does appear to me to have some force. For what can be the meaning of a truly wise man wanting to fly away and lightly leave a master who is better than himself? And I rather imagine that Cebes is referring to you; he thinks that you are too ready to leave us, and too ready to leave the gods who, as you acknowledge, are our good rulers.

Yes, replied Socrates; there is reason in that. And this indictment you think that I ought to answer as if I were in court?

That is what we should like, said Simmias.

Then I must try to make a better impression upon you than I did when defending myself before the judges. For I am quite ready to acknowledge, Simmias and Cebes, that I ought to be grieved at death, if I were not persuaded that I am going to other gods who are wise and good (of this I am as certain as I can be of anything of the sort) and to men departed (though I am not so certain of this), who are better than those whom I leave behind; and therefore I do not grieve as I might have done, for I have good hope that there is yet something remaining for the dead, and, as has been said of old, some far better thing for the good than for the evil.

But do you mean to take away your thoughts with you, Socrates? said Simmias. Will you not communicate them to us?—the benefit is one in which we too may hope to share. Moreover, if you succeed in convincing us, that will be an answer to the charge against yourself.

I will do my best, replied Socrates. But you must first let me hear what Crito wants; he was going to say something to me.

Only this, Socrates, replied Crito: the attendant who is to give you the poison has been telling me that you are not to talk much, and he wants me to let you know this; for that by talking heat is increased, and this interferes with the action of the poison; those who excite themselves are sometimes obliged to drink the poison two or three times.

Then, said Socrates, let him mind his business and be prepared to give the poison two or three times, if necessary; that is all.

I was almost certain that you would say that, replied Crito; but I was obliged to satisfy him.

Never mind him, he said.

The Philosopher Embraces Death

And now I will make answer to you, O my judges, and show that he who has lived as a true philosopher has reason to be of good cheer when he is about to die, and that after death he may hope to receive the greatest good in the other world. And how this may be, Simmias and Cebes, I will endeavor to explain. For I deem that the true disciple of philosophy is likely to be misunderstood by other men; they do not perceive that he is ever pursuing death and dying; and if this is true, why, having had the desire of death all his life long, should he repine at the arrival of that which he has been always pursuing and desiring?

Simmias laughed and said: Though not in a laughing humor, I swear that I cannot help laughing when I think what the wicked world will say when they hear this. They will say that this is very true, and our people at home will agree with them in saying that the life which philosophers desire is truly death, and that they have found them out to be deserving of the death which they desire.

And they are right, Simmias, in saying this, with the exception of the words "They have found them out"; for they have not found out what is the nature of this death which the true philosopher desires, or how he deserves or desires death. But let us leave them and have a word with ourselves: Do we believe that there is such a thing as death?

To be sure, replied Simmias.

And is this anything but the separation of soul and body? And being dead is the attainment of this separation; when the soul exists in herself, and is parted from the body and the body is parted from the soul—that is death?

Exactly: that and nothing else, he replied.

And what do you say of another question, my friend, about which I should like to have your opinion, and the answer to which will probably throw light on our present inquiry: Do you think that the philosopher ought to care about the pleasures—if they are to be called pleasures—of eating and drinking?

Certainly not, answered Simmias.

And what do you say of the pleasures of love—should he care about them?

By no means.

And will he think much of the other ways of indulging the body—for example, the acquisition of costly raiment, or sandals, or other adornments of the body? Instead of caring about them, does he not rather despise anything more than nature needs? What do you say?

I should say the true philosopher would despise them.

Would you not say that he is entirely concerned with the soul and not with the body? He would like, as far as he can, to be quit of the body and turn to the soul.

That is true.

In matters of this sort philosophers, above all other men, may be observed in every sort of way to dissever the soul from the body.

That is true.

Whereas, Simmias, the rest of the world are of opinion that a life which has no bodily pleasures and no part in them is not worth having; but that he who thinks nothing of bodily pleasures is almost as though he were dead.

That is quite true.

Death and Knowledge

What again shall we say of the actual acquirement of knowledge?—is the body, if invited to share in the inquiry, a hinderer or a helper? I mean to say, have sight and hearing any truth in them? Are they not, as the poets are always telling us, inaccurate witnesses? and yet, if even they are inaccurate and indistinct, what is to be said of the other senses?—for you will allow that they are the best of them?

Certainly, he replied.

Then when does the soul attain truth?—for in attempting to consider anything in company with the body she is obviously deceived.

Yes, that is true.

Then must not existence be revealed to her in thought, if at all?

Yes.

And thought is best when the mind is gathered into herself and none of these things trouble her—neither sounds nor sights nor pain nor any pleasure—when she has as little as possible to do with the body, and has no bodily sense or feeling, but is aspiring after being?

That is true.

And in this the philosopher dishonors the body; his soul runs away from the body and desires to be alone and by herself?

That is true.

Well, but there is another thing, Simmias: Is there or is there not an absolute justice?

Assuredly there is.

And an absolute beauty and absolute good?

Of course.

But did you ever behold any of them with your eyes?

Certainly not.

Or did you ever reach them with any other bodily sense? (and I speak not of these alone, but of absolute greatness, and health, and strength, and of the essence or true nature of everything). Has the reality of them ever been perceived by you through the bodily organs? or rather, is not the nearest approach to the knowledge of their several natures made by him who so orders his intellectual vision as to have the most exact conception of the essence of that which he considers?

Certainly.

And he attains to the knowledge of them in their highest purity who goes to each of them with the mind alone, not allowing when in the act of thought the intrusion or introduction of sight or any other sense in the company of reason, but with the very light of the mind in her clearness penetrates into the very fight of truth in each; he has got rid, as far as he can, of eyes and ears and of the whole body, which he conceives of only as a disturbing element, hindering the soul from the acquisition of knowledge when in company with her—is not this the sort of man who, if ever man did, is likely to attain the knowledge of existence?

There is admirable truth in that, Socrates, replied Simmias.

And when they consider all this, must not true philosophers make a reflection, of which they will speak to one another in such words as these: We have found, they will say, a path of speculation which seems to bring us and the argument to the conclusion that while we are in the body, and while the soul is mingled with this mass of evil, our desire will not be satisfied, and our desire is of the truth. For the body is a source of endless trouble to us by reason of the mere requirement of food; and also is liable to diseases which overtake and impede us in the search after truth: and by filling us so full of loves, and lusts, and fears, and fancies, and idols, and every sort of folly, prevents our ever having, as people say, so much as a thought. For whence come wars, and fightings, and factions? whence but from the body and the lusts of the body? For wars are occasioned by the love of money, and money has to be acquired for the sake and in the service of the body; and in consequence of all these things the time which ought to be given to philosophy is lost.

Moreover, if there is time and an inclination toward philosophy, yet the body introduces a turmoil and confusion and fear into the course of speculation, and hinders us from seeing the truth: and all experience shows that if we would have pure knowledge of anything we must be quit of the body, and the soul in herself must behold all things in themselves: then I suppose that we shall attain that which we desire, and of which we say that we are lovers, and that is wisdom, not while we live, but after death, as the argument shows; for if while in company with the body the soul cannot have pure knowledge, one of two things seems to follow—either knowledge is not to be attained at all, or, if at all, after death. For then, and not till then, the soul will be in herself alone and without the body. In this present life, I reckon that we make the nearest approach to knowledge when we have the least possible concern or interest in the body, and are not saturated with the bodily nature, but remain pure until the hour when God himself is pleased to release us. And then the foolishness of the body will be cleared away and we shall be pure and hold converse with other pure souls, and know of ourselves the clear light everywhere; and this is surely the light of truth. For no impure thing is allowed to approach the pure. These are the sort of words, Simmias, which the true lovers of wisdom cannot help saying to one another, and thinking. You will agree with me in that?

Certainly, Socrates.

Death As Purification

But if this is true, O my friend, then there is great hope that, going whither I go, I shall there be satisfied with that which has been the chief concern of you and me in our past lives. And now that the hour of departure is appointed to me, this is the hope with which I depart, and not I only, but every man who believes that he has his mind purified.

Certainly, replied Simmias.

And what is purification but the separation of the soul from the body, as I was saying before; the habit of the soul gathering and collecting herself into herself, out of all the courses of the body; the dwelling in her own place alone, as in another life, so also in this, as far as she can; the release of the soul from the chains of the body?

Very true, he said.

And what is that which is termed death, but this very separation and release of the soul from the body?

To be sure, he said.

And the true philosophers, and they only, study and are eager to release the soul. Is not the separation and release of the soul from the body their especial study?

That is true.

And as I was saying at first, there would be a ridiculous contradiction in men studying to live as nearly as they can in a state of death, and yet repining when death comes.

Certainly.

Then, Simmias, as the true philosophers are ever studying death, to them, of all men, death is the least terrible. Look at the matter in this way: how inconsistent of them to have been always enemies of the body, and wanting to have the soul alone, and when this is granted to them, to be trembling and repining; instead of rejoicing at their departing to that place where, when they arrive, they hope to gain that which in life they loved (and this was wisdom), and at the same time to be rid of the company of their enemy. Many a man has been willing to go to the world below in the hope of seeing there an earthly love, or wife, or son, and conversing with them. And will he who is a true lover of wisdom, and is persuaded in like manner that only in the world below he can worthily enjoy her, still repine at death? Will he not depart with joy? Surely he will, my friend, if he be a true philosopher. For he will have a firm conviction that there only, and nowhere else, he can find wisdom in her purity. And if this be true, he would be very absurd, as I was saying, if he were to fear death.

He would, indeed, replied Simmias....

Cebes' Objection

Cebes answered: I agree, Socrates, in the greater part of what you say. But in what relates to the soul, men are apt to be incredulous; they fear that when she leaves the body her place may be nowhere, and that on the very day of death she may be destroyed and perish—immediately on her release from the body, issuing forth like smoke or air and vanishing away into nothingness. For if she could only hold together and be herself after she was released from the evils of the body, there would be good reason to hope, Socrates, that what you say is true. But much persuasion and many arguments are required in order to prove that when the man is dead the soul yet exists, and has any force of intelligence.

True, Cebes, said Socrates; and shall I suggest that we talk a little of the probabilities of these things?

I am sure, said Cebes, that I should gready like to know your opinion about them.

I reckon, said Socrates, that no one who heard me now, not even if he were one of my old enemies, the comic poets, could accuse me of idle talking about matters in which I have no concern. Let us, then, if you please, proceed with the inquiry....

Body and Soul

...[O]bserve, that after a man is dead, the body, which is the visible part of man, and has a visible framework, which is called a corpse, and which would naturally be dissolved and decomposed and dissipated, is not dissolved or decomposed at once, but may remain for a good while, if the constitution be sound at the time of death, and the season of the year favorable? For the body when shrunk and embalmed, as is the custom in Egypt, may remain almost entire through infinite ages; and even in decay, still there are some portions, such as the bones and ligaments, which are practically indestructible. You allow that?

Yes.

And are we to suppose that the soul, which is invisible, in passing to the true Hades, which like her is invisible, and pure, and noble, and on her way to the good and wise God, whither, if God will, my soul is also soon to go—that the soul, I repeat, if this be her nature and origin, is blown away and perishes immediately on quitting the body as the many say? That can never be, dear Simmias and Cebes. The truth rather is that the soul which is pure at departing draws after her no bodily taint, having never voluntarily had connection with the body, which she is ever avoiding, herself gathered into herself (for such abstraction has been the study of her life). And what does this mean but that she has been a true disciple of philosophy and has practised how to die easily? And is not philosophy the practice of death?

Certainly.

That soul, I say, herself invisible, departs to the invisible world to the divine and immortal and rational: thither arriving, she lives in bliss and is released from the error and folly of men, their fears and wild passions and all other human ills, and forever dwells, as they say of the initiated, in company with the gods. Is not this true, Cebes?

Yes, said Cebes, beyond a doubt.

The "Pollution" of Souls

But the soul which has been polluted, and is impure at the time of her departure, and is the companion and servant of the body always, and is in love with and fascinated by the body and by the desires and pleasures of the body, until she is led to believe that the truth only exists in a bodily form, which a man may touch and see and taste and use for the purposes of his lusts—the soul, I mean, accustomed to hate and fear and avoid the intellectual principle, which to the bodily eye is dark and invisible, and can be attained only by philosophy—do you suppose that such a soul as this will depart pure and unalloyed?

That is impossible, he replied.

She is engrossed by the corporeal, which the continual association and constant care of the body have made natural to her.

Very true.

And this, my friend, may be conceived to be that heavy, weighty, earthy element of sight by which such a soul is depressed and dragged down again into the visible world, because she is afraid of the invisible and of the world below—prowling about tombs and sepulchres, in the neighborhood of which, as they tell us, are seen certain ghostly apparitions of souls which have not departed pure, but are cloyed with sight and therefore visible.

That is very likely, Socrates.

Yes, that is very likely, Cebes; and these must be the souls, not of the good, but of the evil, who are compelled to wander about such places in payment of the penalty of their former evil way of life; and they continue to wander until the desire which haunts them is satisfied and they are imprisoned in another body. And they may be supposed to be fixed in the same natures which they had in their former life.

What natures do you mean, Socrates?

I mean to say that men who have followed after gluttony, and wantonness, and drunkenness, and have had no thought of avoiding them, would pass into asses and animals of that sort. What do you think?

I think that exceedingly probable.

And those who have chosen the portion of injustice, and tyranny, and violence, will pass into wolves, or into hawks and kites; whither else can we suppose them to go?

Yes, said Cebes; that is doubtless the place of natures such as theirs. And there is no difficulty, he said, in assigning to all of them places answering to their several natures and propensities?

There is not, he said.

Even among them some are happier than others; and the happiest both in themselves and their place of abode are those who have practised the civil and social virtues which are called temperance and justice, and are acquired by habit and attention without philosophy and mind.

Why are they the happiest?

Because they may be expected to pass into some gentle, social nature which is like their own, such as that of bees or ants, or even back again into the form of man, and just and moderate men spring from them.

That is not impossible.

Philosophy as Purification of the Soul

But he who is a philosopher or lover of learning, and is entirely pure at departing, is alone permitted to reach the gods. And this is the reason, Simmias and Cebes, why the true votaries of philosophy abstain from all fleshly lusts, and endure and refuse to give themselves up to them -- not because they fear poverty or the ruin of their families, like the lovers of money, and the world in general; nor like the lovers of power and honor, because they dread the dishonor or disgrace of evil deeds.

No, Socrates, that would not become them, said Cebes.

No, indeed, he replied; and therefore they who have a care of their souls, and do not merely live in the fashions of the body, say farewell to all this; they will not walk in the ways of the blind: and when philosophy offers them purification and release from evil, they feel that they ought not to resist her influence, and to her they incline, and whither she leads they follow her.

What do you mean, Socrates?

The Body as Prison of the Soul

I will tell you, he said. The lovers of knowledge are conscious that their souls, when philosophy receives them, are simply fastened and glued to their bodies: the soul is only able to view existence through the bars of a prison, and not in her own nature; she is wallowing in the mire of all ignorance; and philosophy, seeing the terrible nature of her confinement, and that the captive through desire is led to conspire in her own captivity (for the lovers of knowledge are aware that this was the original state of the soul, and that when she was in this state philosophy received and gently counseled her, and wanted to release her, pointing out to her that the eye is full of deceit, and also the ear and other senses, and persuading her to retire from them in all but the necessary use of them and to be gathered up and collected into herself, and to trust only to herself and her own intuitions of absolute existence, and mistrust that which comes to her through others and is subject to vicissitude)—philosophy shows her that this is visible and tangible, but that what she sees in her own nature is intellectual and invisible. And the soul of the true philosopher thinks that she ought not to resist this deliverance, and therefore abstains from pleasures and desires and pains and fears, as far as she is able; reflecting that when a man has great joys or sorrows or fears or desires he suffers from them, not the sort of evil which might be anticipated

—as, for example, the loss of his health or property, which he has sacrificed to his lusts—but he has suffered an evil greater far, which is the greatest and worst of all evils, and one of which he never thinks.

And what is that, Socrates? said Cebes.

Why, this: When the feeling of pleasure or pain in the soul is most intense, all of us naturally suppose that the object of this intense feeling is then plainest and truest: but this is not the case.

Very true.

And this is the state in which the soul is most enthralled by the body.

How is that?

Why, because each pleasure and pain is a sort of nail which nails and rivets the soul to the body, and engrosses her and makes her believe that to be true which the body affirms to be true; and from agreeing with the body and having the same delights she is obliged to have the same habits and ways, and is not likely ever to be pure at her departure to the world below, but is always saturated with the body; so that she soon sinks into another body and there germinates and grows, and has therefore no part in the communion of the divine and pure and simple.

That is most true, Socrates, answered Cebes.

And this, Cebes, is the reason why the true lovers of knowledge are temperate and brave; and not for the reason which the world gives.

Certainly not.

Certainly not! For not in that way does the soul of a philosopher reason; she will not ask philosophy to release her in order that when released she may deliver herself up again to the thraldom of pleasures and pains, doing a work only to be undone again, weaving instead of unweaving her Penelope's web. But she will make herself a calm of passion and follow Reason, and dwell in her, beholding the true and divine (which is not matter of opinion), and thence derive nourishment. Thus she seeks to live while she lives, and after death she hopes to go to her own kindred and to be freed from human ills. Never fear, Simmias and Cebes, that a soul which has been thus nurtured and has had these pursuits, will at her departure from the body be scattered and blown away by the winds and be nowhere and nothing....

The Death of Socrates

When he had done speaking, Crito said: And have you any commands for us, Socrates—anything to say about your children, or any other matter in which we can serve you?

Nothing particular, he said: only, as I have always told you, I would have you look to yourselves; that is a service which you may always be doing to me and mine as well as to yourselves. And you need not make professions; for if you take no thought for yourselves, and walk not according to the precepts which I have given you, not now for the first time, the warmth of your professions will be of no avail.

We will do our best, said Crito. But in what way would you have us bury you?

In any way that you like; only you must get hold of me, and take care that I do not walk away from you. Then he turned to us, and added with a smile: I cannot make Crito believe that I am the same Socrates who have been talking and conducting the argument; he fancies that I am the other Socrates whom he will soon see, a dead body—and he asks, How shall he bury me? And though I have spoken many words in the endeavor to show that when I have drunk the poison I shall leave you and go to the joys of the blessed—these words of mine, with which I comforted you and myself, have had, I perceive, no effect upon Crito. And therefore I want you to be surety for me now, as he was surety for me at the trial: but let the promise be of another sort; for he was my surety to the judges that I would remain, but you must be my surety to him that I shall not remain, but go away and depart; and then he will suffer less at my death, and not be grieved when he sees my body being burned or buried. I would not have him sorrow at my hard lot, or say at the burial, Thus we lay out Socrates, or, Thus we follow him to the grave or bury him; for false words are not only evil in themselves, but they infect the soul with evil. Be of good cheer, then, my dear Crito, and say that you are burying my body only, and do with that as is usual, and as you think best.

When he had spoken these words, he arose and went into the bath chamber with Crito, who bade us wait; and we waited, talking and thinking of the subject of discourse, and also of the greatness of our sorrow; he was like a father of whom we were being bereaved, and we were about to pass the rest of our lives as orphans. When he had taken the bath his children were brought to him—(he had two young sons and an elder one); and the women of his family also came, and he talked to them and gave them a few directions in the presence of Crito; and he then dismissed them and returned to us.

Now the hour of sunset was near, for a good deal of time had passed while he was within. When he came out, he sat down with us again after his bath, but not much was said. Soon the jailer, who was the servant of the Eleven, entered and stood by him, saying: To you, Socrates, whom I know to be the noblest and gentlest and best of all who ever came to this place, I will not impute the angry feelings of other men, who rage and swear at me when, in obedience to the authorities, I bid them drink the poison—indeed, I am sure that you will not be angry with me; for others, as you are aware, and not I, are the guilty cause. And so fare you well, and try to bear lightly what must needs be; you know my errand. Then bursting into tears he turned way and went out.

Socrates looked at him and said: I return your good wishes, and will do as you bid. Then, turning to us, he said, How charming the man is: since I have been in prison he has always been coming to see me, and at times he would talk to me, and was as good as could be to me, and now see how generously he sorrows for me. But we must do as he says, Crito; let the cup be brought, if the poison is prepared: if not, let the attendant prepare some.

Yet, said Crito, the sun is still upon the hilltops, and many a one has taken the draught late, and after the announcement has been made to him, he has eaten and drunk, and indulged in sensual delights; do not hasten then, there is still time.

Socrates said: Yes, Crito, and they of whom you speak are right in doing thus, for they think that they will gain by the delay; but I am right in not doing thus, for I do not think that I should gain anything by drinking the poison a little later; I should be sparing and saving a life which is already gone: I could only laugh at myself for this. Please then to do as I say, and not to refuse me.

Crito, when he heard this, made a sign to the servant, and the servant went in, and remained for some time, and then returned with the jailer carrying a cup of poison. Socrates said: You, my good friend, who are experienced in these matters, shall give me directions how I am to proceed. The man answered: You have only to walk about until your legs are heavy, and then to lie down, and the poison will act. At the same time he handed the cup to Socrates, who in the easiest and gentlest manner, without the least fear or change of color or feature, looking at the man with all his eyes, Echecrates, as his manner was, took the cup and said: What do you say about making a libation out of this cup to any god? May I, or not? The man answered: We only prepare, Socrates, just so much as we deem enough. I understand, he said: yet I may and must pray to the gods to prosper my journey from this to that other world—may this, then, which is my prayer, be granted to me. Then holding the cup to his lips, quite readily and cheerfully he drank off the poison. And hitherto most of us had been able to control our sorrow; but now when we saw him drinking, and saw too that he had finished the draught, we could no longer forbear, and in spite of myself my own tears were flowing fast; so that I covered my face and wept over myself, for certainly I was not weeping over him, but at the thought of my own calamity in having lost such a companion. Nor was I the first, for Crito, when he found himself unable to restrain his tears, had got up and moved away, and I followed; and at that moment. Apollodorus, who had been weeping all the time, broke out in a loud cry which made cowards of us all. Socrates alone retained his calmness: What is this strange outcry? he said. I sent away the women mainly in order that they might not offend in this way, for I have heard that a man should die in peace. Be quiet, then, and have patience.

When we heard that, we were ashamed, and refrained our tears; and he walked about until, as he said, his legs began to fail, and then he lay on his back, according to the directions, and the man who gave him the poison now and then looked at his feet and legs; and after a while he pressed his foot hard and asked him if he could feel; and he said, no; and then his leg, and so upwards and upwards, and showed us that he was cold and stiff. And he felt them himself, and said: When the poison reaches the heart, that will be the end. He was beginning to grow cold about the groin, when he uncovered his face, for he had covered himself up, and said (they were his last words)—he said: Crito, I owe a cock to Asclepius; will you remember to pay the debt? The debt shall be paid, said Crito; is there anything else? There was no answer to this question; but in a minute or two a movement was heard, and the attendants uncovered him; his eyes were set, and Crito closed his eyes and mouth.

Such was the end, Echecrates, of our friend, whom I may truly call the wisest, and justest, and best of all the men whom I have ever known.

Plato. "Phaedo." *The Dialogues of Plato.* Vol. 2. Translated by Benjamin Jowett. Oxford: Oxford University Press, 1892.

The Cave
Plato

AND now, I said, let me show in a figure how far our nature is enlightened or unenlightened: Behold! human beings living in an underground den, which has a mouth open toward the light and reaching all along the den; here they have been from their childhood, and have their legs and necks chained so that they cannot move, and can only see before them, being prevented by the chains from turning round their heads. Above and behind them a fire is blazing at a distance, and between the fire and the prisoners there is a raised way; and you will see, if you look, a low wall built along the way, like the screen which marionette players have in front of them, over which they show the puppets.

I see.

And do you see, I said, men passing along the wall carrying all sorts of vessels, and statues and figures of animals made of wood and stone and various materials, which appear over the wall? Some of them are talking, others silent.

You have shown me a strange image, and they are strange prisoners.

Like ourselves, I replied; and they see only their own shadows, or the shadows of one another, which the fire throws on the opposite wall of the cave?

True, he said; how could they see anything but the shadows if they were never allowed to move their heads?

And of the objects which are being carried in like manner they would only see the shadows?

Yes, he said.

And if they were able to converse with one another, would they not suppose that they were naming what was actually before them?

Very true.

And suppose further that the prison had an echo which came from the other side, would they not be sure to fancy when one of the passersby spoke that the voice which they heard came from the passing shadow?

No question, he replied.

To them, I said, the truth would be literally nothing but the shadows of the images.

That is certain.

And now look again, and see what will naturally follow if the prisoners are released and disabused of their error. At first, when any of them is liberated and compelled suddenly to stand up and turn his neck round and walk and look toward the light, he will suffer sharp pains; the glare will distress him, and he will be unable to see the realities of which in his former state he had seen the shadows; and then conceive someone saying to him, that what he saw before was an illusion, but that now, when he is approaching nearer to being and his eye is turned toward more real existence, he has a clearer vision—what will be his reply? And you may further imagine that his instructor is pointing to the objects as they pass and requiring him to name them—will he not be perplexed? Will he not fancy that the shadows which he formerly saw are truer than the objects which are now shown to him?

Far truer.

And if he is compelled to look straight at the light, will he not have a pain in his eyes which will make him turn away to take refuge in the objects of vision which he can see, and which he will conceive to be in reality clearer than the things which are now being shown to him?

True, he said.

And suppose once more, that he is reluctantly dragged up a steep and rugged ascent, and held fast until he is forced into the presence of the sun himself, is he not likely to be pained and irritated? When he approaches the light his eyes will be dazzled, and he will not be able to see anything at all of what are now called realities.

Not all in a moment, he said.

He will require to grow accustomed to the sight of the upper world. And first he will see the shadows best, next the reflections of men and other objects in the water, and then the objects themselves; then he will gaze upon the light of the moon and the stars and the spangled heaven; and he will see the sky and the stars by night better than the sun or the light of the sun by day?

Certainly.

Last of all he will be able to see the sun, and not mere reflections of him in the water, but he will see him in his own proper place, and not in another; and he will contemplate him as he is.

Certainly.

He will then proceed to argue that this is he who gives the season and the years, and is the guardian of all that is in the visible world, and in a certain way the cause of all things which he and his fellows have been accustomed to behold?

Clearly, he said, he would first see the sun and then reason about him.

And when he remembered his old habitation, and the wisdom of the den and his fellow prisoners, do you not suppose that he would felicitate himself on the change, and pity him?

Certainly, he would.

And if they were in the habit of conferring honors among themselves on those who were quickest to observe the passing shadows and to remark which of them went before, and which followed after, and which were together; and who were therefore best able to draw conclusions as to the future, do you think that he would care for such honors and glories, or envy the possessors of them? Would he not say with Homer,

"Better to be the poor servant of a poor master," and to endure anything, rather than think as they do and live after their manner?

Yes, he said, I think that he would rather suffer anything than entertain these false notions and live in this miserable manner.

Imagine once more, I said, such a one coming suddenly out of the sun to be replaced in his old situation; would he not be certain to have his eyes full of darkness?

To be sure, he said.

And if there were a contest, and he had to compete in measuring the shadows with the prisoners who had never moved out of the den, while his sight was still weak, and before his eyes had become steady (and the time which would be needed to acquire this new habit of sight might be very considerable), would he not be ridiculous? Men would say of him that up he went and down he came without his eyes; and that it was better not even to think of ascending; and if anyone tried to loose another and lead him up to the light, let them only catch the offender, and they would put him to death.

No question, he said.

This entire allegory, I said, you may now append, dear Glaucon, to the previous argument; the prisonhouse is the world of sight, the light of the fire is the sun, and you will not misapprehend me if you interpret the journey upward to be the ascent of the soul into the intellectual world according to my poor belief, which, at your desire, I have expressed—whether rightly or wrongly, God knows. But, whether true or false, my opinion is that in the world of knowledge the idea of good appears last of all, and is seen only with an effort; and, when seen, is also inferred to be the universal author of all things beautiful and right, parent of light and of the lord of light in this visible world, and the immediate source of reason and truth in the intellectual; and that this is the power upon which he who would act rationally either in public or private life must have his eye fixed.

I agree, he said, as far as I am able to understand you.

Moreover, I said, you must not wonder that those who attain to this beatific vision are unwilling to descend to human affairs; for their souls are ever hastening into the upper world where they desire to dwell; which desire of theirs is very natural, if our allegory may be trusted.

Yes, very natural.

Plato. "Republic." *The Dialogues of Plato.* Vol. 2. Translated by Benjamin Jowett. Oxford: Oxford University Press, 1892.

The Ring of Gyges
Plato

They say that to do injustice is, by nature, good; to suffer injustice, evil; but that the evil is greater than the good. And so when men have both done and suffered injustice and have had experience of both, not being able to avoid the one and obtain the other, they think that they had better agree among themselves to have neither; hence there arise laws and mutual covenants; and that which is ordained by law is termed by them lawful and just. This they affirm to be the origin and nature of justice; it is a mean or compromise, between the best of all, which is to do injustice and not be punished, and the worst of all, which is to suffer injustice without the power of retaliation; and justice, being at a middle point between the two, is tolerated not as a good, but as the lesser evil, and honored by reason of the inability of men to do injustice. For no man who is worthy to be called a man would ever submit to such an agreement if he were able to resist; he would be mad if he did. Such is the received account, Socrates, of the nature and origin of justice.

Now that those who practise justice do so involuntarily and because they have not the power to be unjust will best appear if we imagine something of this kind: having given both to the just and the unjust power to do what they will, let us watch and see whither desire will lead them; then we shall discover in the very act the just and unjust man to be proceeding along the same road, following their interest, which all natures deem to be their good, and are only diverted into the path of justice by the force of law. The liberty which we are supposing may be most completely given to them in the form of such a power as is said to have been possessed by Gyges, the ancestor of Croesus the Lydian. According to the tradition, Gyges was a shepherd in the service of the King of Lydia; there was a great storm, and an earthquake made an opening in the earth at the place where he was feeding his flock. Amazed at the sight, he descended into the opening, where, among other marvels, he beheld a hollow brazen horse, having doors, at which he, stooping and looking in, saw a dead body of stature, as appeared to him, more than human and having nothing on but a gold ring; this he took from the finger of the dead and reascended. Now the shepherds met together, according to custom, that they might send their monthly report about the flocks to the King; into their assembly he came having the ring on his finger, and as he was sitting among them he chanced to turn the collet of the ring inside his hand, when instantly he became invisible to the rest of the company and they began to speak of him as if he were no longer present. He was astonished at this, and again touching the ring he turned the collet outward and reappeared; he made several trials of the ring, and always with the same result—when he turned the collet inward he became invisible, when outward he reappeared. Whereupon he contrived to be chosen one of the messengers who were sent to the court; where as soon as he arrived he seduced the Queen, and with her help conspired against the King and slew him and took the kingdom.

Suppose now that there were two such magic rings, and the just put on one of them and the unjust the other; no man can be imagined to be of such an iron nature that he would stand fast in justice. No man would keep his hands off what was not his own when he could safely take what he liked out of the market, or go into houses and lie with anyone at his pleasure, or kill or release from prison whom he would, and in all respects be like a god among men. Then the actions of the just would be as the actions of the unjust; they would both come at last to the same point. And this we may truly affirm to be a great proof that a man is just, not willingly or because he thinks that justice is any good to him individually, but of necessity, for wherever anyone thinks that he can safely be unjust, there he is unjust. For all men believe in their hearts that injustice is far more profitable to the individual than justice, and he who argues as I have been supposing, will say that they are right. If you could imagine anyone obtaining this power of becoming invisible, and never doing any wrong or touching what was another's, he would be thought by the lookerson to be a most wretched idiot, although they would praise him to one another's faces, and keep up appearances with one another from a fear that they too might suffer injustice. Enough of this.

Now, if we are to form a real judgment of the life of the just and un-just, we must isolate them; there is no other way; and how is the isolation to be effected? I answer: Let the unjust man be entirely unjust, and the just man entirely just; nothing is to be taken away from either of them, and both are to be perfectly furnished for the work of their respective lives. First, let the unjust be like other distinguished masters of craft; like the skilful pilot or physician, who knows intuitively his own powers and keeps within their limits, and who, if he fails at any point, is able to recover himself. So let the unjust make his unjust attempts in the right way, and lie hidden if he means to be great in his injustice (he who is found out is nobody): for the highest reach of injustice is, to be deemed just when you are not. Therefore I say that in the perfectly unjust man we must assume the most perfect injustice; there is to be no deduction, but we must allow him, while doing the most unjust acts, to have acquired the greatest reputation for justice. If he have taken a false step he must be able to recover himself; he must be one who can speak with effect, if any of his deeds come to light, and who can force his way where force is required by his courage and strength, and command of money and friends. And at his side let us place the just man in his nobleness and simplic-ity, wishing, as Aeschylus says, to be and not to seem good. There must be no seeming, for if he seem to be just he will be honored and rewarded, and then we shall not know whether he is just for the sake of justice or for the sake of honor and rewards; therefore, let him be clothed in justice only, and have no other covering; and he must be imagined in a state of life the opposite of the former. Let him be the best of men, and let him be thought the worst; then he will have been put to the proof; and we shall see whether he will be affected by the fear of infamy and its consequences. And let him continue thus to the hour of death; being just and seeming to be unjust. When both have reached the uttermost extreme, the one of justice and the other of injustice, let judgment be given which of them is the happier of the two.

Heavens! my dear Glaucon, I said, how energetically you polish them up for the decision, first one and then the other, as if they were two statues.

I do my best, he said. And now that we know what they are like there is no difficulty in tracing out the sort of life which awaits either of them. This I will proceed to describe; but as you may think the description a little too coarse, I ask you to suppose, Socrates, that the words which follow are not mine. Let me put them into the mouths of the eulogists of injustice: They will tell you that the just man who is thought unjust will be scourged, racked, bound—will have his eyes burnt out; and, at last, after suffering every kind of evil, he will be impaled. Then he will understand that he ought to seem only, and not to be, just; the words of Aeschylus may be more truly spoken of the unjust than of the just. For the unjust is pursuing a reality; he does not live with a view to appearances—he wants to be really unjust and not to seem only—"His mind has a soil deep and fertile, Out of which spring his prudent counsels."

In the first place, he is thought just, and therefore bears rule in the city; he can marry whom he will, and give in marriage to whom he will; also he can trade and deal where he likes, and always to his own advantage, because he has no misgivings about injustice; and at every contest, whether in public or private, he gets the better of his antagonists, and gains at their expense, and is rich, and out of his gains he can benefit his friends, and harm his enemies; moreover, he can offer sacrifices, and dedicate gifts to the gods abundantly and magnificently, and can honor the gods or any man whom he wants to honor in a far better style than the just, and therefore he is likely to be dearer than they are to the gods. And thus, Socrates, gods and men are said to unite in making the life of the unjust better than the life of the just.

Plato. "Republic." *The Dialogues of Plato.* Vol. 2. Translated by Benjamin Jowett. Oxford: Oxford University Press, 1892.

Phaedrus
Plato

The soul through all her being is immortal, for that which is ever in motion is immortal; but that which moves another and is moved by another, in ceasing to move ceases also to live. Only the self-moving, never leaving self, never ceases to move, and is the fountain and beginning of motion to all that moves besides. Now, the beginning is unbegotten, for that which is begotten has a beginning; but the beginning is begotten of nothing, for if it were begotten of something, then the begotten would not come from a beginning. But if unbegotten, it must also be indestructible; for if beginning were destroyed, there could be no beginning out of anything, nor anything out of a beginning; and all things must have a beginning. And therefore the self-moving is the beginning of motion; and this can neither be destroyed nor begotten, else the whole heavens and all creation would collapse and stand still, and never again have motion or birth. But if the self-moving is proved to be immortal, he who affirms that self-motion is the very idea and essence of the soul will not be put to confusion. For the body which is moved from without is soulless; but that which is moved from within has a soul, for such is the nature of the soul. But if this be true, must not the soul be the self-moving, and therefore of necessity unbegotten and immortal? Enough of the soul's immortality.

Of the nature of the soul, though her true form be ever a theme of large and more than mortal discourse, let me speak briefly, and in a figure. And let the figure be composite-a pair of winged horses and a charioteer. Now the winged horses and the charioteers of the gods are all of them noble and of noble descent, but those of other races are mixed; the human charioteer drives his in a pair; and one of them is noble and of noble breed, and the other is ignoble and of ignoble breed; and the driving of them of necessity gives a great deal of trouble to him. I will endeavour to explain to you in what way the mortal differs from the immortal creature. The soul in her totality has the care of inanimate being everywhere, and traverses the whole heaven in divers forms appearing--when perfect and fully winged she soars upward, and orders the whole world; whereas the imperfect soul, losing her wings and drooping in her flight at last settles on the solid ground-there, finding a home, she receives an earthly frame which appears to be self-moved, but is really moved by her power; and this composition of soul and body is called a living and mortal creature. For immortal no such union can be reasonably believed to be; although fancy, not having seen nor surely known the nature of God, may imagine an immortal creature having both a body and also a soul which are united throughout all time. Let that, however, be as God wills, and be spoken of acceptably to him. And now let us ask the reason why the soul loses her wings!

The wing is the corporeal element which is most akin to the divine, and which by nature tends to soar aloft and carry that which gravitates downwards into the upper region, which is the habitation of the gods. The divine is beauty, wisdom, goodness, and the like; and by these the wing of the soul is nourished, and grows apace; but when fed upon evil and foulness and the opposite of good, wastes and falls away. Zeus, the mighty lord, holding the reins of a winged chariot, leads the way in heaven, ordering all and taking care of all; and there follows him the array of gods and demigods, marshalled in eleven bands; Hestia alone abides at home in the house of heaven; of the rest they who are reckoned among the princely twelve march in their appointed order. They see many blessed sights in the inner heaven, and there are many ways to and fro, along which the blessed gods are passing, every one doing his own work; he may follow who will and can, for jealousy has no place in the celestial choir. But when they go to banquet and festival, then they move up the steep to the top of the vault of heaven. The chariots of the gods in even poise, obeying the rein, glide rapidly; but the others labour, for the vicious steed goes heavily, weighing down the charioteer to the earth when his steed has not been thoroughly trained:-and this is the hour of agony and extremest conflict for the soul. For the immortals, when they are at the end of their course, go forth and stand upon the outside of heaven, and the revolution of the spheres carries them round, and they behold the things beyond. But of the heaven which is above the heavens, what earthly poet ever did or ever will sing worthily? It is such as I will describe; for I must dare to speak the truth, when truth is my theme. There abides the very being with which true knowledge is concerned; the colourless, formless, intangible essence, visible only to mind, the pilot of the soul. The divine intelligence, being nurtured upon mind and pure knowledge, and the intelligence of every soul which is capable of receiving the food proper to it, rejoices at beholding reality, and once more gazing upon truth, is replenished and made glad, until the revolution of the worlds brings her round again to the same place. In the revolution she beholds justice, and temperance, and knowledge absolute, not in the form of generation or of relation, which men call existence, but knowledge absolute in existence absolute; and beholding the other true existences in like manner, and feasting upon them, she passes down into the interior of the heavens and returns home; and there the charioteer putting up his horses at the stall, gives them ambrosia to eat and nectar to drink.

Such is the life of the gods; but of other souls, that which follows God best and is likest to him lifts the head of the charioteer into the outer world, and is carried round in the revolution, troubled indeed by the steeds, and with difficulty beholding true being; while another only rises and falls, and sees, and again fails to see by reason of the unruliness of the steeds. The rest of the souls are also longing after the upper world and they all follow, but not being strong enough they are carried round below the surface, plunging, treading on one another, each striving to be first; and there is confusion and perspiration and the extremity of effort; and many of them are lamed or have their wings broken through the ill-driving of the charioteers; and all of them after a fruitless toil, not having attained to the mysteries of true being, go away, and feed upon opinion. The reason why the souls exhibit this exceeding eagerness to behold the plain of truth is that pasturage is found there, which is suited to the highest part of the soul; and the wing on which the soul soars is nourished with this. And there is a law of Destiny, that the soul which attains any vision of truth in company with a god is preserved from harm until the next period, and if attaining always is always unharmed. But when she is unable to follow, and fails to behold the truth, and through some ill-hap sinks beneath the double load of forgetfulness and vice, and her wings fall from her and she drops to the ground, then the law ordains that this soul shall at her first birth pass, not into any other animal, but only into man; and the soul which has seen most of truth shall come to the birth as a philosopher, or artist, or some musical and loving nature; that which has seen truth in the second degree shall be some righteous king or warrior chief; the soul which is of the third class shall be a politician, or economist, or trader; the fourth shall be lover of gymnastic toils, or a physician; the fifth shall lead the life of a prophet or hierophant; to the sixth the character of poet or some other imitative artist will be assigned; to the seventh the life of an artisan or husbandman; to the eighth that of a sophist or demagogue; to the ninth that of a tyrant-all these are states of probation, in which he who does righteously improves, and he who does unrighteously, improves, and he who does unrighteously, deteriorates his lot.

Ten thousand years must elapse before the soul of each one can return to the place from whence she came, for she cannot grow her wings in less; only the soul of a philosopher, guileless and true, or the soul of a lover, who is not devoid of philosophy, may acquire wings in the third of the recurring periods of a thousand years; he is distinguished from the ordinary good man who gains wings in three thousand years:-and they who choose this life three times in succession have wings given them, and go away at the end of three thousand years. But the others receive judgment when they have completed their first life, and after the judgment they go, some of them to the houses of correction which are under the earth, and are punished; others to some place in heaven whither they are lightly borne by justice, and there they live in a manner worthy of the life which they led here when in the form of men. And at the end of the first thousand years the good souls and also the evil souls both come to draw lots and choose their second life, and they may take any which they please. The soul of a man may pass into the life of a beast, or from the beast return again into the man. But the soul which has never seen the truth will not pass into the human form. For a man must have intelligence of universals, and be able to proceed from the many particulars of sense to one conception of reason;-this is the recollection of those things which our soul once saw while following God-when regardless of that which we now call being she raised her head up towards the true being. And therefore the mind of the philosopher alone has wings; and this is just, for he is always, according to the measure of his abilities, clinging in recollection to those things in which God abides, and in beholding which He is what He is. And he who employs aright these memories is ever being initiated into perfect mysteries and alone becomes truly perfect. But, as he forgets earthly interests and is rapt in the divine, the vulgar deem him mad, and rebuke him; they do not see that he is inspired.

Thus far I have been speaking of the fourth and last kind of madness, which is imputed to him who, when he sees the beauty of earth, is transported with the recollection of the true beauty; he would like to fly away, but he cannot; he is like a bird fluttering and looking upward and careless of the world below; and he is therefore thought to be mad. And I have shown this of all inspirations to be the noblest and highest and the offspring of the highest to him who has or shares in it, and that he who loves the beautiful is called a lover because he partakes of it. For, as has been already said, every soul of man has in the way of nature beheld true being; this was the condition of her passing into the form of man. But all souls do not easily recall the things of the other world; they may have seen them for a short time only, or they may have been unfortunate in their earthly lot, and, having had their hearts turned to unrighteousness through some corrupting influence, they may have lost the memory of the holy things which once they saw. Few only retain an adequate remembrance of them; and they, when they behold here any image of that other world, are rapt in amazement; but they are ignorant of what this rapture means, because they do not clearly perceive. For there is no light of justice or temperance or any of the higher ideas which are precious to souls in the earthly copies of them: they are seen through a glass dimly; and there are few who, going to the images, behold in them the realities, and these only with difficulty. There was a time when with the rest of the happy band they saw beauty shining in brightness-we philosophers following in the train of Zeus, others in company with other gods; and then we beheld the beatific vision and were initiated into a mystery which may be truly called most blessed, celebrated by us in our state of innocence, before we had any experience of evils to come, when we were admitted to the sight of apparitions innocent and simple and calm and happy, which we beheld shining impure light, pure ourselves and not yet enshrined in that living tomb which we carry about, now that we are imprisoned in the body, like an oyster in his shell. Let me linger over the memory of scenes which have passed away.

But of beauty, I repeat again that we saw her there shining in company with the celestial forms; and coming to earth we find her here too, shining in clearness through the clearest aperture of sense. For sight is the most piercing of our bodily senses; though not by that is wisdom seen; her loveliness would have been transporting if there had been a visible image of her, and the other ideas, if they had visible counterparts, would be equally lovely. But this is the privilege of beauty, that being the loveliest she is also the most palpable to sight. Now he who is not newly initiated or who has become corrupted, does not easily rise out of this world to the sight of true beauty in the other; he looks only at her earthly namesake, and instead of being awed at the sight of her, he is given over to pleasure, and like a brutish beast he rushes on to enjoy and beget; he consorts with wantonness, and is not afraid or ashamed of pursuing pleasure in violation of nature. But he whose initiation is recent, and who has been the spectator of many glories in the other world, is amazed when he sees any one having a godlike face or form, which is the expression of divine beauty; and at first a shudder runs through him, and again the old awe steals over him; then looking upon the face of his beloved as of a god he reverences him, and if he were not afraid of being thought a downright madman, he would sacrifice to his beloved as to the image of a god; then while he gazes on him there is a sort of reaction, and the shudder passes into an unusual heat and perspiration; for, as he receives the effluence of beauty through the eyes, the wing moistens and he warms. And as he warms, the parts out of which the wing grew, and which had been hitherto closed and rigid, and had prevented the wing from shooting forth, are melted, and as nourishment streams upon him, the lower end of the wings begins to swell and grow from the root upwards; and the growth extends under the whole soul-for once the whole was winged.

During this process the whole soul is all in a state of ebullition and effervescence,-which may be compared to the irritation and uneasiness in the gums at the time of cutting teeth,-bubbles up, and has a feeling of uneasiness and tickling; but when in like manner the soul is beginning to grow wings, the beauty of the beloved meets her eye and she receives the sensible warm motion of particles which flow towards her, therefore called emotion (imeros), and is refreshed and warmed by them, and then she ceases from her pain with joy. But when she is parted from her beloved and her moisture fails, then the orifices of the passage out of which the wing shoots dry up and close, and intercept the germ of the wing; which, being shut up with the emotion, throbbing as with the pulsations of an artery, pricks the aperture which is nearest, until at length the entire soul is pierced and maddened and pained, and at the recollection of beauty is again delighted. And from both of them together the soul is oppressed at the strangeness of her condition, and is in a great strait and excitement, and in her madness can neither sleep by night nor abide in her place by day. And wherever she thinks that she will behold the beautiful one, thither in her desire she runs. And when she has seen him, and bathed herself in the waters of beauty, her constraint is loosened, and she is refreshed, and has no more pangs and pains; and this is the sweetest of all pleasures at the time, and is the reason why the soul of the lover will never forsake his beautiful one, whom he esteems above all; he has forgotten mother and brethren and companions, and he thinks nothing of the neglect and loss of his property; the rules and proprieties of life, on which he formerly prided himself, he now despises, and is ready to sleep like a servant, wherever he is allowed, as near as he can to his desired one, who is the object of his worship, and the physician who can alone assuage the greatness of his pain. And this state, my dear imaginary youth to whom I am talking, is by men called love, and among the gods has a name at which you, in your simplicity, may be inclined to mock; there are two lines in the apocryphal writings of Homer in which the name occurs. One of them is rather outrageous, and not altogether metrical. They are as follows:

> Mortals call him fluttering love,
> But the immortals call him winged one,
> Because the growing of wings is a necessity to him. You may believe this, but not unless you like. At any rate the loves of lovers and their causes are such as I have described.

Now the lover who is taken to be the attendant of Zeus is better able to bear the winged god, and can endure a heavier burden; but the attendants and companions of Ares, when under the influence of love, if they fancy that they have been at all wronged, are ready to kill and put an end to themselves and their beloved. And he who follows in the train of any other god, while he is unspoiled and the impression lasts, honours and imitates him, as far as he is able; and after the manner of his god he behaves in his intercourse with his beloved and with the rest of the world during the first period of his earthly existence. Every one chooses his love from the ranks of beauty according to his character, and this he makes his god, and fashions and adorns as a sort of image which he is to fall down and worship. The followers of Zeus desire that their beloved should have a soul like him; and therefore they seek out some one of a philosophical and imperial nature, and when they have found him and loved him, they do all they can to confirm such a nature in him, and if they have no experience of such a disposition hitherto, they learn of any one who can teach them, and themselves follow in the same way. And they have the less difficulty in finding the nature of their own god in themselves, because they have been compelled to gaze intensely on him; their recollection clings to him, and they become possessed of him, and receive from him their character and disposition, so far as man can participate in God. The qualities of their god they attribute to the beloved, wherefore they love him all the more, and if, like the Bacchic Nymphs, they draw inspiration from Zeus, they pour out their own fountain upon him, wanting to make him as like as possible to their own god. But those who are the followers of Here seek a royal love, and when they have found him they do just the same with him; and in like manner the followers of Apollo, and of every other god walking in the ways of their god, seek a love who is to be made like him whom they serve, and when they have found him, they themselves imitate their god, and persuade their love to do the same, and educate him into the manner and nature of the god as far as they each can; for no feelings of envy or jealousy are entertained by them towards their beloved, but they do their utmost to create in him the greatest likeness of themselves and of the god whom they honour. Thus fair and blissful to the beloved is the desire of the inspired lover, and the initiation of which I speak into the mysteries of true love, if he be captured by the lover and their purpose is effected. Now the beloved is taken captive in the following manner:

As I said at the beginning of this tale, I divided each soul into three-two horses and a charioteer; and one of the horses was good and the other bad: the division may remain, but I have not yet explained in what the goodness or badness of either consists, and to that I will proceed. The right-hand horse is upright and cleanly made; he has a lofty neck and an aquiline nose; his colour is white, and his eyes dark; he is a lover of honour and modesty and temperance, and the follower of true glory; he needs no touch of the whip, but is guided by word and admonition only. The other is a crooked lumbering animal, put together anyhow; he has a short thick neck; he is flat-faced and of a dark colour, with grey eyes and blood-red complexion; the mate of insolence and pride, shag-eared and deaf, hardly yielding to whip and spur. Now when the charioteer beholds the vision of love, and has his whole soul warmed through sense, and is full of the prickings and ticklings of desire, the obedient steed, then as always under the government of shame, refrains from leaping on the beloved; but the other, heedless of the pricks and of the blows of the whip, plunges and runs away, giving all manner of trouble to his companion and the charioteer, whom he forces to approach the beloved and to remember the joys of love. They at first indignantly oppose him and will not be urged on to do terrible and unlawful deeds; but at last, when he persists in plaguing them, they yield and agree to do as he bids them.

And now they are at the spot and behold the flashing beauty of the beloved; which when the charioteer sees, his memory is carried to the true beauty, whom he beholds in company with Modesty like an image placed upon a holy pedestal. He sees her, but he is afraid and falls backwards in adoration, and by his fall is compelled to pull back the reins with such violence as to bring both the steeds on their haunches, the one willing and unresisting, the unruly one very unwilling; and when they have gone back a little, the one is overcome with shame and wonder, and his whole soul is bathed in perspiration; the other, when the pain is over which the bridle and the fall had given him, having with difficulty taken breath, is full of wrath and reproaches, which he heaps upon the charioteer and his fellow-steed, for want of courage and manhood, declaring that they have been false to their agreement and guilty of desertion. Again they refuse, and again he urges them on, and will scarce yield to their prayer that he would wait until another time. When the appointed hour comes, they make as if they had forgotten, and he reminds them, fighting and neighing and dragging them on, until at length he, on the same thoughts intent, forces them to draw near again. And when they are near he stoops his head and puts up his tail, and takes the bit in his teeth. and pulls shamelessly. Then the charioteer is. worse off than ever; he falls back like a racer at the barrier, and with a still more violent wrench drags the bit out of the teeth of the wild steed and covers his abusive tongue and-jaws with blood, and forces his legs and haunches to the ground and punishes him sorely. And when this has happened several times and the villain has ceased from his wanton way, he is tamed and humbled, and follows the will of the charioteer, and when he sees the beautiful one he is ready to die of fear. And from that time forward the soul of the lover follows the beloved in modesty and holy fear.

And so the beloved who, like a god, has received every true and loyal service from his lover, not in pretence but in reality, being also himself of a nature friendly to his admirer, if in former days he has blushed to own his passion and turned away his lover, because his youthful companions or others slanderously told him that he would be disgraced, now as years advance, at the appointed age and time, is led to receive him into communion. For fate which has ordained that there shall be no friendship among the evil has also ordained that there shall ever be friendship among the good. And the beloved when he has received him into communion and intimacy, is quite amazed at the good-will of the lover; he recognises that the inspired friend is worth all other friends or kinsmen; they have nothing of friendship in them worthy to be compared with his. And when his feeling continues and he is nearer to him and embraces him, in gymnastic exercises and at other times of meeting, then the fountain of that stream, which Zeus when he was in love with Ganymede named Desire, overflows upon the lover, and some enters into his soul, and some when he is filled flows out again; and as a breeze or an echo rebounds from the smooth rocks and returns whence it came, so does the stream of beauty, passing through the eyes which are the windows of the soul, come back to the beautiful one; there arriving and quickening the passages of the wings, watering. them and inclining them to grow, and filling the soul of the beloved also with love. And thus he loves, but he knows not what; he does not understand and cannot explain his own state; he appears to have caught the infection of blindness from another; the lover is his mirror in whom he is beholding himself, but he is not aware of this. When he is with the lover, both cease from their pain, but when he is away then he longs as he is longed for, and has love's image, love for love (Anteros) lodging in his breast, which he calls and believes to be not love but friendship only, and his desire is as the desire of the other, but weaker; he wants to see him, touch him, kiss him, embrace him, and probably not long afterwards his desire is accomplished. When they meet, the wanton steed of the lover has a word to say to the charioteer; he would like to have a little pleasure in return for many pains, but the wanton steed of the beloved says not a word, for he is bursting with passion which he understands not;-he throws his arms round the lover and embraces him as his dearest friend; and, when they are side by side, he is not in it state in which he can refuse the lover anything, if he ask him; although his fellow-steed and the charioteer oppose him with the arguments of shame and reason.

After this their happiness depends upon their self-control; if the better elements of the mind which lead to order and philosophy prevail, then they pass their life here in happiness and harmony-masters of themselves and orderly-enslaving the vicious and emancipating the virtuous elements of the soul; and when the end comes, they are light and winged for flight, having conquered in one of the three heavenly or truly Olympian victories; nor can human discipline or divine inspiration confer any greater blessing on man than this. If, on the other hand, they leave philosophy and lead the lower life of ambition, then probably, after wine or in some other careless hour, the two wanton animals take the two souls when off their guard and bring them together, and they accomplish that desire of their hearts which to the many is bliss; and this having once enjoyed they continue to enjoy, yet rarely because they have not the approval of the whole soul. They too are dear, but not so dear to one another as the others, either at the time of their love or afterwards. They consider that they have given and taken from each other the most sacred pledges, and they may not break them and fall into enmity. At last they pass out of the body, unwinged, but eager to soar, and thus obtain no mean reward of love and madness. For those who have once begun the heavenward pilgrimage may not go down again to darkness and the journey beneath the earth, but they live in light always; happy companions in their pilgrimage, and when the time comes at which they receive their wings they have the same plumage because of their love.

Thus great are the heavenly blessings which the friendship of a lover will confer upon you, my youth. Whereas the attachment of the non-lover, which is alloyed with a worldly prudence and has worldly and niggardly ways of doling out benefits, will breed in your soul those vulgar qualities which the populace applaud, will send you bowling round the earth during a period of nine thousand years, and leave, you a fool in the world below.

"The Phaedrus." The Dialogues of Plato. Vol. 1. Trans. Benjamin Jowett. Oxford University Press, 1892.

The Four Causes

Aristotle

Now that we have established these distinctions, we must proceed to consider causes, their character and number. Knowledge is the object of our inquiry, and men do not think they know a thing till they have grasped the 'why' of (which is to grasp its primary cause). So clearly we too must do this as regards both coming to be and passing away and every kind of physical change, in order that, knowing their principles, we may try to refer to these principles each of our problems.

In one sense, then, (1) that out of which a thing comes to be and which persists, is called 'cause', e.g. the bronze of the statue, the silver of the bowl, and the genera of which the bronze and the silver are species.

In another sense (2) the form or the archetype, i.e. the statement of the essence, and its genera, are called 'causes' (e.g. of the octave the relation of 2:1, and generally number), and the parts in the definition.

Again (3) the primary source of the change or coming to rest; e.g. the man who gave advice is a cause, the father is cause of the child, and generally what makes of what is made and what causes change of what is changed.

Again (4) in the sense of end or 'that for the sake of which' a thing is done, e.g. health is the cause of walking about. ('Why is he walking about?' we say. 'To be healthy', and, having said that, we think we have assigned the cause.) The same is true also of all the intermediate steps which are brought about through the action of something else as means towards the end, e.g. reduction of flesh, purging, drugs, or surgical instruments are means towards health. All these things are 'for the sake of' the end, though they differ from one another in that some are activities, others instruments.

This then perhaps exhausts the number of ways in which the term 'cause' is used.

As the word has several senses, it follows that there are several causes of the same thing not merely in virtue of a concomitant attribute), e.g. both the art of the sculptor and the bronze are causes of the statue. These are causes of the statue qua statue, not in virtue of anything else that it may be-only not in the same way, the one being the material cause, the other the cause whence the motion comes. Some things cause each other reciprocally, e.g. hard work causes fitness and vice versa, but again not in the same way, but the one as end, the other as the origin of change. Further the same thing is the cause of contrary results. For that which by its presence brings about one result is sometimes blamed for bringing about the contrary by its absence. Thus we ascribe the wreck of a ship to the absence of the pilot whose presence was the cause of its safety.

All the causes now mentioned fall into four familiar divisions. The letters are the causes of syllables, the material of artificial products, fire, &c., of bodies, the parts of the whole, and the premisses of the conclusion, in the sense of 'that from which'. Of these pairs the one set are causes in the sense of substratum, e.g. the parts, the other set in the sense of essence-the whole and the combination and the form. But the seed and the doctor and the adviser, and generally the maker, are all sources whence the change or stationariness originates, while the others are causes in the sense of the end or the good of the rest; for 'that for the sake of which' means what is best and the end of the things that lead up to it. (Whether we say the 'good itself or the 'apparent good' makes no difference.) Such then is the number and nature of the kinds of cause.

Now the modes of causation are many, though when brought under heads they too can be reduced in number. For 'cause' is used in many senses and even within the same kind one may be prior to another (e.g. the doctor and the expert are causes of health, the relation 2:1 and number of the octave), and always what is inclusive to what is particular. Another mode of causation is the incidental and its genera, e.g. in one way 'Polyclitus', in another 'sculptor' is the cause of a statue, because 'being Polyclitus' and 'sculptor' are incidentally conjoined. Also the classes in which the incidental attribute is included; thus 'a man' could be said to be the cause of a statue or, generally, 'a living creature'. An incidental attribute too may be more or less remote, e.g. suppose that 'a pale man' or 'a musical man' were said to be the cause of the statue.

All causes, both proper and incidental, may be spoken of either as potential or as actual; e.g. the cause of a house being built is either 'house-builder' or 'house-builder building'.

Similar distinctions can be made in the things of which the causes are causes, e.g. of 'this statue' or of 'statue' or of 'image' generally, of 'this bronze' or of 'bronze' or of 'material' generally. So too with the incidental attributes. Again we may use a complex expression for either and say, e.g. neither 'Polyclitus' nor 'sculptor' but 'Polyclitus, sculptor'.

All these various uses, however, come to six in number, under each of which again the usage is twofold. Cause means either what is particular or a genus, or an incidental attribute or a genus of that, and these either as a complex or each by itself; and all six either as actual or as potential. The difference is this much, that causes which are actually at work and particular exist and cease to exist simultaneously with their effect, e.g. this healing person with this being-healed person and that house-building man with that being-built house; but this is not always true of potential causes--the house and the housebuilder do not pass away simultaneously.

In investigating the cause of each thing it is always necessary to seek what is most precise (as also in other things): thus man builds because he is a builder, and a builder builds in virtue of his art of building. This last cause then is prior: and so generally. Further, generic effects should be assigned to generic causes, particular effects to particular causes, e.g. statue to sculptor, this statue to this sculptor; and powers are relative to possible effects, actually operating causes to things which are actually being effected.

This must suffice for our account of the number of causes and the modes of causation.

Aristotle. *Physica*, Trans. R. P. Hardie and R. K. Gaye. *The Works of Aristotle*. Vol. II. Oxford: Clarendon Press, 1930.

The Unmoved Mover
Aristotle

Part 4

Now of things that cause motion or suffer motion, to some the motion is accidental, to others essential: thus it is accidental to what merely belongs to or contains as a part a thing that causes motion or suffers motion, essential to a thing that causes motion or suffers motion not merely by belonging to such a thing or containing it as a part.

Of things to which the motion is essential some derive their motion from themselves, others from something else: and in some cases their motion is natural, in others violent and unnatural. Thus in things that derive their motion from themselves, e.g. all animals, the motion is natural (for when an animal is in motion its motion is derived from itself): and whenever the source of the motion of a thing is in the thing itself we say that the motion of that thing is natural. Therefore the animal as a whole moves itself naturally: but the body of the animal may be in motion unnaturally as well as naturally: it depends upon the kind of motion that it may chance to be suffering and the kind of element of which it is composed. And the motion of things that derive their motion from something else is in some cases natural, in other unnatural: e.g. upward motion of earthy things and downward motion of fire are unnatural. Moreover the parts of animals are often in motion in an unnatural way, their positions and the character of the motion being abnormal. The fact that a thing that is in motion derives its motion from something is most evident in things that are in motion unnaturally, because in such cases it is clear that the motion is derived from something other than the thing itself. Next to things that are in motion unnaturally those whose motion while natural is derived from themselves-e.g. animals-make this fact clear: for here the uncertainty is not as to whether the motion is derived from something but as to how we ought to distinguish in the thing between the movent and the moved. It would seem that in animals, just as in ships and things not naturally organized, that which causes motion is separate from that which suffers motion, and that it is only in this sense that the animal as a whole causes its own motion.

The greatest difficulty, however, is presented by the remaining case of those that we last distinguished. Where things derive their motion from something else we distinguished the cases in which the motion is unnatural:

we are left with those that are to be contrasted with the others by reason of the fact that the motion is natural. It is in these cases that difficulty would be experienced in deciding whence the motion is derived, e.g. in the case of light and heavy things. When these things are in motion to positions the reverse of those they would properly occupy, their motion is violent: when they are in motion to their proper positions-the light thing up and the heavy thing down-their motion is natural; but in this latter case it is no longer evident, as it is when the motion is unnatural, whence their motion is derived. It is impossible to say that their motion is derived from themselves: this is a characteristic of life and peculiar to living things. Further, if it were, it would have been in their power to stop themselves (I mean that if e.g. a thing can cause itself to walk it can also cause itself not to walk), and so, since on this supposition fire itself possesses the power of upward locomotion, it is clear that it should also possess the power of downward locomotion. Moreover if things move themselves, it would be unreasonable to suppose that in only one kind of motion is their motion derived from themselves. Again, how can anything of continuous and naturally connected substance move itself? In so far as a thing is one and continuous not merely in virtue of contact, it is impassive: it is only in so far as a thing is divided that one part of it is by nature active and another passive. Therefore none of the things that we are now considering move themselves (for they are of naturally connected substance), nor does anything else that is continuous: in each case the movent must be separate from the moved, as we see to be the case with inanimate things when an animate thing moves them. It is the fact that these things also always derive their motion from something: what it is would become evident if we were to distinguish the different kinds of cause.

The above-mentioned distinctions can also be made in the case of things that cause motion: some of them are capable of causing motion unnaturally (e.g. the lever is not naturally capable of moving the weight), others naturally (e.g. what is actually hot is naturally capable of moving what is potentially hot): and similarly in the case of all other things of this kind.

In the same way, too, what is potentially of a certain quality or of a certain quantity in a certain place is naturally movable when it contains the corresponding principle in itself and not accidentally (for the same thing may be both of a certain quality and of a certain quantity, but the one is an accidental, not an essential property of the other). So when fire or earth is moved by something the motion is violent when it is unnatural, and natural when it brings to actuality the proper activities that they potentially possess. But the fact that the term 'potentially' is used in more than one sense is the reason why it is not evident whence such motions as the upward motion of fire and the downward motion of earth are derived. One who is learning a science potentially knows it in a different sense from one who while already possessing the knowledge is not actually exercising it. Wherever we have something capable of acting and something capable of being correspondingly acted on, in the event of any such pair being in contact what is potential becomes at times actual: e.g. the learner becomes from one potential something another potential something: for one who possesses knowledge of a science but is not actually exercising it knows the science potentially in a sense, though not in the same sense as he knew it potentially before he learnt it. And when he is in this condition, if something does not prevent him, he actively exercises his knowledge: otherwise he would be in the contradictory state of not knowing. In regard to natural bodies also the case is similar. Thus what is cold is potentially hot: then a change takes place and it is fire, and it burns, unless something prevents and hinders it. So, too, with heavy and light: light is generated from heavy, e.g. air from water (for water is the first thing that is potentially light), and air is actually light, and will at once realize its proper activity as such unless something prevents it. The activity of lightness consists in the light thing being in a certain situation, namely high up: when it is in the contrary situation, it is being prevented from rising. The case is similar also in regard to quantity and quality. But, be it noted, this is the question we are trying to answer-how can we account for the motion of light things and heavy things to their proper situations? The reason for it is that they have a natural tendency respectively towards a certain position: and this constitutes the essence of lightness and heaviness, the former being determined by an upward, the latter by a downward, tendency. As we have said, a thing may be potentially light or heavy in more senses than one. Thus not only when a thing is water is it in a sense potentially light, but when it has become air it may be still potentially light: for it may be that through some hindrance it does not occupy an upper position, whereas, if what hinders it is removed, it realizes its activity and continues to rise higher. The process whereby what is of a certain quality changes to a condition of active existence is similar: thus the exercise of knowledge follows at once upon the possession of it unless something prevents it. So, too, what is of a certain quantity extends itself over a certain space unless something prevents it. The thing in a sense is and in a sense is not moved by one who moves what is obstructing and preventing its motion (e.g. one who pulls away a pillar from under a roof or one who removes a stone from a wineskin in the water is the accidental cause of motion): and in the same way the real cause of the motion of a ball rebounding from a wall is not the wall but the thrower. So it is clear that in all these cases the thing does not move itself, but it contains within itself the source of motion-not of moving something or of causing motion, but of suffering it.

If then the motion of all things that are in motion is either natural or unnatural and violent, and all things whose motion is violent and unnatural are moved by something, and something other than themselves, and again all things whose motion is natural are moved by something-both those that are moved by themselves and those that are not moved by themselves (e.g. light things and heavy things, which are moved either by that which brought the thing into existence as such and made it light and heavy, or by that which released what was hindering and preventing it); then all things that are in motion must be moved by something.

Part 5

Now this may come about in either of two ways. Either the movent is not itself responsible for the motion, which is to be referred to something else which moves the movent, or the movent is itself responsible for the motion. Further, in the latter case, either the movent immediately precedes the last thing in the series, or there may be one or more intermediate links: e.g. the stick moves the stone and is moved by the hand, which again is moved by the man: in the man, however, we have reached a movent that is not so in virtue of being moved by something else. Now we say that the thing is moved both by the last and by the first movent in the series, but more strictly by the first, since the first movent moves the last, whereas the last does not move the first, and the first will move the thing without the last, but the last will not move it without the first: e.g. the stick will not move anything unless it is itself moved by the man. If then everything that is in motion must be moved by something, and the movent must either itself be moved by something else or not, and in the former case there must be some first movent that is not itself moved by anything else, while in the case of the immediate movent being of this kind there is no need of an intermediate movent that is also moved (for it is impossible that there should be an infinite series of movents, each of which is itself moved by something else, since in an infinite series there is no first term)-if then everything that is in motion is moved by something, and the first movent is moved but not by anything else, it much be moved by itself.

This same argument may also be stated in another way as follows. Every movent moves something and moves it with something, either with itself or with something else: e.g. a man moves a thing either himself or with a stick, and a thing is knocked down either by the wind itself or by a stone propelled by the wind. But it is impossible for that with which a thing is moved to move it without being moved by that which imparts motion by its own agency: on the other hand, if a thing imparts motion by its own agency, it is not necessary that there should be anything else with which it imparts motion, whereas if there is a different thing with which it imparts motion, there must be something that imparts motion not with something else but with itself, or else there will be an infinite series. If, then, anything is a movent while being itself moved, the series must stop somewhere and not be infinite. Thus, if the stick moves something in virtue of being moved by the hand, the hand moves the stick: and if something else moves with the hand, the hand also is moved by something different from itself. So when motion by means of an instrument is at each stage caused by something different from the instrument, this must always be preceded by something else which imparts motion with itself. Therefore, if this last movent is in motion and there is nothing else that moves it, it must move itself. So this reasoning also shows that when a thing is moved, if it is not moved immediately by something that moves itself, the series brings us at some time or other to a movent of this kind.

And if we consider the matter in yet a third wa Ly we shall get this same result as follows. If everything that is in motion is moved by something that is in motion, ether this being in motion is an accidental attribute of the movents in question, so that each of them moves something while being itself in motion, but not always because it is itself in motion, or it is not accidental but an essential attribute. Let us consider the former alternative. If then it is an accidental attribute, it is not necessary that that is in motion should be in motion: and if this is so it is clear that there may be a time when nothing that exists is in motion, since the accidental is not necessary but contingent. Now if we assume the existence of a possibility, any conclusion that we thereby reach will not be an impossibility though it may be contrary to fact. But the nonexistence of motion is an impossibility: for we have shown above that there must always be motion.

Moreover, the conclusion to which we have been led is a reasonable one. For there must be three things-the moved, the movent, and the instrument of motion. Now the moved must be in motion, but it need not move anything else: the instrument of motion must both move something else and be itself in motion (for it changes together with the moved, with which it is in contact and continuous, as is clear in the case of things that move other things locally, in which case the two things must up to a certain point be in contact): and the movent-that is to say, that which causes motion in such a manner that it is not merely the instrument of motion-must be unmoved. Now we have visual experience of the last term in this series, namely that which has the capacity of being in motion, but does not contain a motive principle, and also of that which is in motion but is moved by itself and not by anything else: it is reasonable, therefore, not to say necessary, to suppose the existence of the third term also, that which causes motion but is itself unmoved. So, too, Anaxagoras is right when he says that Mind is impassive and unmixed, since he makes it the principle of motion: for it could cause motion in this sense only by being itself unmoved, and have supreme control only by being unmixed.

We will now take the second alternative. If the movement is not accidentally but necessarily in motion-so that, if it were not in motion, it would not move anything-then the movent, in so far as it is in motion, must be in motion in one of two ways: it is moved either as that is which is moved with the same kind of motion, or with a different kind-either that which is heating, I mean, is itself in process of becoming hot, that which is making healthy in process of becoming healthy, and that which is causing locomotion in process of locomotion, or else that which is making healthy is, let us say, in process of locomotion, and that which is causing locomotion in process of, say, increase. But it is evident that this is impossible. For if we adopt the first assumption we have to make it apply within each of the very lowest species into which motion can be divided: e.g. we must say that if some one is teaching some lesson in geometry, he is also in process of being taught that same lesson in geometry, and that if he is throwing he is in process of being thrown in just the same manner. Or if we reject this assumption we must say that one kind of motion is derived from another; e.g. that that which is causing locomotion is in process of increase, that which is causing this increase is in process of being altered by something else, and that which is causing this alteration is in process of suffering some different kind of motion. But the series must stop somewhere, since the kinds of motion are limited; and if we say that the process is reversible, and that that which is causing alteration is in process of locomotion, we do no more than if we had said at the outset that that which

is causing locomotion is in process of locomotion, and that one who is teaching is in process of being taught: for it is clear that everything that is moved
is moved by the movent that is further back in the series as well as by that
which immediately moves it: in fact the earlier movent is that which more
strictly moves it. But this is of course impossible: for it involves the consequence that one who is teaching is in process of learning what he is teaching,
whereas teaching necessarily implies possessing knowledge, and learning
not possessing it. Still more unreasonable is the consequence involved that,
since everything that is moved is moved by something that is itself moved by
something else, everything that has a capacity for causing motion has as such
a corresponding capacity for being moved: i.e. it will have a capacity for
being moved in the sense in which one might say that everything that has a
capacity for making healthy, and exercises that capacity, has as such a capacity for being made healthy, and that which has a capacity for building has as
such a capacity for being built. It will have the capacity for being thus moved
either immediately or through one or more links (as it will if, while everything that has a capacity for causing motion has as such a capacity for being
moved by something else, the motion that it has the capacity for suffering is
not that with which it affects what is next to it, but a motion of a different
kind; e.g. that which has a capacity for making healthy might as such have a
capacity for learn. the series, however, could be traced back, as we said before, until at some time or other we arrived at the same kind of motion). Now
the first alternative is impossible, and the second is fantastic: it is absurd that
that which has a capacity for causing alteration should as such necessarily
have a capacity, let us say, for increase. It is not necessary, therefore, that
that which is moved should always be moved by something else that is itself
moved by something else: so there will be an end to the series. Consequently
the first thing that is in motion will derive its motion either from something
that is at rest or from itself. But if there were any need to consider which of
the two, that which moves itself or that which is moved by something else,
is the cause and principle of motion, every one would decide the former: for
that which is itself independently a cause is always prior as a cause to that
which is so only in virtue of being itself dependent upon something else that
makes it so.

We must therefore make a fresh start and consider the question; if a thing
moves itself, in what sense and in what manner does it do so? Now everything that is in motion must be infinitely divisible, for it has been shown
already in our general course on Physics, that everything that is essentially
in motion is continuous. Now it is impossible that that which moves itself
should in its entirety move itself: for then, while being specifically one and
indivisible, it would as a Whole both undergo and cause the same locomotion
or alteration: thus it would at the same time be both teaching and being taught
(the same thing), or both restoring to and being restored to the same health.
Moreover, we have established the fact that it is the movable that is moved;
and this is potentially, not actually, in motion, but the potential is in process to actuality, and motion is an incomplete actuality of the movable. The
movent on the other hand is already in activity: e.g. it is that which is hot that

produces heat: in fact, that which produces the form is always something that possesses it. Consequently (if a thing can move itself as a whole), the same thing in respect of the same thing may be at the same time both hot and not hot. So, too, in every other case where the movent must be described by the same name in the same sense as the moved. Therefore when a thing moves itself it is one part of it that is the movent and another part that is moved. But it is not self-moving in the sense that each of the two parts is moved by the other part: the following considerations make this evident. In the first place, if each of the two parts is to move the other, there will be no first movent. If a thing is moved by a series of movents, that which is earlier in the series is more the cause of its being moved than that which comes next, and will be more truly the movent: for we found that there are two kinds of movent, that which is itself moved by something else and that which derives its motion from itself: and that which is further from the thing that is moved is nearer to the principle of motion than that which is intermediate. In the second place, there is no necessity for the movent part to be moved by anything but itself: so it can only be accidentally that the other part moves it in return. I take then the possible case of its not moving it: then there will be a part that is moved and a part that is an unmoved movent. In the third place, there is no necessity for the movent to be moved in return: on the contrary the necessity that there should always be motion makes it necessary that there should be some movent that is either unmoved or moved by itself. In the fourth place we should then have a thing undergoing the same motion that it is causing-that which is producing heat, therefore, being heated. But as a matter of fact that which primarily moves itself cannot contain either a single part that moves itself or a number of parts each of which moves itself. For, if the whole is moved by itself, it must be moved either by some part of itself or as a whole by itself as a whole. If, then, it is moved in virtue of some part of it being moved by that part itself, it is this part that will be the primary self-movent, since, if this part is separated from the whole, the part will still move itself, but the whole will do so no longer. If on the other hand the whole is moved by itself as a whole, it must be accidentally that the parts move themselves: and therefore, their self-motion not being necessary, we may take the case of their not being moved by themselves. Therefore in the whole of the thing we may distinguish that which imparts motion without itself being moved and that which is moved: for only in this way is it possible for a thing to be self-moved. Further, if the whole moves itself we may distinguish in it that which imparts the motion and that which is moved: so while we say that AB is moved by itself, we may also say that it is moved by A. And since that which imparts motion may be either a thing that is moved by something else or a thing that is unmoved, and that which is moved may be either a thing that imparts motion to something else or a thing that does not, that which moves itself must be composed of something that is unmoved but imparts motion and also of something that is moved but does not necessarily impart motion but may or may not do so. Thus let A be something that imparts motion but is unmoved, B something that is moved by A and moves G, G something that is moved by B but moves nothing (granted that we eventually arrive at

G we may take it that there is only one intermediate term, though there may be more). Then the whole ABG moves itself. But if I take away G, AB will move itself, A imparting motion and B being moved, whereas G will not move itself or in fact be moved at all. Nor again will BG move itself apart from A: for B imparts motion only through being moved by something else, not through being moved by any part of itself. So only AB moves itself. That which moves itself, therefore, must comprise something that imparts motion but is unmoved and something that is moved but does not necessarily move anything else: and each of these two things, or at any rate one of them, must be in contact with the other. If, then, that which imparts motion is a continuous substance-that which is moved must of course be so-it is clear that it is not through some part of the whole being of such a nature as to be capable of moving itself that the whole moves itself: it moves itself as a whole, both being moved and imparting motion through containing a part that imparts motion and a part that is moved. It does not impart motion as a whole nor is it moved as a whole: it is A alone that imparts motion and B alone that is moved. It is not true, further, that G is moved by A, which is impossible.

Here a difficulty arises: if something is taken away from A (supposing that that which imparts motion but is unmoved is a continuous substance), or from B the part that is moved, will the remainder of A continue to impart motion or the remainder of B continue to be moved? If so, it will not be AB primarily that is moved by itself, since, when something is taken away from AB, the remainder of AB will still continue to move itself. Perhaps we may state the case thus: there is nothing to prevent each of the two parts, or at any rate one of them, that which is moved, being divisible though actually undivided, so that if it is divided it will not continue in the possession of the same capacity: and so there is nothing to prevent self-motion residing primarily in things that are potentially divisible.

From what has been said, then, it is evident that that which primarily imparts motion is unmoved: for, whether the series is closed at once by that which is in motion but moved by something else deriving its motion directly from the first unmoved, or whether the motion is derived from what is in motion but moves itself and stops its own motion, on both suppositions we have the result that in all cases of things being in motion that which primarily imparts motion is unmoved

Part 6

Since there must always be motion without intermission, there must necessarily be something, one thing or it may be a plurality, that first imparts motion, and this first movent must be unmoved. Now the question whether each of the things that are unmoved but impart motion is eternal is irrelevant to our present argument: but the following considerations will make it clear that there must necessarily be some such thing, which, while it has the capacity of moving something else, is itself unmoved and exempt from all change, which can affect it neither in an unqualified nor in an accidental sense. Let us suppose, if any one likes, that in the case of certain things it is possible for them at different times to be and not to be, without any process of becoming and perishing (in fact it would seem to be necessary, if a thing that has not parts at one time is and at another time is not, that any such thing should without undergoing any process of change at one time be and at another time not be). And let us further suppose it possible that some principles that are unmoved but capable of imparting motion at one time are and at another time are not. Even so, this cannot be true of all such principles, since there must clearly be something that causes things that move themselves at one time to be and at another not to be. For, since nothing that has not parts can be in motion, that which moves itself must as a whole have magnitude, though nothing that we have said makes this necessarily true of every movent. So the fact that some things become and others perish, and that this is so continuously, cannot be caused by any one of those things that, though they are unmoved, do not always exist: nor again can it be caused by any of those which move certain particular things, while others move other things. The eternity and continuity of the process cannot be caused either by any one of them singly or by the sum of them, because this causal relation must be eternal and necessary, whereas the sum of these movents is infinite and they do not all exist together. It is clear, then, that though there may be countless instances of the perishing of some principles that are unmoved but impart motion, and though many things that move themselves perish and are succeeded by others that come into being, and though one thing that is unmoved moves one thing while another moves another, nevertheless there is something that comprehends them all, and that as something apart from each one of them, and this it is that is the cause of the fact that some things are and others are not and of the continuous process of change: and this causes the motion of the other movents, while they are the causes of the motion of other things. Motion, then, being eternal, the first movent, if there is but one, will be eternal also: if there are more than one, there will be a plurality of such eternal movents. We ought, however, to suppose that there is one rather than many, and a finite rather than an infinite number. When the consequences of either assumption are the same, we should always assume that things are finite rather than infinite in number, since in things constituted by nature that which is finite and that which is better ought, if possible, to be present rather than the reverse: and here it is sufficient to assume only one movent, the first of unmoved things, which being eternal will be the principle of motion to everything else.

The following argument also makes it evident that the first movent must be something that is one and eternal. We have shown that there must always be motion. That being so, motion must also be continuous, because what is always is continuous, whereas what is merely in succession is not continuous. But further, if motion is continuous, it is one: and it is one only if the movent and the moved that constitute it are each of them one, since in the event of a thing's being moved now by one thing and now by another the whole motion will not be continuous but successive.

Moreover a conviction that there is a first unmoved something may be reached not only from the foregoing arguments, but also by considering again the principles operative in movents. Now it is evident that among existing things there are some that are sometimes in motion and sometimes at rest. This fact has served above to make it clear that it is not true either that all things are in motion or that all things are at rest or that some things are always at rest and the remainder always in motion: on this matter proof is supplied by things that fluctuate between the two and have the capacity of being sometimes in motion and sometimes at rest. The existence of things of this kind is clear to all: but we wish to explain also the nature of each of the other two kinds and show that there are some things that are always unmoved and some things that are always in motion. In the course of our argument directed to this end we established the fact that everything that is in motion is moved by something, and that the movent is either unmoved or in motion, and that, if it is in motion, it is moved either by itself or by something else and so on throughout the series: and so we proceeded to the position that the first principle that directly causes things that are in motion to be moved is that which moves itself, and the first principle of the whole series is the unmoved. Further it is evident from actual observation that there are things that have the characteristic of moving themselves, e.g. the animal kingdom and the whole class of living things. This being so, then, the view was suggested that perhaps it may be possible for motion to come to be in a thing without having been in existence at all before, because we see this actually occurring in animals: they are unmoved at one time and then again they are in motion, as it seems. We must grasp the fact, therefore, that animals move themselves only with one kind of motion, and that this is not strictly originated by them. The cause of it is not derived from the animal itself: it is connected with other natural motions in animals, which they do not experience through their own instrumentality, e.g. increase, decrease, and respiration: these are experienced by every animal while it is at rest and not in motion in respect of the motion set up by its own agency: here the motion is caused by the atmosphere and by many things that enter into the animal: thus in some cases the cause is nourishment: when it is being digested animals sleep, and when it is being distributed through the system they awake and move themselves, the first principle of this motion being thus originally derived from outside. Therefore animals are not always in continuous motion by their own agency: it is something else that moves them, itself being in motion and changing as it comes into relation with each several thing that moves itself. (Moreover in all these self-moving things the first movent and cause of their self-motion is itself moved by itself, though in an accidental sense: that is to say, the body changes its place, so that that which is in the body changes its place also and is a self-movent through its exercise of leverage.) Hence we may confidently conclude that if a thing belongs to the class of unmoved movents that are also themselves moved accidentally, it is impossible that it should cause continuous motion. So the necessity that there should be motion continuously requires that there should be a first movent that is unmoved even accidentally, if, as we have said, there is to be in the world of things an unceasing and undying motion, and the world is to remain permanently self-contained and within the same limits: for if the first principle is permanent, the universe must also be permanent, since it is continuous with the first principle. (We must distinguish, however, between accidental motion of a thing by itself and such motion by something else, the former being confined to perishable things, whereas the latter belongs also to certain first principles of heavenly bodies, of all those, that is to say, that experience more than one locomotion.)

And further, if there is always something of this nature, a movent that is itself unmoved and eternal, then that which is first moved by it must be eternal. Indeed this is clear also from the consideration that there would otherwise be no becoming and perishing and no change of any kind in other things, which require something that is in motion to move them: for the motion imparted by the unmoved will always be imparted in the same way and be one and the same, since the unmoved does not itself change in relation to that which is moved by it. But that which is moved by something that, though it is in motion, is moved directly by the unmoved stands in varying relations to the things that it moves, so that the motion that it causes will not be always the same: by reason of the fact that it occupies contrary positions or assumes contrary forms at different times it will produce contrary motions in each several thing that it moves and will cause it to be at one time at rest and at another time in motion.

The foregoing argument, then, has served to clear up the point about which we raised a difficulty at the outset-why is it that instead of all things being either in motion or at rest, or some things being always in motion and the remainder always at rest, there are things that are sometimes in motion and sometimes not? The cause of this is now plain: it is because, while some things are moved by an eternal unmoved movent and are therefore always in motion, other things are moved by a movent that is in motion and changing, so that they too must change. But the unmoved movent, as has been said, since it remains permanently simple and unvarying and in the same state, will cause motion that is one and simple.

Aristotle. *Physica*, Trans. R. P. Hardie and R. K. Gaye. *The Works of Aristotle*. Vol. II. Oxford: Clarendon Press, 1930.

Athens and Jerusalem
Tertullian of Carthage

These are the doctrines of men and of demons (1 Timothy 4:1) produced for itching ears of the spirit of this world's wisdom: this the Lord called foolishness, and chose the foolish things of the world to confound even philosophy itself. For (philosophy) it is which is the material of the world's wisdom, the rash interpreter of the nature and the dispensation of God. Indeed heresies are themselves instigated by philosophy. From this source came the Aeons, and I know not what infinite forms, and the trinity of man in the system of Valentinus, who was of Plato's school. From the same source came Marcion's better god, with all his tranquillity; he came of the Stoics. Then, again, the opinion that the soul dies is held by the Epicureans; while the denial of the restoration of the body is taken from the aggregate school of all the philosophers; also, when matter is made equal to God, then you have the teaching of Zeno; and when any doctrine is alleged touching a god of fire, then Heraclitus comes in. The same subject-matter is discussed over and over again by the heretics and the philosophers; the same arguments are involved. Whence comes evil? Why is it permitted? What is the origin of man? And in what way does he come? Besides the question which Valentinus has very lately proposed—Whence comes God? Which he settles with the answer: From enthymesis and ectroma. Unhappy Aristotle! Who invented for these men dialectics, the art of building up and pulling down; an art so evasive in its propositions, so far-fetched in its conjectures, so harsh, in its arguments, so productive of contentions—embarrassing even to itself, retracting everything, and really treating of nothing! Whence spring those fables and endless genealogies (1 Timothy 1:4) and unprofitable questions (Titus 3:9) and words which spread like a cancer (2 Timothy 2:17)?

From all these, when the apostle would restrain us, he expressly names philosophy as that which he would have us be on our guard against. Writing to the Colossians, he says, See that no one beguile you through philosophy and vain deceit, after the tradition of men, and contrary to the wisdom of the Holy Ghost. He had been at Athens, and had in his interviews (with its philosophers) become acquainted with that human wisdom which pretends to know the truth, while it only corrupts it, and is itself divided into its own manifold heresies, by the variety of its mutually repugnant sects.

What indeed has Athens to do with Jerusalem? What concord is there between the Academy and the Church? What between heretics and Christians? Our instruction comes from the porch of Solomon, who had himself taught that the Lord should be sought in simplicity of heart (Wisdom 1:1). Away with all attempts to produce a mottled Christianity of Stoic, Platonic, and dialectic composition! We want no curious disputation after possessing Christ Jesus, no inquisition after enjoying the gospel! With our faith, we desire no further belief. For this is our palmary faith, that there is nothing which we ought to believe besides.

Tertullian. "Perscription Against Heresies." *The Ante-Nicene Fathers*. Vol. 3. Trans. Alexander Roberts and James Donaldson. Edinburgh: T & T Clark, 1889.

Philosophy: Handmaiden of Theology
Clement of Alexandria

Accordingly, before the advent of the Lord, philosophy was necessary to the Greeks for righteousness. And now it becomes conducive to piety; being a kind of preparatory training to those who attain to faith through demonstration. "For thy foot," it is said, "will not stumble, if thou refer what is good, whether belonging to the Greeks or to us, to Providence." For God is the cause of all good things; but of some primarily, as of the Old and the New Testament; and of others by consequence, as philosophy. Perchance, too, philosophy was given to the Greeks directly and primarily, till the Lord should call the Greeks. For this was a schoolmaster to bring "the Hellenic mind," as the law, the Hebrews, "to Christ." Philosophy, therefore, was a preparation, paving the way for him who is perfected in Christ.

"Now," says Solomon, "defend wisdom, and it will exalt thee, and it will shield thee with a crown of pleasure." For when thou hast strengthened wisdom with a cope by philosophy, and with right expenditure, thou wilt preserve it unassailable by sophists. The way of truth is therefore one. But into it, as into a perennial river, streams flow from all sides. It has been therefore said by inspiration: "Hear, my son, and receive my words; that thine may be the many ways of life. For I teach thee the ways of wisdom; that the fountains fail thee not," which gush forth from the earth itself. Not only did He enumerate several ways of salvation for any one righteous man, but He added many other ways of many righteous, speaking thus: "The paths of the righteous shine like the light." The commandments and the modes of preparatory training are to be regarded as the ways and appliances of life.

"Jerusalem, Jerusalem, how often would I have gathered thy children, as a hen her chickens!" And Jerusalem is, when interpreted, "a vision of peace." He therefore shows prophetically, that those who peacefully contemplate sacred things are in manifold ways trained to their calling. What then? He "would," and could not. How often, and where? Twice; by p. 306 the prophets, and by the advent. The expression, then, "How often," shows wisdom to be manifold; every mode of quantity and quality, it by all means saves some, both in time and in eternity. "For the Spirit of the Lord fills the earth." And if any should violently say that the reference is to the Hellenic culture, when it is said, "Give not heed to an evil woman; for honey drops from the lips of a harlot," let him hear what follows: "who lubricates thy throat for the time." But philosophy does not flatter. Who, then, does He allude to as having committed fornication? He adds expressly, "For the feet of folly lead those who use her, after death, to Hades. But her steps are not supported." Therefore remove thy way far from silly pleasure. "Stand not at the doors of her house, that thou yield not thy life to others." And He testifies, "Then shall thou repent in old age, when the flesh of thy body is consumed." For this is the end of foolish pleasure. Such, indeed, is the case. And when He says, "Be not much with a strange woman," He admonishes us to use indeed, but not to linger and spend time with, secular culture. For what was bestowed on each generation advantageously, and at seasonable times, is a preliminary training for the word of the Lord. "For already some men, ensnared by the charms of handmaidens, have despised their consort philosophy, and have grown old, some of them in music, some in geometry, others in grammar, the most in rhetoric."

"But as the encyclical branches of study contribute to philosophy, which is their mistress; so also philosophy itself co-operates for the acquisition of wisdom. For philosophy is the study of wisdom, and wisdom is the knowledge of things divine and human; and their causes." Wisdom is therefore queen of philosophy, as philosophy is of preparatory culture. For if philosophy "professes control of the tongue, and the belly, and the parts below the belly, it is to be chosen on its own account. But it appears more worthy of respect and pre-eminence, if cultivated for the honour and knowledge of God." And Scripture will afford a testimony to what has been said in what follows. Sarah was at one time barren, being Abraham's wife. Sarah having no child, assigned her maid, by name Hagar, the Egyptian, to Abraham, in order to get children. Wisdom, therefore, who dwells with the man of faith (and Abraham was reckoned faithful and righteous), was still barren and without child in that generation, not having brought forth to Abraham aught allied to virtue. And she, as was proper, thought that he, being now in the time of progress, should have intercourse with secular culture first (by Egyptian the world is designated figuratively); and afterwards should approach to her according to divine providence, and beget Isaac."

And Philo interprets Hagar to mean "sojourning." For it is said in connection with this, "Be not much with a strange woman." Sarah he interprets to mean "my princedom." He, then, who has received previous training is at liberty to approach to wisdom, which is supreme, from which grows up the race of Israel. These things show that that wisdom can be acquired through instruction, to which Abraham attained, passing from the contemplation of heavenly things to the faith and righteousness which are according to God. And Isaac is shown to mean "self-taught;" wherefore also he is discovered to be a type of Christ. He was the husband of one wife Rebecca, which they translate "Patience." And Jacob is said to have consorted with several, his name being interpreted "Exerciser." And exercises are engaged in by means of many and various dogmas. Whence, also, he who is really "endowed with the power of seeing" is called Israel, having much experience, and being fit for exercise.

Something else may also have been shown by the three patriarchs, namely, that the sure seal of knowledge is composed of nature, of education, and exercise.

You may have also another image of what has been said, in Thamar sitting by the way, and presenting the appearance of a harlot, on whom the studious Judas (whose name is interpreted "powerful"), who left nothing unexamined and uninvestigated, looked; and turned aside to her, preserving his profession towards God. Wherefore also, when Sarah was jealous at Hagar being preferred to her, Abraham, as choosing only what was profitable in secular philosophy, said, "Behold, thy maid is in thine hands: deal with her as it pleases thee;" manifestly meaning, "I embrace secular culture as youthful, and a handmaid; but thy knowledge I honour and reverence as true wife." And Sarah afflicted her; which is equivalent to corrected and admonished her. It has therefore been well said, "My son, despise not thou the correction of God; nor faint when thou art rebuked of Him. For whom the LORD loveth He chasteneth, and scourgeth every son whom He receiveth." And the foresaid Scriptures, when examined in other places, will be seen to exhibit other mysteries. We merely therefore assert here, that philosophy is characterized by investigation into truth and the nature of things (this is the truth of which the Lord Himself said, "I am the truth"); and that, again, the preparatory training for rest in Christ exercises the mind, rouses the intelligence, and begets an inquiring shrewdness, by means of the true philosophy, which the initiated possess, having found it, or rather received it, from the truth itself.

Clement of Alexandria. "Stromata." *The Ante-Nicene Fathers*. Vol. 2. Trans. William Wilson. Edinburgh: T & T Clark, 1889.

Confessions
Augustine of Hippo

1. In a spirit of gratitude, O my God, let me remember and confess to you the mercies that you bestowed upon me. Let my bones be penetrated with your love, and let them cry out to you, "Who is like you, O Lord?" You have completely broken my bonds; let me offer you a sacrifice of praise. I will tell how you have severed these shackles, so that all who worship you, when they hear my tale will say, "Blessed be the Lord, in heaven and in earth, for great and wonderful is his name."

Your words had now firmly fixed themselves in my heart, and I was besieged on all sides by you. Of your eternal life, I was now quite certain, though I saw it obscurely, as through a looking glass. But I no longer doubted that there was an incorruptible substance from which all other substances were derived. And I no longer desired to be more certain of you, but only to stand more firmly in you. As for my temporal life, everything was in a state of flux, and my heart needed to be purged of its old ways. The Way—the Savior Himself—pleased me, but I still hesitated to enter the narrowness of that path....

The Two Wills

5. The enemy held my will, and made a chain out of it, and bound me with it. For from a perverse will came lust, and lust given into became habit, and habit not resisted became necessity. These links, as it were, joined together—for this reason I called it a chain—and held me fast in harsh slavery. But that new will, which had begun to develop in me, freely to serve you and to enjoy you, O God, was not yet able to overcome the old will, which had become strengthened by long custom. And so, my two wills—one new and the other old, one carnal and the other spiritual—struggled within me; and they laid waste to my soul by their discord.

Thus, I understood by my own experience what I had read—that the flesh lusts against the spirit and the spirit against the flesh. I certainly was on both sides, but more when I was on that side which I approved in myself than on that side which I disapproved. For the latter was not really "me," because, for the most part, I suffered things against my will rather than doing them willingly. And yet it was my own fault that custom became more powerful against me, since I had come willingly where I now wished not to be. And who has any right to complain when just punishment overtakes the sinner?

Nor had I any longer my former excuse that the reason I continued to hesitate to turn my back to the world and serve you was because I could not see the truth clearly. For now I could see it with perfect clarity. But I was still bound to the earth and refused to be your soldier. I was as much afraid of being freed of my encumbrances as I was of being encumbered by them.

So I was held down by the pleasant burdens of this world, like one who is asleep, and the thoughts in which I attempted to meditate on you were like the efforts of one who tries to wake up but who sinks back again into sleep. No one, of course, wants to sleep forever, and sensible people all agree that it is better to be awake; yet a man, feeling the sleepiness of his limbs, generally puts off waking up and, even after it is time to arise, often defers to shake off sleep, though he knows he should not be doing so. In the same way, I was quite sure that it was much better to give myself up to your charity than to give myself over to my own desires; but though the former course satisfied me and was beginning to gain mastery over me, the latter pleased me and ensnared me. Nor had I any answer to give to you as you called out to me, "Awake, you who sleep, and arise from the dead, and Christ shall give you light." And when you showed me in every possible way that what you said was true, I had no answer, except the dull and drowsy words, "A minute. Just a minute. Let me have just a little while longer." But these minutes never ended, and my little while went on for a very long while.

In vain, I tried to delight in your law according to the inner man, while another law in my members rebelled against the law of my mind and led me captive under the law of sin which was in my members. For the law of sin is the strong force of habit, whereby the mind is drawn and held, even against its will—but deservedly, for the mind fell into the habit willingly. Who then shall deliver me, wretched man that I am, from the body of this death, but only your grace, through Jesus Christ our Lord?...

[Augustine goes to visit the priest Simplicianus, who recounts the tales of several men and women who had converted to the Christian faith, thus inflaming Augustine with the strong desire to do likewise.]

The Struggle in the Garden

8. In the midst, then, of this great quarrel of my inner dwelling,...disturbed both in mind and appearance, I rushed to Alypius and cried: "What is wrong with us? What is this that you have just heard? The unlearned are rising up and taking heaven, while we, with all our learning, are wallowing in the world of flesh and blood! Are we ashamed to follow because they have gone ahead of us? And aren't we ashamed of not having the courage to follow at all?" I spoke words like these, and the disturbance of my mind tore me away from him, while he gazed on in silent bewilderment. For I spoke in strange tones, and my forehead, cheeks, eyes, color, and tone of voice all expressed my emotions more fully than the words I had uttered.

There was a small garden attached to the house where we were staying. We were free to make use of it as well as the house, since the owner of the house, our host, was not living there. The turmoil in my heart had driven me to this garden, and no one would interfere with the debate I had started within myself until it could be resolved—the outcome of which you knew, though I did not. I only knew that I was going mad so that I might be whole, and dying that I might have life, knowing what an evil thing I was, but not knowing what a good thing I was soon to become.

So I retired into the garden, and Alypius followed behind me. My privacy was not lessened by his presence, and, in any event, how could he have abandoned me in the state that I was in? We sat down as far from the house as possible. I was troubled in spirit for not entering into your will and covenant, my God, which all my bones cried out to me to enter, and praised it to the heavens. And the way to go there is not by ships, or chariots, or feet; nor did it even demand going so far as the short distance I had come from the house to the place where we were sitting. For to go there, all I had had to do was to will to go, but to will it resolutely and sincerely; not to toss and turn, this way and that of a will half-maimed by the struggle, with one part falling as another rose.

While still consumed by the fever of my irresoluteness, I made many bodily movements—the kind that people often want to perform, but cannot, either because they lack limbs, or because they are bound, or weakened by sickness, or in some other way prevented from acting. If I tore out my hair, beat my forehead, locked my fingers together around my knee, I did so because I willed it. But I might have willed to do so and not have done it, if the power of motion in my limbs had not obeyed. So I did many things where "willing" was not the same as "being able." And yet I was not able to do the thing that I longed to do so much more, and which very shortly, when I willed it, would be able to do, because when I willed, I should will thoroughly. For in this particular instance the ability was one with the will, and to will was to do. And yet it was not done. It was much easier for my body to obey the weakest willing of my soul to move my limbs than it was for the soul to carry out its own major act of willing, which could be accomplished in the will alone.

9. What is the cause of this absurd situation? Let your mercy illuminate my inquiry, so that an answer can be found in the mysterious punishment of humanity and the darkest pains of the children of Adam. What is the cause, then, of this absurd situation? The mind commands the body, and the body obeys immediately; the mind commands itself, and is resisted. The mind commands the hand to move, and so complete is the compliance that the command is hardly to be distinguished from its execution. Yet the mind is mind and the hand is body. The mind commands the mind—its own self—to will, and yet it does not. Again, what is the cause of this absurd situation? The mind, I say, commands itself to will something, and it would not command, unless it willed, and yet what it commands is not done. But it does not will the thing entirely, and therefore it does not command entirely. Insofar as it commands the thing, it does will it, but insofar as the thing is not done, it

does not will it. For the will commands that there be a will—not a different will, but itself. But it does not command entirely, and therefore the command is not obeyed. For if the will was entire, it would not command itself to act, since the will would already be there. This partial willing and partial non-willing is not quite so absurd, but is rather a sickness of the soul, which was so weighed down by habit that it cannot be raised up by the truth. There are two wills, then, and neither is entire, because one has what the other lacks.

Rejection of the Manichaean Solution

10. There are those who, having perceived two deliberating wills, conclude that there are two natures within us—one good and one evil. Let them perish from your presence, O God, as do all those idle talkers who lead our minds astray. They themselves are truly evil when they assert such things, and yet these same people could become good if they would just assent to the truth, so that your Apostle may say to them, "You were in darkness once, but now light in the Lord." Unfortunately, they want to be light, not in the Lord, but in themselves, and, imagining the nature of the soul to be that what God is, are made more gross darkness still through their dreadful arrogance; for they have moved further away from you, the true light that enlightens everyone who comes into the world. I say to these men, be wary of what you say and blush for shame; but draw near to him and be enlightened, and you shall no longer be ashamed.

When I was deliberating about whether to serve the Lord my God now, as I had long intended, I was the one who wanted to do it and I was also the one who wanted not to do it. I was the only one involved. But I neither willed this course entirely nor rejected it entirely. I was at war with myself and was torn apart by myself. This tearing apart took place against my will, but what it indicated was not the presence of an alien mind, but a punishment that I was suffering in my own mind. Therefore, it was not I who caused it, but the sin that dwelled within me—the penalty for a sin more freely committed, for I was a son of Adam.

For, if there are as many conflicting natures as there are conflicting wills, there would not be two such natures only, but many. Suppose a man is wondering whether he should go to the Manichaean conventicler or to the theater. These Manichaeans will say, "You see, here are two natures, one good, pulling him in one direction, the other evil, pulling him in another. For what else could this indecision be except a conflict between wills?" But I say that both are equally bad—that which pulls towards them and that which pulls towards the theater. But they believe that a will which pulls towards them must be good.

But suppose one of us should deliberate, and through a conflict of his two wills, should be in confusion as to whether he should go to the theater or to our Church. Wouldn't these same Manichaeans be perplexed as to what to say on this point? For they must either confess that the will which leads to our Church is good as well as theirs (something they would not be willing to do)…; or they must assume that in the same man there are two evil natures and two evil souls, and that it is not true, as they say, that there is one good and another bad; or they must be converted to the truth, and no longer deny that when a person is deliberating there is a soul fluctuating between two conflicting wills.

Let them stop saying, therefore, when they perceive two conflicting wills in the same man, that the conflict is between two opposing souls, of two opposing substances, from two opposing principles, one good and the other bad. For you, O God of truth, have disproved, checked, and overthrown them. Such is the case when both wills being bad, one debates whether he should kill a man by poison or by the sword; whether he should seize this or that part of a man's property, when he cannot have both; whether he should squander his money for pleasure or hoard his money like a miser; whether he should go to the circus or the theater, if both are opened on the same day (a third option being to rob another's house if he has the opportunity and a fourth being to commit adultery)—assuming he has the means to do all these things at the time, and all are equally desired, although impossible to enact at the same time. The mind is then torn apart by four or even more…conflicting wills. But the Manichaeans do not hold that there are a similar number of conflicting substances.

The same holds true in wills which are good. Let me ask: Is it a good thing to take pleasure in reading the apostle? Or a good thing to take pleasure in a sober psalm? Or a good thing to discuss the Gospel? For each of these, they will answer, "It is good." But what if all of these give equal pleasure at the same time? Doesn't this mean that different wills distract the mind, while he deliberates which to select? Yet they are all good, but they compete among themselves until one is chosen….It is likewise the case when eternity delights us from above and the pleasure of temporal goods holds us down from below: our one soul is not ready to embrace either with its entire will. And so the soul is torn apart with great distress, with truth pulling in one direction and habit pulling in the other.

Inner Debate

11. So I was soul-sick and tormented. And I accused myself far more severely than I usually did, tossing and turning in my chain, as I strove to break free from it completely. I was held by it only slightly, but I was still held. And you, O Lord, pressed upon me in my innermost being by a severe mercy, redoubling the lashes of fear and shame, so that I would not give way once more, and that small piece of chain that still bound me would not get stronger and bind me even more. I said to myself, "Let it be done now, let it be done now." And as I spoke these words, I was all but moving in that direction. I nearly did it, but yet did not do it. But I didn't slip back into my own ways, but took a breath and kept my stand. And I tried again…and all but touched and grasped it; and yet still I did not come to it, or touch it, or grasp it; for I hesitated to die to death and to live to life….At that very moment in which I was to become something other than I was, the nearer it approached me, the greater was my horror, but it did not strike me back, nor turn me away, but

held me in suspense.

The very toys of toys and vanities of vanities, my ancient mistresses, were still holding me back, as they plucked the garment of my flesh and whispered softly, "Do you think you can be done with us? From this moment shall we no longer be with you forever? And from his moment shall this-and-that no longer be lawful for you forever?" And what did they suggest to me by "this" and "that"? What did they suggest, O my God? Let your mercy turn it away from the soul of your servant. What foul deed were they suggesting? What shameful acts? But now their voices were half as loud, and they did not openly show themselves to contradict me, but muttered, as it were, behind my back, and slyly grasping at me as I walked away to make me look back at them. And yet they did delay me as I hesitated to tear free and shake them off and move in the direction in which I was being called. They had an aggressive habit of taunting me by saying, "Do you really think that you can live without them?"

But now it spoke very faintly. For on that side where I had turned my face and where I hesitated to go, there appeared to me the chaste, dignified figure of Continence. She was serene and calm, honestly beckoning me to come and doubt no longer. As she stretched forth to receive and embrace me, her holy hands filled with multitudes of good examples of all ages, there were some young men and women here and grave widows and aged virgins. And in them all was Continence herself, not barren, but a fruitful mother of children, her joys given by you, her husband, O Lord. She smiled on me with encouraging prodding, as though to say, "Can't you do what these youths and maidens have done? Or do you think that they did it all by themselves and without the help of the Lord their God? The Lord their God gave me to them. Why do you insist upon standing by yourself, and so not really stand firm at all? Cast yourself upon him and fear not. He will not draw away and let you fall. Lean fearlessly upon him and he will receive you and heal you." And I was blushing with shame, for I could still hear the whisperings of those vanities of mine, and hung back in suspense. And yet again she seemed to say, "Close your ears to those unclean parts of you that belong to the earth, so that they might be mortified. They might tell you of delights, but nothing like the delights that are told by the law of the Lord your God."

And so continued the debate in my heart, waged between myself and myself. But Alypius, sitting by my side, silently waited to see how this extreme agitation within me would end.

Augustine's Conversion

12. But this deep reflection, from the secret depths of my soul, drew together and heaped up all my misery…, and there arose a great storm within me, bringing with it a mighty shower of tears. So that I might be free to give vent to these feelings without self-consciousness, I left Alypius, since solitude was more appropriate for the act of weeping. So I went far enough away that even his presence would not be a burden to me. This was how I was feeling, and he understood it; for I suppose that I had said something, and the tones

of my voice must have appeared choked with tears. And so I arose to leave and he remained where we were sitting, filled with extreme astonishment. I threw myself down—I don't really know how—under a certain fig tree, and gave full reign to my tears. They poured out from my eyes like a flood, an acceptable sacrifice to you. And, I said to you, not in these exact words, but in this sense, "And you, O Lord, how long? How long, Lord? Will you be angry forever? O do not remember our former sins." For I felt it was these that were holding me back. I uttered these cries of despair to you: "How long, how long this "tomorrow and tomorrow? Why not now? Why can't my depravity be put to an end at this every hour?"

So I was saying words of this sort and crying in the bitter contrition of my heart, when suddenly a voice reached my ears from a nearby house. It was the voice of a boy or girl—I don't know which—and it kept repeating, "Take it and read. Take it and read." Immediately, my expression changed. I began to reflect upon whether words like these were ever used in the kinds of games that children play, but couldn't remember ever before hearing words of that kind. So I stemmed the flood of my tears and arose, interpreting it to be nothing other than a command from God to open the book and read the first chapter I came upon. For I had once heard that Anthony, coming in during the reading of the Gospels, believed the words to be directed to him, when he heard, "Go and sell all you have, and give the money to the poor, and you will have treasure in heaven, and come follow me." By such a divine message was he converted to you. Eagerly, I then returned to the place where Alypius was sitting, since it was in that spot that I had left the book of the Apostle when I had gotten up. Snatching it up and opening it, in silence I read that section upon which my eyes first fell: "Not in rioting and drunkenness, not in debauchery and wantonness, not in strife and envy-ing; but put on the Lord Jesus Christ, and make not provision for the flesh, in concupiscence." I didn't need to read any further, for immediately at the end of this sentence, the light of certainty flooded my heart, and the darkness of doubt vanished away.

I closed the book, and either using my fingers or some other means to mark the page, and with complete calmness told Alypius what had happened. And he told me in his turn what had been going on with him, which I didn't know anything about. He asked to see what I had read and I showed him. And he looked beyond even what I had read. I didn't know the words that followed, which were, "He that is weak in faith, receive"—which he applied to himself and interpreted for me. He became strengthened by the admoni-tion; and he joined me with the kind of strong resolution and commitment that was totally in keeping with his character (for in this respect he was quite superior to me).

We then went inside to my mother and told her what had transpired, and she rejoiced. We described to her what took place and she leapt with joyful triumph, and blessed you, who have the power to do much more than we ask for or understand. For she understood that you had given her much more in my regard than she had even asked for in her pitiful and sorrowful pleadings. For you had converted me to yourself, so that I no longer sought a wife or any worldly ambitions. I was now standing in that rule of faith that many years earlier you had shown to her in a vision of me. And, in doing so, you converted her sorrow into joy—a joy far more plentiful than she could have hoped for, and much more precious and purer than she desired by having grandchildren from my flesh.

Augustine. *Confessions*. Trans. by Michael S. Russo, 2012. Used with permission.

The Ontological Argument
Anselm of Canterbury

Chapter 1: Encouraging the Mind to Contemplate God

Come on now little man, get away from your worldly occupations for a while, escape from your tumultuous thoughts. Lay aside your burdensome cares and put off your laborious exertions. Give yourself over to God for a little while, and rest for a while in Him. Enter into the cell of your mind, shut out everything except God and whatever helps you to seek Him once the door is shut. Speak now, my heart, and say to God, "I seek your face; your face, Lord, I seek."

Come on then, my Lord God, teach my heart where and how to seek you, where and how to find you. Lord, if you are not here, where shall I find you? If, however, you are everywhere, why do I not see you here? But certainly you dwell in inaccessible light. And where is that inaccessible light? Or how do I reach it? Or who will lead me to it and into it, so that I can see you in it? And then by what signs, under what face shall I seek you? I have never seen you, my Lord God, or known your face. What shall I do, Highest Lord, what shall this exile do, banished far from you as he is? What should your servant do, desperate as he is for your love yet cast away from your face? He longs to see you, and yet your face is too far away from him. He wants to come to you, and yet your dwelling place is unreachable. He yearns to discover you, and he does not know where you are. He craves to seek you, and does not know how to recognize you. Lord, you are my Lord and my God, and I have never seen you. You have made me and nurtured me, given me every good thing I have ever received, and I still do not know you. I was created for the purpose of seeing you, and I still have not done the thing I was made to do.

Oh, how miserable man's lot is when he has lost what he was made for! Oh how hard and dire was that downfall! Alas, what did he lose and what did he find? What was taken away and what remains? He has lost beatitude for which he was made, and he has found misery for which he was not made. That without which he cannot be happy has been taken away, and that remains which in itself can only make him miserable. Back then man ate the bread of angels for which he now hungers, and now he eats the bread of griefs which he did not even know back then. Alas for the common grief of man, the universal lamentation of Adam's sons! He belched in his satiety, while we sigh in our want. He was rich, we are beggars. He happily possessed and miserably abandoned, we unhappily lack and miserably desire, yet alas, we remain empty. Why, since it would have been easy for him, did he not keep what we so disastrously lack? Why did he deprive us of light, and cover us with darkness instead? Why did he take life away from us and inflict death instead? From what have we poor wretches been expelled, and toward what are we being driven? From what have we been cast down, in what buried? From our fatherland into exile, from the vision of God into blindness. From the happiness of immortality into the bitterness and horror of death. What a miserable transformation! From so much good into so much evil! A heavy injury, a heavy, heavy grief.

I have come to you as a poor man to a rich one, as a poor rich to a merciful giver. May I not return empty and rejected! And if "I sigh before I eat" (Job 3:4), once I have sighed give me something to eat. Lord, turned in (incurvatus) as I am I can only look down, so raise me up so that I can look up. "My iniquities heaped on my head" cover me over and weigh me down "like a heavy load" (Ps. 37:5). Dig me out and set me free before "the pit" created by them "shuts its jaws over me" (Ps. 67:16).Let me see your light, even if I see it from afar or from the depths. Teach me to seek you, and reveal yourself to this seeker. For I cannot seek you unless you teach me how, nor can I find you unless you show yourself to me. Let me seek you in desiring you, and desire you in seeking you. Let me find you in loving you and love you in finding you.

I acknowledge, Lord, and I give thanks that you have created in me this your image, so that I can remember you, think about you and love you. But it is so worn away by sins, so smudged over by the smoke of sins, that it cannot do what it was created to do unless you renew and reform it. I do not even try, Lord, to rise up to your heights, because my intellect does not measure up to that task; but I do want to understand in some small measure your truth, which my heart believes in and loved. Nor do I seek to understand so that I can believe, but rather I believe so that I can understand. For I believe this too, that "unless I believe I shall not understand" (Isa. 7:9).

Chapter 2: That God Really Exists

Therefore, Lord, you who give knowledge of the faith, give me as much knowledge as you know to be fitting for me, because you are as we believe and that which we believe. And indeed we believe you are something greater than which cannot be thought. Or is there no such kind of thing, for "the fool said in his heart, 'there is no God'" (Ps. 13:1, 52:1)? But certainly that same fool, having heard what I just said, "something greater than which cannot be thought," understands what he heard, and what he understands is in his thought, even if he does not think it exists. For it is one thing for something to exist in a person's thought and quite another for the person to think that thing exists. For when a painter thinks ahead to what he will paint, he has that picture in his thought, but he does not yet think it exists, because he has not done it yet. Once he has painted it he has it in his thought and thinks it exists because he has done it. Thus even the fool is compelled to grant that something greater than which cannot be thought exists in thought, because he understands what he hears, and whatever is understood exists in thought. And certainly that greater than which cannot be understood cannot exist only in thought, for if it exists only in thought it could also be thought of as existing in reality as well, which is greater. If, therefore, that than which greater cannot be thought exists in thought alone, then that than which greater cannot be thought turns out to be that than which something greater actually can be thought, but that is obviously impossible. Therefore something than which greater cannot be thought undoubtedly exists both in thought and in reality.

Chapter 3: That God Cannot be Thought Not to Exist

In fact, it so undoubtedly exists that it cannot be thought of as not existing. For one can think there exists something that cannot be thought of as not existing, and that would be greater than something which can be thought of as not existing. For if that greater than which cannot be thought can be thought of as not existing, then that greater than which cannot be thought is not that greater than which cannot be thought, which does not make sense. Thus that than which nothing can be thought so undoubtedly exists that it cannot even be thought of as not existing.

And you, Lord God, are this being. You exist so undoubtedly, my Lord God, that you cannot even be thought of as not existing. And deservedly, for if some mind could think of something greater than you, that creature would rise above the creator and could pass judgment on the creator, which is absurd. And indeed whatever exists except you alone can be thought of as not existing. You alone of all things most truly exists and thus enjoy existence to the fullest degree of all things, because nothing else exists so undoubtedly, and thus everything else enjoys being in a lesser degree. Why therefore did the fool say in his heart "there is no God," since it is so evident to any rational mind that you above all things exist? Why indeed, except precisely because he is stupid and foolish?

Chapter 4: How the Fool Managed to Say in His Heart That Which Cannot be Thought

How in the world could he have said in his heart what he could not think? Or how indeed could he not have thought what he said in his heart, since saying it in his heart is the same as thinking it? But if he really thought it because he said it in his heart, and did not say it in his heart because he could not possibly have thought it - and that seems to be precisely what happened - then there must be more than one way in which something can be said in one's heart or thought. For a thing is thought in one way when the words signifying it are thought, and it is thought in quite another way when the thing signified is understood. God can be thought not to exist in the first way but not in the second. For no one who understands what God is can think that he does not exist. Even though he may say those words in his heart he will give them some other meaning or no meaning at all. For God is that greater than which cannot be thought. Whoever understands this also understands that God exists in such a way that one cannot even think of him as not existing.

Thank you, my good God, thank you, because what I believed earlier through your gift I now understand through your illumination in such a way that I would be unable not to understand it even if I did not want to believe you existed.

Anselm of Canterbury. *Proslogion.* Trans. David Burrr. 1996. Used with permission.

The Cosmological Argument
Thomas Aquinas

Question 2: On the Existence of God

First Article: Whether the Existence of God is Self-Evident?

Objection 1: It seems that the existence of God is self-evident. Now those things are said to be self-evident to us the knowledge of which is naturally implanted in us, as we can see in regard to first principles. But as Damascene says (De Fide Orth. i, 1,3), "the knowledge of God is naturally implanted in all." Therefore the existence of God is self-evident.

Objection 2: Further, those things are said to be self-evident which are known as soon as the terms are known, which the Philosopher (1 Poster. iii) says is true of the first principles of demonstration. Thus, when the nature of a whole and of a part is known, it is at once recognized that every whole is greater than its part. But as soon as the signification of the word "God" is understood, it is at once seen that God exists. For by this word is signified that thing than which nothing greater can be conceived. But that which exists actually and mentally is greater than that which exists only mentally. Therefore, since as soon as the word "God" is understood it exists mentally, it also follows that it exists actually. Therefore the proposition "God exists" is self-evident.

Objection 3: Further, the existence of truth is self-evident. For whoever denies the existence of truth grants that truth does not exist: and, if truth does not exist, then the proposition "Truth does not exist" is true: and if there is anything true, there must be truth. But God is truth itself: "I am the way, the truth, and the life" (Jn. 14:6) Therefore "God exists" is self-evident.

On the contrary, No one can mentally admit the opposite of what is self-evident; as the Philosopher (Metaph. iv, lect. vi) states concerning the first principles of demonstration. But the opposite of the proposition "God is" can be mentally admitted: "The fool said in his heart, There is no God" (Ps. 52:1). Therefore, that God exists is not self-evident.

*I answer tha*t, A thing can be self-evident in either of two ways: on the one hand, self-evident in itself, though not to us; on the other, self-evident in itself, and to us. A proposition is self-evident because the predicate is included in the essence of the subject, as "Man is an animal," for animal is contained in the essence of man. If, therefore the essence of the predicate and subject be known to all, the proposition will be self-evident to all; as is clear with regard to the first principles of demonstration, the terms of which are common things that no one is ignorant of, such as being and non-being, whole and part, and such like. If, however, there are some to whom the essence of the predicate and subject is unknown, the proposition will be self-evident in itself, but not to those who do not know the meaning of the predicate and subject of the proposition. Therefore, it happens, as Boethius says (Hebdom., the title of which is: "Whether all that is, is good"), "that there are some mental concepts self-evident only to the learned, as that incorporeal substances are not in space."

Therefore I say that this proposition, "God exists," of itself is self-evident, for the predicate is the same as the subject, because God is His own existence as will be hereafter shown (Q[3], A[4]). Now because we do not know the essence of God, the proposition is not self-evident to us; but needs to be demonstrated by things that are more known to us, though less known in their nature---namely, by effects.

Reply to Objection 1: To know that God exists in a general and confused way is implanted in us by nature, inasmuch as God is man's beatitude. For man naturally desires happiness, and what is naturally desired by man must be naturally known to him. This, however, is not to know absolutely that God exists; just as to know that someone is approaching is not the same as to know that Peter is approaching, even though it is Peter who is approaching; for many there are who imagine that man's perfect good which is happiness, consists in riches, and others in pleasures, and others in something else.

Reply to Objection 2: Perhaps not everyone who hears this word "God" understands it to signify something than which nothing greater can be thought, seeing that some have believed God to be a body. Yet, granted that everyone understands that by this word "God" is signified something than which nothing greater can be thought, nevertheless, it does not therefore follow that he understands that what the word signifies exists actually, but only that it exists mentally. Nor can it be argued that it actually exists, unless it be admitted that there actually exists something than which nothing greater can be thought; and this precisely is not admitted by those who hold that God does not exist.

Reply to Objection 3: The existence of truth in general is self-evident but the existence of a Primal Truth is not self-evident to us.

Second Article: Whether it can be Demonstrated that God Exists?

Objection 1: It seems that the existence of God cannot be demonstrated. For it is an article of faith that God exists. But what is of faith cannot be demonstrated, because a demonstration produces scientific knowledge; whereas faith is of the unseen (Heb. 11:1). Therefore it cannot be demonstrated that God exists.

Objection 2: Further, the essence is the middle term of demonstration. But we cannot know in what God's essence consists, but solely in what it does not consist; as Damascene says (De Fide Orth. i, 4). Therefore we cannot demonstrate that God exists.

Objection 3: Further, if the existence of God were demonstrated, this could only be from His effects. But His effects are not proportionate to Him, since He is infinite and His effects are finite; and between the finite and infinite there is no proportion. Therefore, since a cause cannot be demonstrated by an effect not proportionate to it, it seems that the existence of God cannot be demonstrated.

On the contrary, The Apostle says: "The invisible things of Him are clearly seen, being understood by the things that are made" (Rom. 1:20). But this would not be unless the existence of God could be demonstrated through the things that are made; for the first thing we must know of anything is whether it exists.

I answer that, Demonstration can be made in two ways: One is through the cause, and is called "a priori," and this is to argue from what is prior absolutely. The other is through the effect, and is called a demonstration "a posteriori"; this is to argue from what is prior relatively only to us. When an effect is better known to us than its cause, from the effect we proceed to the knowledge of the cause. And from every effect the existence of its proper cause can be demonstrated, so long as its effects are better known to us; because since every effect depends upon its cause, if the effect exists, the cause must pre-exist. Hence the existence of God, in so far as it is not self-evident to us, can be demonstrated from those of His effects which are known to us.

Reply to Objection 1: The existence of God and other like truths about God, which can be known by natural reason, are not articles of faith, but are preambles to the articles; for faith presupposes natural knowledge, even as grace presupposes nature, and perfection supposes something that can be perfected. Nevertheless, there is nothing to prevent a man, who cannot grasp a proof, accepting, as a matter of faith, something which in itself is capable of being scientifically known and demonstrated.

Reply to Objection 2: When the existence of a cause is demonstrated from an effect, this effect takes the place of the definition of the cause in proof of the cause's existence. This is especially the case in regard to God, because, in order to prove the existence of anything, it is necessary to accept as a middle term the meaning of the word, and not its essence, for the question of its essence follows on the question of its existence. Now the names given to God are derived from His effects; consequently, in demonstrating the existence of God from His effects, we may take for the middle term the meaning of the word "God".

Reply to Objection 3: From effects not proportionate to the cause no perfect knowledge of that cause can be obtained. Yet from every effect the existence of the cause can be clearly demonstrated, and so we can demonstrate the existence of God from His effects; though from them we cannot perfectly know God as He is in His essence.

Third Article: Whether God exists?

Objection 1: It seems that God does not exist; because if one of two contraries be infinite, the other would be altogether destroyed. But the word "God" means that He is infinite goodness. If, therefore, God existed, there would be no evil discoverable; but there is evil in the world. Therefore God does not exist.

Objection 2: Further, it is superfluous to suppose that what can be accounted for by a few principles has been produced by many. But it seems that everything we see in the world can be accounted for by other principles, supposing God did not exist. For all natural things can be reduced to one principle which is nature; and all voluntary things can be reduced to one principle which is human reason, or will. Therefore there is no need to suppose God's existence.

On the contrary, It is said in the person of God: "I am Who am." (Ex. 3:14)

I answer that, The existence of God can be proved in five ways.

The first and more manifest way is the argument from motion. It is certain, and evident to our senses, that in the world some things are in motion. Now whatever is in motion is put in motion by another, for nothing can be in motion except it is in potentiality to that towards which it is in motion; whereas a thing moves inasmuch as it is in act. For motion is nothing else than the reduction of something from potentiality to actuality. But nothing can be reduced from potentiality to actuality, except by something in a state of actuality. Thus that which is actually hot, as fire, makes wood, which is potentially hot, to be actually hot, and thereby moves and changes it. Now it is not possible that the same thing should be at once in actuality and potentiality in the same respect, but only in different respects. For what is actually hot cannot simultaneously be potentially hot; but it is simultaneously potentially cold. It is therefore impossible that in the same respect and in the same way a thing should be both mover and moved, i.e. that it should move itself. Therefore, whatever is in motion must be put in motion by another. If that by which it is put in motion be itself put in motion, then this also must needs be put in motion by another, and that by another again. But this cannot go on to infinity, because then there would be no first mover, and, consequently, no other mover; seeing that subsequent movers move only inasmuch as they are put in motion by the first mover; as the staff moves only because it is put in motion by the hand. Therefore it is necessary to arrive at a first mover, put in motion by no other; and this everyone understands to be God.

The second way is from the nature of the efficient cause. In the world of sense we find there is an order of efficient causes. There is no case known (neither is it, indeed, possible) in which a thing is found to be the efficient cause of itself; for so it would be prior to itself, which is impossible. Now in efficient causes it is not possible to go on to infinity, because in all efficient causes following in order, the first is the cause of the intermediate cause, and the intermediate is the cause of the ultimate cause, whether the intermediate cause be several, or only one. Now to take away the cause is to take away the effect. Therefore, if there be no first cause among efficient causes, there will be no ultimate, nor any intermediate cause. But if in efficient causes it is possible to go on to infinity, there will be no first efficient cause, neither will there be an ultimate effect, nor any intermediate efficient causes; all of which is plainly false. Therefore it is necessary to admit a first efficient cause, to which everyone gives the name of God.

The third way is taken from possibility and necessity, and runs thus. We find in nature things that are possible to be and not to be, since they are found to be generated, and to corrupt, and consequently, they are possible to be and not to be. But it is impossible for these always to exist, for that which is possible not to be at some time is not. Therefore, if everything is possible not to be, then at one time there could have been nothing in existence. Now if this were true, even now there would be nothing in existence, because that which does not exist only begins to exist by something already existing. Therefore, if at one time nothing was in existence, it would have been impossible for anything to have begun to exist; and thus even now nothing would be in existence—which is absurd. Therefore, not all beings are merely possible, but there must exist something the existence of which is necessary. But every necessary thing either has its necessity caused by another, or not. Now it is impossible to go on to infinity in necessary things which have their necessity caused by another, as has been already proved in regard to efficient causes. Therefore we cannot but postulate the existence of some being having of itself its own necessity, and not receiving it from another, but rather causing in others their necessity. This all men speak of as God.

The fourth way is taken from the gradation to be found in things. Among beings there are some more and some less good, true, noble and the like. But "more" and "less" are predicated of different things, according as they resemble in their different ways something which is the maximum, as a thing is said to be hotter according as it more nearly resembles that which is hottest; so that there is something which is truest, something best, something noblest and, consequently, something which is uttermost being; for those things that are greatest in truth are greatest in being, as it is written in Metaph. ii. Now the maximum in any genus is the cause of all in that genus; as fire, which is the maximum heat, is the cause of all hot things. Therefore there must also be something which is to all beings the cause of their being, goodness, and every other perfection; and this we call God.

The fifth way is taken from the governance of the world. We see that things which lack intelligence, such as natural bodies, act for an end, and this is evident from their acting always, or nearly always, in the same way, so as to obtain the best result. Hence it is plain that not fortuitously, but designedly, do they achieve their end. Now whatever lacks intelligence cannot move towards an end, unless it be directed by some being endowed with knowledge and intelligence; as the arrow is shot to its mark by the archer. Therefore some intelligent being exists by whom all natural things are directed to their end; and this being we call God.

Reply to Objection 1: As Augustine says (Enchiridion xi): "Since God is the highest good, He would not allow any evil to exist in His works, unless His omnipotence and goodness were such as to bring good even out of evil." This is part of the infinite goodness of God, that He should allow evil to exist, and out of it produce good.

Reply to Objection 2: Since nature works for a determinate end under the direction of a higher agent, whatever is done by nature must needs be traced back to God, as to its first cause. So also whatever is done voluntarily must also be traced back to some higher cause other than human reason or will, since these can change or fail; for all things that are changeable and capable of defect must be traced back to an immovable and self-necessary first principle, as was shown in the body of the Article.

Translated by the Fathers of the English Dominican Provience (1947). This text is in the public domain.

Critique of Catholicism
Martin Luther

Address to the Christian Nobility
of the German Nation

The Romanists have, with great adroitness, drawn three walls round themselves, with which they have hitherto protected themselves, so that no one could reform them, whereby all Christendom has fallen terribly.

First, if pressed by the temporal power, they have affirmed and maintained that the temporal power has no jurisdiction over them, but, on the contrary, that the spiritual power is above the temporal.

Secondly, if it were proposed to admonish them with the Scriptures, they objected that no one may interpret the Scriptures but the Pope.

Thirdly, if they are threatened with a council, they pretend that no one may call a council but the Pope ...

Now may God help us, and give us one of those trumpets that overthrew the walls of Jericho, so that we may blow down these walls of straw and paper, and that we may set free our Christian rods for the chastisement of sin, and expose the craft and deceit of the devil, so that we may amend ourselves by punishment and again obtain God's favour.

Let us, in the first place, attack the first wall.

It has been devised that the Pope, bishops, priests, and monks are called the spiritual estate; princes, lords, artificers, and peasants, are the temporal estate. This is an artful lie and hypocritical device, but let no one be made afraid by it, and that for this reason: that all Christians are truly of the spiritual estate, and there is no difference among them, save of office alone. As St. Paul says (i Cor. xii), we are all one body, though each member does its own work, to serve the others, This is because we have one baptism, one Gospel, one faith, and are all Christians alike; for baptism, Gospel, and faith, these alone make spiritual and Christian people.

As for the unction by a pope or a bishop, tonsure, ordination, consecration, and clothes differing from those of laymen-all this may make a hypocrite or an anointed puppet, but never a Christian or a spiritual man. Thus we are all consecrated as, priests by baptism, as St. Peter says: 'Ye are a royal priesthood, a holy nation (i Pet. ii. 9); and in the book of Revelation: 'and hast made us unto our God (by Thy blood) kings and priests' (Rev. v. io). For, if we had not a higher consecration in us than pope or bishop can give, no priest could ever be made by the consecration of pope or bishop, nor could he say the mass or preach or absolve. Therefore the bishop's consecration is just as if in the name of the whole congregation he took one person out of the community; each member of which has equal power, and commanded him to exercise this power for the rest; in the same way as if ten brothers, co-heirs as king's sons, were to choose one from among them to rule over their'inheritance, they would all of them still remain- kings and have equal power, although one is ordered to govern. And to put the matter more plainly, if a little company of pious Christian laymen were taken prisoners and carried away to a desert, and had not among them a priest consecrated by a bishop, and were there to agree to elect one of them and were to order him to baptise, to celebrate the mass, to absolve and to preach, this man would as truly be a priest, as if all the bishops and all the popes had consecrated him. That is why, in cases of necessity, every man can baptise and absolve, which would not be possible if we were not all priests. This great grace and virtue of baptism and of the Christian estate they have quite destroyed and made us forget by their ecclesiastical law . . .

Since then the temporal power is baptized as we are, and has the same faith and Gospel, we must allow it to be priest and bishop, and account its office an office that is proper and useful to the Christian community. For whatever issues from baptism may boast that it has been consecrated priest, bishop, and pope, although it does not beseem every one to exercise these offices. For, since we are all priests alike, no man may put himself forward or take upon himself without our consent and election, to do that which we have all alike power to do. For if a thing is common to all, no man may take it to himself without the wish and command of the community. And if it should happen that a man were appointed to one of these offices and deposed for abuses, he would be just what he was before. Therefore a priest should be nothing in Christendom but a functionary; as long as he holds his office, he has precedence of others; if he is deprived of it, he is a peasant or a citizen like the rest. Therefore a priest is verily no longer a priest after deposition. But now they have invented characteres indelibiles, and pretend that a priest after deprivation still differs from a simple layman. They even imagine that a priest can never be anything but a priest-that is, that he become a layman. All this is nothing but mere ordinance of human invention.

It follows then, that between laymen and priests, princes and bishops, or, as they call it, between spiritual and temporal sons, the only real difference is one of office and function, and not of estate. . . .

. . .Therefore I say, Forasmuch as the temporal power has been ordained by God for the punishment of the bad and the protection of the good, we must let it do its duty throughout the whole Christian body, without respect of persons, whether it strike popes, bishops, priests, monks, nuns, or whoever it may be....

Whatever the ecclesiastical law has said in opposition to this is merely the invention of Romanist arrogance. . . .

Now, I imagine the first paper wall is overthrown, inasmuch the temporal power has become a member of the Christian body; although its work relates to the body, yet does it belong to the spritual estate. . . .

The second wall is even more tottering and weak: that they end to be considered masters of the Scriptures. . . . If of our faith is right, 'I believe in the holy Christian church,' the.Pope cannot alone be right; else we must say, 'I believe in the Pope of Rome,' and reduce the Christian Church to one man, which is a devilish and damnable heresy. Besides that, we are all priests, as I have said, and have all one faith, one Gospel, one Sacrament ; how then should we not have the power of discerning and judging what is right or wrong in matters of faith ? ...

The third wall falls of itself, as soon as the first two have fallen; for if the Pope acts contrary to the Scriptures, we are bound to stand by the Scriptures to punish and to constrain him, according to Christ's commandment . 'tell it unto the Church' (Matt. xviii. 15-17). . . . If then I am to accuse him before the Church, I must collect the Church together. . . .Therefore when need requires, and the Pope is a cause of offence to Christendom, in these cases whoever can best do so, as a faithful member of the whole body, must do what he can to procure a true free council. This no one can do so we as the temporal authorities, especially since they are fellow-Christians, fellow-priests. . . .

Against Catholicism

The chief cause that I fell out with the pope was this: the pope boasted that he was the head of the Church, and condemned all that would not be under his power and authority; for he said, although Christ be the head of the Church, yet, notwithstanding, there must be a corporal head of the Church upon earth. With this I could have been content, had he but taught the gospel pure and clear, and not introduced human inventions and lies in its stead. Further, he took upon him power, rule, and authority over the Christian Church, and over the Holy Scriptures, the Word of God; no man must presume to expound the Scriptures, but only he, and according to his ridiculous conceits; so that he made himself lord over the Church, proclaiming her at the same time a powerful mother, and empress over the Scriptures, to which we must yield and be obedient; this was not to be endured. They who, against God's Word, boast of the Church's authority, are mere idiots. The pope attributes more power to the Church, which is begotten and born, than to the Word, which has begotten, conceived, and born the Church.

We, through God's grace, are not heretics, but schismatics, causing, indeed, separation and division, wherein we are not to blame, but our adversaries, who gave occasion thereto, because they remain not by God's Word alone, which we have, hear, and follow. When our Lord God intends to plague and punish one, He leaves him in blindness, so that he regards not God's Word, but condemns the same, as the papists now do. They know that our doctrine is God's Word, but they will not allow of this syllogism and conclusion: When God speaks, we must hear him; now God speaks through the doctrine of the gospel; therefore we must hear Him. But the papists, against their own consciences, say, No; we must hear the Church. It is very strange: they admit propositions, but will not allow of the consequences, or permit the conclusions to be right. They urge some decree or other of the Council of Constance, and say, though Christ speak, who is the truth itself, yet an ancient custom must be preferred, and observed for law. Thus do they answer, when they seek to wrest and pervert the truth.

If this sin of antichrist be not a sin against the Holy Ghost, then I do not know how to define and distinguish sins. They sin herein wilfully against the revealed truth of God's Word, in a most stubborn and stiff-necked manner. I pray, who would not, in this case, resist these devilish and shameless lying lips? I marvel not John Hus died so joyfully, seeing he heard of such abominable impieties and wickedness of the papists. I pray, how holds the pope concerning the Church? He preserves her, but only in an external luster, pomp, and succession. But we judge her according to her essence, as she is in herself, in her own substance, that is, according to God's Word and sacraments. The pope is reserved for God's judgment, therefore only by God's judgment he shall be destroyed. Henry VIII, king of England, is now also an enemy to the pope's person, but not to his essence and substance; he would only kill the body of the pope, but suffer his soul, that is, his false doctrine, to live; the pope can well endure such an enemy; he hopes within the space of twenty years to recover his rule and government again. But I fall upon the pope's soul, his doctrine, with God's word, not regarding his body, that is, his wicked person and life. I not only pluck out his feathers, as the king of England and prince Georg of Saxony do, but I set the knife to his throat, and cut his windpipe asunder. We put the goose on the spit; did we but pluck her, the feathers would soon grow again. Therefore is Satan so bitter an enemy unto us, because we cut the pope's throat, as does also the king of Denmark, who aims at the essence of popery.

'Tis wonderful how, in this our time, the majesty of the pope is fallen. Heretofore, all monarchs, emperors, kings, and princes feared the pope's power, who held them all at his nod; none durst so much as mutter a word against him. This great god is now fallen; his own creatures, the friars and monks, are his enemies, who, if they still continue with him, do so for the sake of gain; otherwise they would oppose him more fiercely than we do. The pope's crown is named regnum mundi, the kingdom of the world. I have heard it credibly reported at Rome, that this crown is worth more than all the princedoms of Germany. God placed popedom in Italy not without cause, for the Italians can make out many things to be real and true, which in truth are not so: they have crafty and subtle brains.

If the pope were the head of the Christian Church, then the Church were a monster with two heads, seeing that St. Paul says that Christ is her head. The pope may well be, and is, the head of the false Church. Where the linnet is, there is also the cuckoo, for he thinks his song a thousand times better than the linnet's. Even thus, the pope places himself in the Church, and so that his song may be heard, overcrows the Church. The cuckoo is good for something, in that its appearance gives tidings that summer is at hand; so the pope serves to show us that the last day of judgment approaches. There are many that think I am too fierce against popedom; on the contrary, I complain that I am, alas! too mild; I wish I could breathe out lightning against pope and popedom, and that every word were a thunderbolt.

'Tis an idle dream the papists entertain of antichrist; they suppose he should be a single person, that should govern, scatter money amongst them, do miracles, carry a fiery oven about him, and kill the saints. In popedom they make priests, not to preach and teach God's Word, but only to celebrate mass, and to gad about with the sacrament. For, when a bishop ordains a man, he says: Take unto thee power to celebrate mass, and to offer for the living and the dead. But we ordain priests according to the command of Christ and St. Paul, namely, to preach the pure gospel and God's Word. The papists in their ordinations make no mention of preaching and teaching God's Word, therefore their consecrating and ordaining is false and unright, for all worshiping which is not ordained of God, or erected by God's Word and command, is nothing worth, yea, mere idolatry.

Next unto my just cause the small repute and mean aspect of my person gave the blow to the pope. For when I began to preach and write, the pope scorned and contemned me; he thought: 'Tis but one poor friar; what can he do against me? I have maintained and defended this doctrine in popedom, against many emperors, kings, and princes, what then shall this one man do? If he had condescended to regard me, he might easily have suppressed me in the beginning.

A German, making his confession to a priest at Rome, promised, on oath, to keep secret whatsoever the priest should impart unto him, until he reached home; whereupon the priest gave him a leg of the ass on which Christ rode into Jerusalem, very neatly bound up in silk, and said: This is the holy relic on which the Lord Christ corporally did sit, with his sacred legs touching this ass's leg. Then was the German wondrous glad, and carried the said holy relic with him into Germany. When he got to the borders, he bragged of his holy relic in the presence of four others, his comrades, when, lo! it turned out that each of them had likewise received from the same priest a leg, after promising the same secrecy. Thereupon, all exclaimed, with great wonder: Lord! had that ass five legs?

A picture being brought to Luther, in which the pope, with Judas the traitor, were represented hanging on the purse and keys, he said: 'Twill vex the pope horribly, that he, whom emperors and kings have worshiped, should now be figured hanging on his false pick-locks. It will also grieve the papists, for their consciences will be touched. The purse accords well with the cardinal's hats and their incomes, for the pope's covetousness has been so gross, that in all kingdoms he has not only raked to himself Annates, Pallium-money, &c., but has also sold for money the holy sacrament, indulgences, fraternities, Christ's blood, matrimony, etc. Therefore, his purse is filled with robberies, upon which justly ought to be exclaimed, as in the Revelations; "Recompense them as they have done to you, and make it double unto them, according to their works." Therefore, seeing the pope has damned me and given me over to the devil, so will I, in requital, hang him on his own keys.

It is abominable that in so many of the pope's decrees, there is not one single sentence of Holy Scripture, or one article of the Catechism mentioned. The pope intending to conduct the government of his Church in an external way, his teachings were blasphemous; such as that a stinking friar's hood, put upon a dead body, procured remission of sins, and was of equal value with the merits of our blessed Savior Christ Jesus.

It is no marvel that the papists hate me so vehemently, for I have well deserved it at their hands. Christ more mildly reproved the Jews than I the papists, yet they killed him. These, therefore, think they justly persecute me, but, according to God's laws and will, they shall find their mistake. In the day of the last judgment I will denounce the pope and his tyrants, who scorn and assail the Word of God, and his sacraments. The pope destroys poor married priests, that receive and observe God's Word and statutes, whereas by all their laws they are only to be displaced from their office. So Prince Georg has banished and driven away from Oschitz ten citizens and householders, with twenty-seven children, martyrs to the Word. Their sighs will rise up to heaven against him.

The pope and his crew can in nowise endure the idea of reformation; the mere word creates more alarm at Rome, than thunderbolts from heaven, or the day of judgment. A cardinal said, the other day: Let them eat, and drink, and do what they will; but as to reforming us, we think that is a vain idea; we will not endure it. Neither will we Protestants be satisfied, though they administer the sacrament in both kinds, and permit priests to marry; we will also have doctrine of the faith pure and unfalsified, and the righteousness that justifies and saves before God, and which expels and drives away all idolatry and false-worshiping; these gone and banished, the foundation on which popedom is built falls also.

We will have the holy sacrament administered in both kinds, that it shall be free for priests to marry, or to forbear, and we will in no way suffer ourselves to be bereaved of the article of justification: "That by faith only in Jesus Christ we are justified and saved before God; without any works, merits and deserts, merely by grace and mercy." This we must keep and preserve, pure and unfalsified, if we intend to be saved. As to private mass, we cannot hinder it, but must leave it to God, to be acted by those over whom we have neither power nor command; yet, nevertheless, we will openly teach and preach against it, and show that it is abominable blasphemy and idolatry. Either we must go together by the ears, or else they, in our countries, must yield unto us in this particular; if it come to pass that herein they yield unto us, then must we be contented; for, like as the Christians dealt with the Arians, and as St. Paul was constrained to carry himself towards the Jews, even so must we also leave the papists to their own consciences, and seeing they will not follow us, so we neither can nor will force them, but must let them go and commit it to God's judgment; and truly, sincerely, and diligently hold unto and maintain our doctrine, let the same vex, anger, and displease whom it will.

The papists see they have an ill cause, and, therefore, labor to maintain it with very poor arguments, that can not endure the proof, and may be easily confuted. They say: "The praising of anything is an invocation; the saints are to be praised, therefore they are to be invoked." I answer: No, in nowise;

for every praising is not invoking: married people are to be praised, but not to be invoked; for invocation belongs only to God and not to any creature, either in heaven or on earth; no, not to any angel. They say: "The doctrine of the remission of sins is necessary: indulgences, pardons, and graces are remissions of sins; therefore they are necessary." No: the pope's pardons are not remissions of sins, but satisfactions of sins, but satisfactions for remitting the punishments: mere fables and fictions.

When I was in Rome, a disputation was held, at which were present thirty learned doctors besides myself, against the pope's power; he boasting, that with his right hand he commands the angels in heaven, and with his left draws souls out of purgatory, and that his person is mingled with the godhead. Calixtus disputed against these assertions, and showed that it was only on earth that power was given to the pope to bind and to loose. The other doctors hereupon assailed him with exceeding vehemence, and Calixtus discontinued his arguments, saying, he had only spoken by way of disputation, and that his real opinions were far otherwise.

For the space of many hundreds years there has not been a single bishop that has shown any zeal on the subject of schools, baptism, and preaching; 'twould have been too great trouble for them, such enemies were they to God. I have heard divers worthy doctors affirm, that the Church has long since stood in need of reformation; but no man was so bold as to assail popedom; for the pope had on his banner, Noli me tangere; therefore every man was silent. Dr. Staupitz said once to me: "If you meddle with popedom, you will have the whole world against you;" and he added "yet the Church is built on blood, and with blood must be sprinkled."

I would have all those who intend to preach the gospel, diligently read the popish abominations, their decrees and books; and, above all things, thoroughly consider the horrors of the mass--on account of which idol God might justly have drowned and destroyed the whole earth--to the end their consciences may be armed and confirmed against their adversaries.

The fasting of the friars is more easy to them than our eating to us. For one day of fasting there are three of feasting. Every friar for his supper has two quarts of beer, a quart of wine, and spice-cakes, or bread prepared with spice and salt, the better to relish their drink. Thus go on these poor fasting brethren; getting so pale and wan, they are like the fiery angels. If the emperor would merit immortal praise, he would utterly root out the order of the Capuchins, and, for an everlasting remembrance of their abominations, cause their books to remain in safe custody. 'Tis the worst and most poisonous sect. The Augustine and Bernardine friars are no way comparable with these confounded lice.

Francis was an Italian, born in the city of Assisi, doubtless an honest and just man. He little thought that such superstition and unbelief would proceed out of his life. There have been so many of those grey friars, that they offered to send forty thousand of their number against the Turks, and yet leave their monasteries sufficiently provided for. The Franciscan and grey friars came up under the emperor Frederick II, at the time St. Elisabeth was canonized, in the year 1207. Francis worked his game eighteen years; two years under the emperor Philip, four years under the emperor Otho, and twelve years under the emperor Frederick II. They feign, that after his death he appeared to the pope in a dream, held a cup in his hand, and filled the same with blood that ran out of his side. Is not this, think ye, a fine and proper piece of government, that began with dreams and with lies? The pope is not God's image, but his ape. He will be both God and emperor; as pope Innocent III said: I will either take the crown from the emperor Philip, or he shall take mine from me. Oh, such histories ought diligently to be written, to the end posterity may know upon what grounds popedom was erected and founded; namely, upon mere lies and fables. If I were younger, I would write a chronicle of the popes.

If the pope should seek to suppress the mendicant friars, he would find fine sport; he has made them fat, and cherished them in his bosom, and assigned them the greatest and most powerful princes for protectors. If he should attempt to abolish them, they would all combine and instigate the princes against him, for many kings and princes, and the emperor himself, have friars for confessors. The friars were the pope's columns, they carried him as the rats carry their king; I was our Lord God's quicksilver, which he threw into the fishpond; that is, which he cast among the friars. A friar is evil every way, whether in the monastery or out of it. For as Aristotle gives an example touching fire, that burns whether it be in Ethiopia or in Germany, even so is it likewise with the friars. Nature is not changed by any circumstances of time or place.

In Italy was a particular order of friars, called Fratres Ignorantiae, that is, Brethren of Ignorance, who took a solemn oath, that they would neither know, learn, nor understand anything at all, but answer all questions with Nescio. Truly, all friars are well worthy of this title, for they only read and babble out the words, but regard not their meaning. The pope and cardinals think: should these brethren study and be learned, they would master us. Therefore, saccum per neccum, that is, hang a bag about their necks, and send them a-begging through cities, towns and countries.

An honest matron here in Wittenberg, widow of the consul Horndorff, complained of the covetousness of the Capuchins, one of whom pressed her father, upon his deathbed, to bequeath something to their monastery, and got from him four hundred florins, for the use of the monastery, the friar constraining herself to make a vow, that she would mention the matter to no person. The man kept the money, which course he usually took, to the great hurt of all the children and orphans in that city. At last, by command of the magistrate, she told how the friar had acted. Many such examples have been, yet no creature dared complain. There was no end of the robbing, filching, and stealing, of those insatiable, money-diseased wretches.

When I was in the monastery at Erfurt, a preaching friar and a bare-foot friar wandered into the country to beg for the brethren, and to gather alms. These two played upon each other in their sermons. The bare-foot friar preaching first, said: "Loving country people, and good friends! take heed of that bird the swallow, for it is white within, but upon the back it is black; it is an evil bird, always chirping, but profitable for nothing; and when angered, is altogether mad," hereby describing the preaching friar, who wear on the outside black coats, and inside white linen. Now, in the afternoon, the preaching friar came into the pulpit and played upon the bare-foot friar: "Indeed, loving friends, I neither may nor can well defend the swallow; but the grey sparrow is far a worse and more hurtful bird than the swallow; for it bites the kine, and when it fouls into people's eyes, makes them blind, as ye may see in the book of Tobit. He robs, steals, and devours all he can get, as oats, barley, wheat, rye, apples, pears, peas, cherries, &c. Moreover, he is a lascivious bird: his greatest art is to cry: 'Scrip, scrip,'" etc. The bare-foot friar might in better colors have painted the preaching friars, for they are proud buzzards and right epicureans; while the bare-foot friars, under color of sanctity and humility, are more proud and haughty than kings or princes, and, most of all, have imagined and devised monstrous lies.

St. Bernard was the best monk that ever was, whom I love beyond all the rest put together; yet he dared to say, it were a sign of damnation if a man quitted his monastery. He had under him three thousand monks, not one of whom was damned, if his opinion be true, sed vix credo. St. Bernard lived in dangerous times, under the emperors Henry IV and V, Conrad and Lothaire. He was a learned and able monk, but he gave evil example. The friars, especially the Minorites and Franciscans, had easy days by their hypocrisy; they touched no money, yet they were vastly rich, and lived in luxury. The evil friar's life began betimes, when people, under color of piety, abandoned temporal matters. The vocation and condition of a true Christian, such as God ordained and founded it, consists in three hierarchies---domestic, temporal, and Church government.

The state of celibacy is great hypocrisy and wickedness. Augustine, though he lived in a good and acceptable time, was deceived through the exaltation of nuns. And although he gave them leave to marry, yet he said they did wrong to marry, and sinned against God. Afterwards, when the time of wrath and blindness came, and the truth was hunted away, and lying got the upper hand, the generation of poor women was contemned, under the color of great holiness, but which, in truth, was mere hypocrisy. Christ with one sentence confutes all their arguments: God created them male and female.

Martin Luther. "Address to the Christian Nobility of the German Nation." J.H. Robinson, ed. *Readings in European History*. Boston: Ginn, 1906.

—. "Against Catholicism." Oliver J. Thatcher, ed., *The Library of Original Sources*. Milwaukee: University Research Extension Co., 1907.

Meditations on First Philosophy
René Descartes

MEDITATION I
OF THE THINGS OF WHICH WE MAY DOUBT.

1. Several years have now elapsed since I first became aware that I had accepted, even from my youth, many false opinions for true, and that consequently what I afterward based on such principles was highly doubtful; and from that time I was convinced of the necessity of undertaking once in my life to rid myself of all the opinions I had adopted, and of commencing anew the work of building from the foundation, if I desired to establish a firm and abiding superstructure in the sciences. But as this enterprise appeared to me to be one of great magnitude, I waited until I had attained an age so mature as to leave me no hope that at any stage of life more advanced I should be better able to execute my design. On this account, I have delayed so long that I should henceforth consider I was doing wrong were I still to consume in deliberation any of the time that now remains for action. To-day, then, since I have opportunely freed my mind from all cares [and am happily disturbed by no passions], and since I am in the secure possession of leisure in a peaceable retirement, I will at length apply myself earnestly and freely to the general overthrow of all my former opinions.

2. But, to this end, it will not be necessary for me to show that the whole of these are false--a point, perhaps, which I shall never reach; but as even now my reason convinces me that I ought not the less carefully to withhold belief from what is not entirely certain and indubitable, than from what is manifestly false, it will be sufficient to justify the rejection of the whole if I shall find in each some ground for doubt. Nor for this purpose will it be necessary even to deal with each belief individually, which would be truly an endless labor; but, as the removal from below of the foundation necessarily involves the downfall of the whole edifice, I will at once approach the criticism of the principles on which all my former beliefs rested.

3. All that I have, up to this moment, accepted as possessed of the highest

truth and certainty, I received either from or through the senses. I observed, however, that these sometimes misled us; and it is the part of prudence not to place absolute confidence in that by which we have even once been deceived.

4. But it may be said, perhaps, that, although the senses occasionally mislead us respecting minute objects, and such as are so far removed from us as to be beyond the reach of close observation, there are yet many other of their informations (presentations), of the truth of which it is manifestly impossible to doubt; as for example, that I am in this place, seated by the fire, clothed in a winter dressing gown, that I hold in my hands this piece of paper, with other intimations of the same nature. But how could I deny that I possess these hands and this body, and withal escape being classed with persons in a state of insanity, whose brains are so disordered and clouded by dark bilious vapors as to cause them pertinaciously to assert that they are monarchs when they are in the greatest poverty; or clothed [in gold] and purple when destitute of any covering; or that their head is made of clay, their body of glass, or that they are gourds? I should certainly be not less insane than they, were I to regulate my procedure according to examples so extravagant.

5. Though this be true, I must nevertheless here consider that I am a man, and that, consequently, I am in the habit of sleeping, and representing to myself in dreams those same things, or even sometimes others less probable, which the insane think are presented to them in their waking moments. How often have I dreamt that I was in these familiar circumstances, that I was dressed, and occupied this place by the fire, when I was lying undressed in bed? At the present moment, however, I certainly look upon this paper with eyes wide awake; the head which I now move is not asleep; I extend this hand consciously and with express purpose, and I perceive it; the occurrences in sleep are not so distinct as all this. But I cannot forget that, at other times I have been deceived in sleep by similar illusions; and, attentively considering those cases, I perceive so clearly that there exist no certain marks by which the state of waking can ever be distinguished from sleep, that I feel greatly astonished; and in amazement I almost persuade myself that I am now dreaming.

6. Let us suppose, then, that we are dreaming, and that all these particulars—namely, the opening of the eyes, the motion of the head, the forth-putting of the hands--are merely illusions; and even that we really possess neither an entire body nor hands such as we see. Nevertheless it must be admitted at least that the objects which appear to us in sleep are, as it were, painted representations which could not have been formed unless in the likeness of realities; and, therefore, that those general objects, at all events, namely, eyes, a head, hands, and an entire body, are not simply imaginary, but really existent. For, in truth, painters themselves, even when they study to represent sirens and satyrs by forms the most fantastic and extraordinary, cannot bestow upon them natures absolutely new, but can only make a certain medley of the members of different animals; or if they chance to imagine something so novel that nothing at all similar has ever been seen before,

and such as is, therefore, purely fictitious and absolutely false, it is at least certain that the colors of which this is composed are real. And on the same principle, although these general objects, viz. [a body], eyes, a head, hands, and the like, be imaginary, we are nevertheless absolutely necessitated to admit the reality at least of some other objects still more simple and universal than these, of which, just as of certain real colors, all those images of things, whether true and real, or false and fantastic, that are found in our consciousness (cogitatio),are formed.

7. To this class of objects seem to belong corporeal nature in general and its extension; the figure of extended things, their quantity or magnitude, and their number, as also the place in, and the time during, which they exist, and other things of the same sort.

8. We will not, therefore, perhaps reason illegitimately if we conclude from this that Physics, Astronomy, Medicine, and all the other sciences that have for their end the consideration of composite objects, are indeed of a doubtful character; but that Arithmetic, Geometry, and the other sciences of the same class, which regard merely the simplest and most general objects, and scarcely inquire whether or not these are really existent, contain somewhat that is certain and indubitable: for whether I am awake or dreaming, it remains true that two and three make five, and that a square has but four sides; nor does it seem possible that truths so apparent can ever fall under a suspicion of falsity [or incertitude].

9. Nevertheless, the belief that there is a God who is all powerful, and who created me, such as I am, has, for a long time, obtained steady possession of my mind. How, then, do I know that he has not arranged that there should be neither earth, nor sky, nor any extended thing, nor figure, nor magnitude, nor place, providing at the same time, however, for [the rise in me of the perceptions of all these objects, and] the persuasion that these do not exist otherwise than as I perceive them ? And further, as I sometimes think that others are in error respecting matters of which they believe themselves to possess a perfect knowledge, how do I know that I am not also deceived each time I add together two and three, or number the sides of a square, or form some judgment still more simple, if more simple indeed can be imagined? But perhaps Deity has not been willing that I should be thus deceived, for he is said to be supremely good. If, however, it were repugnant to the goodness of Deity to have created me subject to constant deception, it would seem likewise to be contrary to his goodness to allow me to be occasionally deceived; and yet it is clear that this is permitted.

10. Some, indeed, might perhaps be found who would be disposed rather to deny the existence of a Being so powerful than to believe that there is nothing certain. But let us for the present refrain from opposing this opinion, and grant that all which is here said of a Deity is fabulous: nevertheless, in whatever way it be supposed that I reach the state in which I exist, whether by fate, or chance, or by an endless series of antecedents and consequents, or by any other means, it is clear (since to be deceived and to err is a certain defect) that the probability of my being so imperfect as to be the constant victim of

deception, will be increased exactly in proportion as the power possessed by the cause, to which they assign my origin, is lessened. To these reasonings I have assuredly nothing to reply, but am constrained at last to avow that there is nothing of all that I formerly believed to be true of which it is impossible to doubt, and that not through thoughtlessness or levity, but from cogent and maturely considered reasons; so that henceforward, if I desire to discover anything certain, I ought not the less carefully to refrain from assenting to those same opinions than to what might be shown to be manifestly false.

11. But it is not sufficient to have made these observations; care must be taken likewise to keep them in remembrance. For those old and customary opinions perpetually recur—long and familiar usage giving them the right of occupying my mind, even almost against my will, and subduing my belief; nor will I lose the habit of deferring to them and confiding in them so long as I shall consider them to be what in truth they are, viz, opinions to some extent doubtful, as I have already shown, but still highly probable, and such as it is much more reasonable to believe than deny. It is for this reason I am persuaded that I shall not be doing wrong, if, taking an opposite judgment of deliberate design, I become my own deceiver, by supposing, for a time, that all those opinions are entirely false and imaginary, until at length, having thus balanced my old by my new prejudices, my judgment shall no longer be turned aside by perverted usage from the path that may conduct to the perception of truth. For I am assured that, meanwhile, there will arise neither peril nor error from this course, and that I cannot for the present yield too much to distrust, since the end I now seek is not action but knowledge.

12. I will suppose, then, not that Deity, who is sovereignly good and the fountain of truth, but that some malignant demon, who is at once exceedingly potent and deceitful, has employed all his artifice to deceive me; I will suppose that the sky, the air, the earth, colors, figures, sounds, and all external things, are nothing better than the illusions of dreams, by means of which this being has laid snares for my credulity; I will consider myself as without hands, eyes, flesh, blood, or any of the senses, and as falsely believing that I am possessed of these; I will continue resolutely fixed in this belief, and if indeed by this means it be not in my power to arrive at the knowledge of truth, I shall at least do what is in my power, viz, [suspend my judgment], and guard with settled purpose against giving my assent to what is false, and being imposed upon by this deceiver, whatever be his power and artifice. But this undertaking is arduous, and a certain indolence insensibly leads me back to my ordinary course of life; and just as the captive, who, perchance, was enjoying in his dreams an imaginary liberty, when he begins to suspect that it is but a vision, dreads awakening, and conspires with the agreeable illusions that the deception may be prolonged; so I, of my own accord, fall back into the train of my former beliefs, and fear to arouse myself from my slumber, lest the time of laborious wakefulness that would succeed this quiet rest, in place of bringing any light of day, should prove inadequate to dispel the darkness that will arise from the difficulties that have now been raised.

MEDITATION II.
OF THE NATURE OF THE HUMAN MIND; AND THAT IT IS MORE EASILY KNOWN THAN THE BODY.

1. The Meditation of yesterday has filled my mind with so many doubts, that it is no longer in my power to forget them. Nor do I see, meanwhile, any principle on which they can be resolved; and, just as if I had fallen all of a sudden into very deep water, I am so greatly disconcerted as to be unable either to plant my feet firmly on the bottom or sustain myself by swimming on the surface. I will, nevertheless, make an effort, and try anew the same path on which I had entered yesterday, that is, proceed by casting aside all that admits of the slightest doubt, not less than if I had discovered it to be absolutely false; and I will continue always in this track until I shall find something that is certain, or at least, if I can do nothing more, until I shall know with certainty that there is nothing certain. Archimedes, that he might transport the entire globe from the place it occupied to another, demanded only a point that was firm and immovable; so, also, I shall be entitled to entertain the highest expectations, if I am fortunate enough to discover only one thing that is certain and indubitable.

2. I suppose, accordingly, that all the things which I see are false (fictitious); I believe that none of those objects which my fallacious memory represents ever existed; I suppose that I possess no senses; I believe that body, figure, extension, motion, and place are merely fictions of my mind. What is there, then, that can be esteemed true ? Perhaps this only, that there is absolutely nothing certain.

3. But how do I know that there is not something different altogether from the objects I have now enumerated, of which it is impossible to entertain the slightest doubt? Is there not a God, or some being, by whatever name I may designate him, who causes these thoughts to arise in my mind ? But why suppose such a being, for it may be I myself am capable of producing them? Am I, then, at least not something? But I before denied that I possessed senses or a body; I hesitate, however, for what follows from that? Am I so dependent on the body and the senses that without these I cannot exist? But I had the persuasion that there was absolutely nothing in the world, that there was no sky and no earth, neither minds nor bodies; was I not, therefore, at the same time, persuaded that I did not exist? Far from it; I assuredly existed, since I was persuaded. But there is I know not what being, who is possessed at once of the highest power and the deepest cunning, who is constantly employing all his ingenuity in deceiving me. Doubtless, then, I exist, since I am deceived; and, let him deceive me as he may, he can never bring it about that I am nothing, so long as I shall be conscious that I am something. So that it must, in fine, be maintained, all things being maturely and carefully considered, that this proposition (pronunciatum) I am, I exist, is necessarily true each time it is expressed by me, or conceived in my mind.

4. But I do not yet know with sufficient clearness what I am, though assured that I am; and hence, in the next place, I must take care, lest perchance

I inconsiderately substitute some other object in room of what is properly myself, and thus wander from truth, even in that knowledge (cognition) which I hold to be of all others the most certain and evident. For this reason, I will now consider anew what I formerly believed myself to be, before I entered on the present train of thought; and of my previous opinion I will retrench all that can in the least be invalidated by the grounds of doubt I have adduced, in order that there may at length remain nothing but what is certain and indubitable.

5. What then did I formerly think I was? Undoubtedly I judged that I was a man. But what is a man ? Shall I say a rational animal ? Assuredly not; for it would be necessary forthwith to inquire into what is meant by animal, and what by rational, and thus, from a single question, I should insensibly glide into others, and these more difficult than the first; nor do I now possess enough of leisure to warrant me in wasting my time amid subtleties of this sort. I prefer here to attend to the thoughts that sprung up of themselves in my mind, and were inspired by my own nature alone, when I applied myself to the consideration of what I was. In the first place, then, I thought that I possessed a countenance, hands, arms, and all the fabric of members that appears in a corpse, and which I called by the name of body. It further occurred to me that I was nourished, that I walked, perceived, and thought, and all those actions I referred to the soul; but what the soul itself was I either did not stay to consider, or, if I did, I imagined that it was something extremely rare and subtile, like wind, or flame, or ether, spread through my grosser parts. As regarded the body, I did not even doubt of its nature, but thought I distinctly knew it, and if I had wished to describe it according to the notions I then entertained, I should have explained myself in this manner: By body I understand all that can be terminated by a certain figure; that can be comprised in a certain place, and so fill a certain space as therefrom to exclude every other body; that can be perceived either by touch, sight, hearing, taste, or smell; that can be moved in different ways, not indeed of itself, but by something foreign to it by which it is touched [and from which it receives the impression]; for the power of self-motion, as likewise that of perceiving and thinking, I held as by no means pertaining to the nature of body; on the contrary, I was somewhat astonished to find such faculties existing in some bodies.

6. But [as to myself, what can I now say that I am], since I suppose there exists an extremely powerful, and, if I may so speak, malignant being, whose whole endeavors are directed toward deceiving me? Can I affirm that I possess any one of all those attributes of which I have lately spoken as belonging to the nature of body? After attentively considering them in my own mind, I find none of them that can properly be said to belong to myself. To recount them were idle and tedious. Let us pass, then, to the attributes of the soul. The first mentioned were the powers of nutrition and walking; but, if it be true that I have no body, it is true likewise that I am capable neither of walking nor of being nourished. Perception is another attribute of the soul; but perception too is impossible without the body; besides, I have frequently, during sleep, believed that I perceived objects which I afterward observed I did not in reality perceive. Thinking is another attribute of the soul; and here I dis-

cover what properly belongs to myself. This alone is inseparable from me. I am--I exist: this is certain; but how often? As often as I think; for perhaps it would even happen, if I should wholly cease to think, that I should at the same time altogether cease to be. I now admit nothing that is not necessarily true. I am therefore, precisely speaking, only a thinking thing, that is, a mind (mens sive animus), understanding, or reason, terms whose signification was before unknown to me. I am, however, a real thing, and really existent; but what thing? The answer was, a thinking thing.

7. The question now arises, am I aught besides ? I will stimulate my imagination with a view to discover whether I am not still something more than a thinking being. Now it is plain I am not the assemblage of members called the human body; I am not a thin and penetrating air diffused through all these members, or wind, or flame, or vapor, or breath, or any of all the things I can imagine; for I supposed that all these were not, and, without changing the supposition, I find that I still feel assured of my existence. But it is true, perhaps, that those very things which I suppose to be non-existent, because they are unknown to me, are not in truth different from myself whom I know. This is a point I cannot determine, and do not now enter into any dispute regarding it. I can only judge of things that are known to me: I am conscious that I exist, and I who know that I exist inquire into what I am. It is, however, perfectly certain that the knowledge of my existence, thus precisely taken, is not dependent on things, the existence of which is as yet unknown to me: and consequently it is not dependent on any of the things I can feign in imagination. Moreover, the phrase itself, I frame an image (efffingo), reminds me of my error; for I should in truth frame one if I were to imagine myself to be anything, since to imagine is nothing more than to contemplate the figure or image of a corporeal thing; but I already know that I exist, and that it is possible at the same time that all those images, and in general all that relates to the nature of body, are merely dreams [or chimeras]. From this I discover that it is not more reasonable to say, I will excite my imagination that I may know more distinctly what I am, than to express myself as follows: I am now awake, and perceive something real; but because my perception is not sufficiently clear, I will of express purpose go to sleep that my dreams may represent to me the object of my perception with more truth and clearness. And, therefore, I know that nothing of all that I can embrace in imagination belongs to the knowledge which I have of myself, and that there is need to recall with the utmost care the mind from this mode of thinking, that it may be able to know its own nature with perfect distinctness.

8. But what, then, am I? A thinking thing, it has been said. But what is a thinking thing? It is a thing that doubts, understands, [conceives], affirms, denies, wills, refuses; that imagines also, and perceives....

11. Let us now accordingly consider the objects that are commonly thought to be [the most easily, and likewise] the most distinctly known, viz, the bodies we touch and see; not, indeed, bodies in general, for these general notions are usually somewhat more confused, but one body in particular. Take, for example, this piece of wax; it is quite fresh, having been but recently taken from the beehive; it has not yet lost the sweetness of the honey

it contained; it still retains somewhat of the odor of the flowers from which it was gathered; its color, figure, size, are apparent (to the sight); it is hard, cold, easily handled; and sounds when struck upon with the finger. In fine, all that contributes to make a body as distinctly known as possible, is found in the one before us. But, while I am speaking, let it be placed near the fire—what remained of the taste exhales, the smell evaporates, the color changes, its figure is destroyed, its size increases, it becomes liquid, it grows hot, it can hardly be handled, and, although struck upon, it emits no sound. Does the same wax still remain after this change ? It must be admitted that it does remain; no one doubts it, or judges otherwise. What, then, was it I knew with so much distinctness in the piece of wax? Assuredly, it could be nothing of all that I observed by means of the senses, since all the things that fell under taste, smell, sight, touch, and hearing are changed, and yet the same wax remains.

12. It was perhaps what I now think, viz, that this wax was neither the sweetness of honey, the pleasant odor of flowers, the whiteness, the figure, nor the sound, but only a body that a little before appeared to me conspicuous under these forms, and which is now perceived under others. But, to speak precisely, what is it that I imagine when I think of it in this way? Let it be attentively considered, and, retrenching all that does not belong to the wax, let us see what remains. There certainly remains nothing, except something extended, flexible, and movable. But what is meant by flexible and movable? Is it not that I imagine that the piece of wax, being round, is capable of becoming square, or of passing from a square into a triangular figure? Assuredly such is not the case, because I conceive that it admits of an infinity of similar changes; and I am, moreover, unable to compass this infinity by imagination, and consequently this conception which I have of the wax is not the product of the faculty of imagination. But what now is this extension? Is it not also unknown ? for it becomes greater when the wax is melted, greater when it is boiled, and greater still when the heat increases; and I should not conceive [clearly and] according to truth, the wax as it is, if I did not suppose that the piece we are considering admitted even of a wider variety of extension than I ever imagined, I must, therefore, admit that I cannot even comprehend by imagination what the piece of wax is, and that it is the mind alone (mens, Lat., entendement, F.) which perceives it. I speak of one piece in particular; for as to wax in general, this is still more evident. But what is the piece of wax that can be perceived only by the [understanding or] mind? It is certainly the same which I see, touch, imagine; and, in fine, it is the same which, from the beginning, I believed it to be. But (and this it is of moment to observe) the perception of it is neither an act of sight, of touch, nor of imagination, and never was either of these, though it might formerly seem so, but is simply an intuition (inspectio) of the mind, which may be imperfect and confused, as it formerly was, or very clear and distinct, as it is at present, according as the attention is more or less directed to the elements which it contains, and of which it is composed.

13. But, meanwhile, I feel greatly astonished when I observe [the weakness of my mind, and] its proneness to error. For although, without at all

giving expression to what I think, I consider all this in my own mind, words yet occasionally impede my progress, and I am almost led into error by the terms of ordinary language. We say, for example, that we see the same wax when it is before us, and not that we judge it to be the same from its retaining the same color and figure: whence I should forthwith be disposed to conclude that the wax is known by the act of sight, and not by the intuition of the mind alone, were it not for the analogous instance of human beings passing on in the street below, as observed from a window. In this case I do not fail to say that I see the men themselves, just as I say that I see the wax; and yet what do I see from the window beyond hats and cloaks that might cover artificial machines, whose motions might be determined by springs ? But I judge that there are human beings from these appearances, and thus I comprehend, by the faculty of judgment alone which is in the mind, what I believed I saw with my eyes....

MEDITATION III.
OF GOD: THAT HE EXISTS.

1. I will now close my eyes, I will stop my ears, I will turn away my senses from their objects, I will even efface from my consciousness all the images of corporeal things; or at least, because this can hardly be accomplished, I will consider them as empty and false; and thus, holding converse only with myself, and closely examining my nature, I will endeavor to obtain by degrees a more intimate and familiar knowledge of myself. I am a thinking (conscious) thing, that is, a being who doubts, affirms, denies, knows a few objects, and is ignorant of many,-- [who loves, hates], wills, refuses, who imagines likewise, and perceives; for, as I before remarked, although the things which I perceive or imagine are perhaps nothing at all apart from me [and in themselves], I am nevertheless assured that those modes of consciousness which I call perceptions and imaginations, in as far only as they are modes of consciousness, exist in me.

2. And in the little I have said I think I have summed up all that I really know, or at least all that up to this time I was aware I knew. Now, as I am endeavoring to extend my knowledge more widely, I will use circumspection, and consider with care whether I can still discover in myself anything further which I have not yet hitherto observed. I am certain that I am a thinking thing; but do I not therefore likewise know what is required to render me certain of a truth ? In this first knowledge, doubtless, there is nothing that gives me assurance of its truth except the clear and distinct perception of what I affirm, which would not indeed be sufficient to give me the assurance that what I say is true, if it could ever happen that anything I thus clearly and distinctly perceived should prove false; and accordingly it seems to me that I may now take as a general rule, that all that is very clearly and distinctly apprehended (conceived) is true....

7. But among these ideas, some appear to me to be innate, others adventitious, and others to be made by myself (factitious); for, as I have the power of conceiving what is called a thing, or a truth, or a thought, it seems to me

that I hold this power from no other source than my own nature; but if I now hear a noise, if I see the sun, or if I feel heat, I have all along judged that these sensations proceeded from certain objects existing out of myself; and, in fine, it appears to me that sirens, hippogryphs, and the like, are inventions of my own mind. But I may even perhaps come to be of opinion that all my ideas are of the class which I call adventitious, or that they are all innate, or that they are all factitious; for I have not yet clearly discovered their true origin.

8. What I have here principally to do is to consider, with reference to those that appear to come from certain objects without me, what grounds there are for thinking them like these objects. The first of these grounds is that it seems to me I am so taught by nature; and the second that I am conscious that those ideas are not dependent on my will, and therefore not on myself, for they are frequently presented to me against my will, as at present, whether I will or not, I feel heat; and I am thus persuaded that this sensation or idea (sensum vel ideam) of heat is produced in me by something different from myself, viz., by the heat of the fire by which I sit. And it is very reasonable to suppose that this object impresses me with its own likeness rather than any other thing.

9. But I must consider whether these reasons are sufficiently strong and convincing. When I speak of being taught by nature in this matter, I understand by the word nature only a certain spontaneous impetus that impels me to believe in a resemblance between ideas and their objects, and not a natural light that affords a knowledge of its truth. But these two things are widely different; for what the natural light shows to be true can be in no degree doubtful, as, for example, that I am because I doubt, and other truths of the like kind; inasmuch as I possess no other faculty whereby to distinguish truth from error, which can teach me the falsity of what the natural light declares to be true, and which is equally trustworthy; but with respect to [seemingly] natural impulses, I have observed, when the question related to the choice of right or wrong in action, that they frequently led me to take the worse part; nor do I see that I have any better ground for following them in what relates to truth and error.

10. Then, with respect to the other reason, which is that because these ideas do not depend on my will, they must arise from objects existing without me, I do not find it more convincing than the former, for just as those natural impulses, of which I have lately spoken, are found in me, notwithstanding that they are not always in harmony with my will, so likewise it may be that I possess some power not sufficiently known to myself capable of producing ideas without the aid of external objects, and, indeed, it has always hitherto appeared to me that they are formed during sleep, by some power of this nature, without the aid of aught external.

11. And, in fine, although I should grant that they proceeded from those objects, it is not a necessary consequence that they must be like them. On the contrary, I have observed, in a number of instances, that there was a great difference between the object and its idea. Thus, for example, I find in my mind two wholly diverse ideas of the sun; the one, by which it appears to me extremely small draws its origin from the senses, and should be placed in the

class of adventitious ideas; the other, by which it seems to be many times larger than the whole earth, is taken up on astronomical grounds, that is, elicited from certain notions born with me, or is framed by myself in some other manner. These two ideas cannot certainly both resemble the same sun; and reason teaches me that the one which seems to have immediately emanated from it is the most unlike.

12. And these things sufficiently prove that hitherto it has not been from a certain and deliberate judgment, but only from a sort of blind impulse, that I believed existence of certain things different from myself, which, by the organs of sense, or by whatever other means it might be, conveyed their ideas or images into my mind [and impressed it with their likenesses]....

17. But, among these my ideas, besides that which represents myself, respecting which there can be here no difficulty, there is one that represents a God; others that represent corporeal and inanimate things; others angels; others animals; and, finally, there are some that represent men like myself.

18. But with respect to the ideas that represent other men, or animals, or angels, I can easily suppose that they were formed by the mingling and composition of the other ideas which I have of myself, of corporeal things, and of God, although they were, apart from myself, neither men, animals, nor angels.

19. And with regard to the ideas of corporeal objects, I never discovered in them anything so great or excellent which I myself did not appear capable of originating....

22. There only remains, therefore, the idea of God, in which I must consider whether there is anything that cannot be supposed to originate with myself. By the name God, I understand a substance infinite, [eternal, immutable], independent, all-knowing, all-powerful, and by which I myself, and every other thing that exists, if any such there be, were created. But these properties are so great and excellent, that the more attentively I consider them the less I feel persuaded that the idea I have of them owes its origin to myself alone. And thus it is absolutely necessary to conclude, from all that I have before said, that God exists.

23. For though the idea of substance be in my mind owing to this, that I myself am a substance, I should not, however, have the idea of an infinite substance, seeing I am a finite being, unless it were given me by some substance in reality infinite.

24. And I must not imagine that I do not apprehend the infinite by a true idea, but only by the negation of the finite, in the same way that I comprehend repose and darkness by the negation of motion and light: since, on the contrary, I clearly perceive that there is more reality in the infinite substance than in the finite, and therefore that in some way I possess the perception (notion) of the infinite before that of the finite, that is, the perception of God before that of myself, for how could I know that I doubt, desire, or that something is wanting to me, and that I am not wholly perfect, if I possessed no idea of a being more perfect than myself, by comparison of which I knew the deficiencies of my nature?....

39. But before I examine this with more attention, and pass on to the

consideration of other truths that may be evolved out of it, I think it proper to remain here for some time in the contemplation of God himself--that I may ponder at leisure his marvelous attributes--and behold, admire, and adore the beauty of this light so unspeakably great, as far, at least, as the strength of my mind, which is to some degree dazzled by the sight, will permit. For just as we learn by faith that the supreme felicity of another life consists in the contemplation of the Divine majesty alone, so even now we learn from experience that a like meditation, though incomparably less perfect, is the source of the highest satisfaction of which we are susceptible in this life.

MEDITATION IV
OF TRUTH AND ERROR

1. I have been habituated these bygone days to detach my mind from the senses, and I have accurately observed that there is exceedingly little which is known with certainty respecting corporeal objects, that we know much more of the human mind, and still more of God himself. I am thus able now without difficulty to abstract my mind from the contemplation of [sensible or] imaginable objects, and apply it to those which, as disengaged from all matter, are purely intelligible. And certainly the idea I have of the human mind in so far as it is a thinking thing, and not extended in length, breadth, and depth, and participating in none of the properties of body, is incomparably more distinct than the idea of any corporeal object; and when I consider that I doubt, in other words, that I am an incomplete and dependent being, the idea of a complete and independent being, that is to say of God, occurs to my mind with so much clearness and distinctness, and from the fact alone that this idea is found in me, or that I who possess it exist, the conclusions that God exists, and that my own existence, each moment of its continuance, is absolutely dependent upon him, are so manifest, as to lead me to believe it impossible that the human mind can know anything with more clearness and certitude. And now I seem to discover a path that will conduct us from the contemplation of the true God, in whom are contained all the treasures of science and wisdom, to the knowledge of the other things in the universe.

2. For, in the first place, I discover that it is impossible for him ever to deceive me, for in all fraud and deceit there is a certain imperfection: and although it may seem that the ability to deceive is a mark of subtlety or power, yet the will testifies without doubt of malice and weakness; and such, accordingly, cannot be found in God.

3. In the next place, I am conscious that I possess a certain faculty of judging [or discerning truth from error], which I doubtless received from God, along with whatever else is mine; and since it is impossible that he should will to deceive me, it is likewise certain that he has not given me a faculty that will ever lead me into error, provided I use it aright.

4. And there would remain no doubt on this head, did it not seem to follow from this, that I can never therefore be deceived; for if all I possess be from God, and if he planted in me no faculty that is deceitful, it seems to follow that I can never fall into error. Accordingly, it is true that when I think

only of God and turn wholly to him, I discover [in myself] no cause of error or falsity: but immediately thereafter, recurring to myself, experience assures me that I am nevertheless subject to innumerable errors. When I come to inquire into the cause of these, I observe that there is not only present to my consciousness a real and positive idea of God, or of a being supremely perfect, but also, so to speak, a certain negative idea of nothing, in other words, of that which is at an infinite distance from every sort of perfection, and that I am, as it were, a mean between God and nothing, or placed in such a way between absolute existence and non-existence, that there is in truth nothing in me to lead me into error, in so far as an absolute being is my creator; but that, on the other hand, as I thus likewise participate in some degree of nothing or of nonbeing, in other words, as I am not myself the supreme Being, and as I am wanting in many perfections, it is not surprising I should fall into error. And I hence discern that error, so far as error is not something real, which depends for its existence on God, but is simply defect; and therefore that, in order to fall into it, it is not necessary God should have given me a faculty expressly for this end, but that my being deceived arises from the circumstance that the power which God has given me of discerning truth from error is not infinite.

5. Nevertheless this is not yet quite satisfactory; for error is not a pure negation, [in other words, it is not the simple deficiency or want of some knowledge which is not due], but the privation or want of some knowledge which it would seem I ought to possess. But, on considering the nature of God, it seems impossible that he should have planted in his creature any faculty not perfect in its kind, that is, wanting in some perfection due to it: for if it be true, that in proportion to the skill of the maker the perfection of his work is greater, what thing can have been produced by the supreme Creator of the universe that is not absolutely perfect in all its parts? And assuredly there is no doubt that God could have created me such as that I should never be deceived; it is certain, likewise, that he always wills what is best: is it better, then, that I should be capable of being deceived than that I should not?

6. Considering this more attentively the first thing that occurs to me is the reflection that I must not be surprised if I am not always capable of comprehending the reasons why God acts as he does; nor must I doubt of his existence because I find, perhaps, that there are several other things besides the present respecting which I understand neither why nor how they were created by him; for, knowing already that my nature is extremely weak and limited, and that the nature of God, on the other hand, is immense, incomprehensible, and infinite, I have no longer any difficulty in discerning that there is an infinity of things in his power whose causes transcend the grasp of my mind: and this consideration alone is sufficient to convince me, that the whole class of final causes is of no avail in physical [or natural] things; for it appears to me that I cannot, without exposing myself to the charge of temerity, seek to discover the (impenetrable) ends of Deity.

7. It further occurs to me that we must not consider only one creature apart from the others, if we wish to determine the perfection of the works of Deity, but generally all his creatures together; for the same object that might

perhaps, with some show of reason, be deemed highly imperfect if it were alone in the world, may for all that be the most perfect possible, considered as forming part of the whole universe: and although, as it was my purpose to doubt of everything, I only as yet know with certainty my own existence and that of God, nevertheless, after having remarked the infinite power of Deity, I cannot deny that we may have produced many other objects, or at least that he is able to produce them, so that I may occupy a place in the relation of a part to the great whole of his creatures.

8. Whereupon, regarding myself more closely, and considering what my errors are (which alone testify to the existence of imperfection in me), I observe that these depend on the concurrence of two causes, viz, the faculty of cognition, which I possess, and that of election or the power of free choice,--in other words, the understanding and the will. For by the understanding alone, I [neither affirm nor deny anything but] merely apprehend (percipio) the ideas regarding which I may form a judgment; nor is any error, properly so called, found in it thus accurately taken. And although there are perhaps innumerable objects in the world of which I have no idea in my understanding, it cannot, on that account be said that I am deprived of those ideas [as of something that is due to my nature], but simply that I do not possess them, because, in truth, there is no ground to prove that Deity ought to have endowed me with a larger faculty of cognition than he has actually bestowed upon me; and however skillful a workman I suppose him to be, I have no reason, on that account, to think that it was obligatory on him to give to each of his works all the perfections he is able to bestow upon some. Nor, moreover, can I complain that God has not given me freedom of choice, or a will sufficiently ample and perfect, since, in truth, I am conscious of will so ample and extended as to be superior to all limits. And what appears to me here to be highly remarkable is that, of all the other properties I possess, there is none so great and perfect as that I do not clearly discern it could be still greater and more perfect. For, to take an example, if I consider the faculty of understanding which I possess, I find that it is of very small extent, and greatly limited, and at the same time I form the idea of another faculty of the same nature, much more ample and even infinite, and seeing that I can frame the idea of it, I discover, from this circumstance alone, that it pertains to the nature of God. In the same way, if I examine the faculty of memory or imagination, or any other faculty I possess, I find none that is not small and circumscribed, and in God immense [and infinite]. It is the faculty of will only, or freedom of choice, which I experience to be so great that I am unable to conceive the idea of another that shall be more ample and extended; so that it is chiefly my will which leads me to discern that I bear a certain image and similitude of Deity. For although the faculty of will is incomparably greater in God than in myself, as well in respect of the knowledge and power that are conjoined with it, and that render it stronger and more efficacious, as in respect of the object, since in him it extends to a greater number of things, it does not, nevertheless, appear to me greater, considered in itself formally and precisely: for the power of will consists only in this, that we are able to do or not to do the same thing (that is, to affirm or deny, to pursue or shun it), or

rather in this alone, that in affirming or denying, pursuing or shunning, what is proposed to us by the understanding, we so act that we are not conscious of being determined to a particular action by any external force. For, to the possession of freedom, it is not necessary that I be alike indifferent toward each of two contraries; but, on the contrary, the more I am inclined toward the one, whether because I clearly know that in it there is the reason of truth and goodness, or because God thus internally disposes my thought, the more freely do I choose and embrace it; and assuredly divine grace and natural knowledge, very far from diminishing liberty, rather augment and fortify it. But the indifference of which I am conscious when I am not impelled to one side rather than to another for want of a reason, is the lowest grade of liberty, and manifests defect or negation of knowledge rather than perfection of will; for if I always clearly knew what was true and good, I should never have any difficulty in determining what judgment I ought to come to, and what choice I ought to make, and I should thus be entirely free without ever being indifferent.

9. From all this I discover, however, that neither the power of willing, which I have received from God, is of itself the source of my errors, for it is exceedingly ample and perfect in its kind; nor even the power of understanding, for as I conceive no object unless by means of the faculty that God bestowed upon me, all that I conceive is doubtless rightly conceived by me, and it is impossible for me to be deceived in it. Whence, then, spring my errors ? They arise from this cause alone, that I do not restrain the will, which is of much wider range than the understanding, within the same limits, but extend it even to things I do not understand, and as the will is of itself indifferent to such, it readily falls into error and sin by choosing the false in room of the true, and evil instead of good.

10. For example, when I lately considered whether aught really existed in the world, and found that because I considered this question, it very manifestly followed that I myself existed, I could not but judge that what I so clearly conceived was true, not that I was forced to this judgment by any external cause, but simply because great clearness of the understanding was succeeded by strong inclination in the will; and I believed this the more freely and spontaneously in proportion as I was less indifferent with respect to it. But now I not only know that I exist, in so far as I am a thinking being, but there is likewise presented to my mind a certain idea of corporeal nature; hence I am in doubt as to whether the thinking nature which is in me, or rather which I myself am, is different from that corporeal nature, or whether both are merely one and the same thing, and I here suppose that I am as yet ignorant of any reason that would determine me to adopt the one belief in preference to the other; whence it happens that it is a matter of perfect indifference to me which of the two suppositions I affirm or deny, or whether I form any judgment at all in the matter.

11. This indifference, moreover, extends not only to things of which the understanding has no knowledge at all, but in general also to all those which it does not discover with perfect clearness at the moment the will is deliberating upon them; for, however probable the conjectures may be that dispose me

to form a judgment in a particular matter, the simple knowledge that these are merely conjectures, and not certain and indubitable reasons, is sufficient to lead me to form one that is directly the opposite. Of this I lately had abundant experience, when I laid aside as false all that I had before held for true, on the single ground that I could in some degree doubt of it.

12. But if I abstain from judging of a thing when I do not conceive it with sufficient clearness and distinctness, it is plain that I act rightly, and am not deceived; but if I resolve to deny or affirm, I then do not make a right use of my free will; and if I affirm what is false, it is evident that I am deceived; moreover, even although I judge according to truth, I stumble upon it by chance, and do not therefore escape the imputation of a wrong use of my freedom; for it is a dictate of the natural light, that the knowledge of the understanding ought always to precede the determination of the will. And it is this wrong use of the freedom of the will in which is found the privation that constitutes the form of error. Privation, I say, is found in the act, in so far as it proceeds from myself, but it does not exist in the faculty which I received from God, nor even in the act, in so far as it depends on him.

13. For I have assuredly no reason to complain that God has not given me a greater power of intelligence or more perfect natural light than he has actually bestowed, since it is of the nature of a finite understanding not to comprehend many things, and of the nature of a created understanding to be finite; on the contrary, I have every reason to render thanks to God, who owed me nothing, for having given me all the perfections I possess, and I should be far from thinking that he has unjustly deprived me of, or kept back, the other perfections which he has not bestowed upon me.

14. I have no reason, moreover, to complain because he has given me a will more ample than my understanding, since, as the will consists only of a single element, and that indivisible, it would appear that this faculty is of such a nature that nothing could be taken from it [without destroying it]; and certainly, the more extensive it is, the more cause I have to thank the goodness of him who bestowed it upon me.

15. And, finally, I ought not also to complain that God concurs with me in forming the acts of this will, or the judgments in which I am deceived, because those acts are wholly true and good, in so far as they depend on God; and the ability to form them is a higher degree of perfection in my nature than the want of it would be. With regard to privation, in which alone consists the formal reason of error and sin, this does not require the concurrence of Deity, because it is not a thing [or existence], and if it be referred to God as to its cause, it ought not to be called privation, but negation [according to the signification of these words in the schools]. For in truth it is no imperfection in Deity that he has accorded to me the power of giving or withholding my assent from certain things of which he has not put a clear and distinct knowledge in my understanding; but it is doubtless an imperfection in me that I do not use my freedom aright, and readily give my judgment on matters which I only obscurely and confusedly conceive. I perceive, nevertheless, that it was easy for Deity so to have constituted me as that I should never be deceived, although I still remained free and possessed of a limited knowledge, viz.,

by implanting in my understanding a clear and distinct knowledge of all the objects respecting which I should ever have to deliberate; or simply by so deeply engraving on my memory the resolution to judge of nothing without previously possessing a clear and distinct conception of it, that I should never forget it. And I easily understand that, in so far as I consider myself as a single whole, without reference to any other being in the universe, I should have been much more perfect than I now am, had Deity created me superior to error; but I cannot therefore deny that it is not somehow a greater perfection in the universe, that certain of its parts are not exempt from defect, as others are, than if they were all perfectly alike. And I have no right to complain because God, who placed me in the world, was not willing that I should sustain that character which of all others is the chief and most perfect.

16. I have even good reason to remain satisfied on the ground that, if he has not given me the perfection of being superior to error by the first means I have pointed out above, which depends on a clear and evident knowledge of all the matters regarding which I can deliberate, he has at least left in my power the other means, which is, firmly to retain the resolution never to judge where the truth is not clearly known to me: for, although I am conscious of the weakness of not being able to keep my mind continually fixed on the same thought, I can nevertheless, by attentive and oft-repeated meditation, impress it so strongly on my memory that I shall never fail to recollect it as often as I require it, and I can acquire in this way the habitude of not erring.

17. And since it is in being superior to error that the highest and chief perfection of man consists, I deem that I have not gained little by this day's meditation, in having discovered the source of error and falsity. And certainly this can be no other than what I have now explained: for as often as I so restrain my will within the limits of my knowledge, that it forms no judgment except regarding objects which are clearly and distinctly represented to it by the understanding, I can never be deceived; because every clear and distinct conception is doubtless something, and as such cannot owe its origin to nothing, but must of necessity have God for its author-- God, I say, who, as supremely perfect, cannot, without a contradiction, be the cause of any error; and consequently it is necessary to conclude that every such conception [or judgment] is true. Nor have I merely learned to-day what I must avoid to escape error, but also what I must do to arrive at the knowledge of truth; for I will assuredly reach truth if I only fix my attention sufficiently on all the things I conceive perfectly, and separate these from others which I conceive more confusedly and obscurely; to which for the future I shall give diligent heed.

René Descartes. *Meditations on First Philosophy.* Trans. John Veitch, 1901

Of Mircales
David Hume

...A miracle is a violation of the laws of nature; and as a firm and unalterable experience has established these laws, the proof against a miracle, from the very nature of the fact, is as entire as any argument from experience can possibly be imagined. Why is it more than probable, that all men must die; that lead cannot, of itself, remain suspended in the air; that fire consumes wood, and is extinguished by water; unless it be, that these events are found agreeable to the laws of nature, and there is required a violation of these laws, or in other words, a miracle to prevent them? Nothing is esteemed a miracle, if it ever happen in the common course of nature. It is no miracle that a man, seemingly in good health, should die on a sudden: because such a kind of death, though more unusual than any other, has yet been frequently observed to happen. But it is a miracle, that a dead man should come to life; because that has never been observed in any age or country. There must, therefore, be a uniform experience against every miraculous event, otherwise the event would not merit that appellation....

The plain consequence is (and it is a general maxim worthy of our attention), 'That no testimony is sufficient to establish a miracle, unless the testimony be of such a kind, that its falsehood would be more miraculous, than the fact, which it endeavours to establish....' When anyone tells me, that he saw a dead man restored to life, I immediately consider with myself, whether it be more probable, that this person should either deceive or be deceived, or that the fact, which he relates, should really have happened. I weigh the one miracle against the other; and according to the superiority, which I discover, I pronounce my decision, and always reject the greater miracle. If the falsehood of his testimony would be more miraculous, than the event which he relates; then, and not till then, can he pretend to command my belief or opinion.

In the foregoing reasoning we have supposed, that the testimony, upon which a miracle is founded, may possibly amount to an entire proof, and that the falsehood of that testimony would be a real prodigy: But it is easy to shew, that we have been a great deal too liberal in our concession, and that there never was a miraculous event established on so full an evidence.

For first, there is not to be found, in all history, any miracle attested by a sufficient number of men, of such unquestioned good-sense, education, and learning, as to secure us against all delusion in themselves; of such undoubted integrity, as to place them beyond all suspicion of any design to deceive others; of such credit and reputation in the eyes of mankind, as to have a great deal to lose in case of their being detected in any falsehood; and at the same time, attesting facts performed in such a public manner and in so celebrated a part of the world, as to render the detection unavoidable: all which circumstances are requisite to give us a full assurance in the testimony of men.

Secondly. We may observe in human nature a principle which, if strictly examined, will be found to diminish extremely the assurance, which we might, from human testimony, have in any kind of prodigy. The maxim, by which we commonly conduct ourselves in our reasonings, is, that the objects, of which we have no experience, resembles those, of which we have; that what we have found to be most usual is always most probable; and that where there is an opposition of arguments, we ought to give the preference to such as are founded on the greatest number of past observations. But though, in proceeding by this rule, we readily reject any fact which is unusual and incredible in an ordinary degree; yet in advancing farther, the mind observes not always the same rule; but when anything is affirmed utterly absurd and miraculous, it rather the more readily admits of such a fact, upon account of that very circumstance, which ought to destroy all its authority. The passion of surprise and wonder, arising from miracles, being an agreeable emotion, gives a sensible tendency towards the belief of those events, from which it is derived. And this goes so far, that even those who cannot enjoy this pleasure immediately, nor can believe those miraculous events, of which they are informed, yet love to partake of the satisfaction at second-hand or by rebound, and place a pride and delight in exciting the admiration of others.

With what greediness are the miraculous accounts of travellers received, their descriptions of sea and land monsters, their relations of wonderful adventures, strange men, and uncouth manners? But if the spirit of religion join itself to the love of wonder, there is an end of common sense; and human testimony, in these circumstances, loses all pretensions to authority. A religionist may be an enthusiast, and imagine he sees what has no reality: he may know his narrative to be false, and yet persevere in it, with the best intentions in the world, for the sake of promoting so holy a cause: or even where this delusion has not place, vanity, excited by so strong a temptation, operates on him more powerfully than on the rest of mankind in any other circumstances; and self-interest with equal force. His auditors may not have, and commonly have not, sufficient judgement to canvass his evidence: what judgement they have, they renounce by principle, in these sublime and mysterious subjects: or if they were ever so willing to employ it, passion and a heated imagination disturb the regularity of its operations. their credulity increases his impudence: and his impudence overpowers their credulity....

Thirdly. It forms a strong presumption against all supernatural and miraculous relations, that they are observed chiefly to abound among ignorant and barbarous nations; or if a civilized people has ever given admission to any of them, that people will be found to have received them from ignorant and barbarous ancestors, who transmitted them with that inviolable sanction and authority, which always attend received opinions. When we peruse the first histories of all nations, we are apt to imagine ourselves transported into some new world; where the whole frame of nature is disjointed, and every element performs its operations in a different manner, from what it does at present. Battles, revolutions, pestilence, famine and death, are never the effect of those natural causes, which we experience. Prodigies, omens, oracles, judgements, quite obscure the few natural events, that are intermingled with them. But as the former grow thinner every page, in proportion as we advance nearer the enlightened ages, we soon learn, that there is nothing mysterious or supernatural in the case, but that all proceeds from the usual propensity of mankind towards the marvellous, and that, though this inclination may at intervals receive a check from sense and learning, it can never be thoroughly extirpated from human nature....

I may add as a fourth reason, which diminishes the authority of prodigies, that there is no testimony for any, even those which have not been expressly detected, that is not opposed by an infinite number of witnesses; so that not only the miracle destroys the credit of testimony, but the testimony destroys itself. ...

Upon the whole, then, it appears, that no testimony for any kind of miracle has ever amounted to a probability, much less to a proof; and that, even supposing it amounted to a proof, it would be opposed by another proof; derived from the very nature of the fact, which it would endeavour to establish. It is experience only, which gives authority to human testimony; and it is the same experience, which assures us of the laws of nature. When, therefore, these two kinds of experience are contrary, we have nothing to do but subtract the one from the other, and embrace an opinion, either on one side or the other, with that assurance which arises from the remainder. But according to the principle here explained, this subtraction, with regard to all popular religions, amounts to an entire annihilation; and therefore we may establish it as a maxim, that no human testimony can have such force as to prove a miracle, and make it a just foundation for any such system of religion....

David Hume, *An Enquiry Concerning Human Understanding, Ed. L. A.* Selby Bigge. Oxford: Clarendon Press, 1902.

The Death of God
Friedrich Nietzsche

THE MADMAN—Have you not heard of that madman who lit a lantern in the bright morning hours, ran to the market place, and cried incessantly: "I seek God! I seek God!"—As many of those who did not believe in God were standing around just then, he provoked much laughter. Has he got lost? asked one. Did he lose his way like a child? asked another. Or is he hiding? Is he afraid of us? Has he gone on a voyage? emigrated?—Thus they yelled and laughed

The madman jumped into their midst and pierced them with his eyes. "Whither is God?" he cried; "I will tell you. *We have killed him*—you and I. All of us are his murderers. But how did we do this? How could we drink up the sea? Who gave us the sponge to wipe away the entire horizon? What were we doing when we unchained this earth from its sun? Whither is it moving now? Whither are we moving? Away from all suns? Are we not plunging continually? Backward, sideward, forward, in all directions? Is there still any up or down? Are we not straying, as through an infinite nothing? Do we not feel the breath of empty space? Has it not become colder? Is not night continually closing in on us? Do we not need to light lanterns in the morning? Do we hear nothing as yet of the noise of the gravediggers who are burying God? Do we smell nothing as yet of the divine decomposition? Gods, too, decompose. God is dead. God remains dead. And we have killed him.

"How shall we comfort ourselves, the murderers of all murderers? What was holiest and mightiest of all that the world has yet owned has bled to death under our knives: who will wipe this blood off us? What water is there for us to clean ourselves? What festivals of atonement, what sacred games shall we have to invent? Is not the greatness of this deed too great for us? Must we ourselves not become gods simply to appear worthy of it? There has never been a greater deed; and whoever is born after us—for the sake of this deed he will belong to a higher history than all history hitherto."

Here the madman fell silent and looked again at his listeners; and they, too, were silent and stared at him in astonishment. At last he threw his lantern on the ground, and it broke into pieces and went out. "I have come too early," he said then; "my time is not yet. This tremendous event is still on its way, still wandering; it has not yet reached the ears of men. Lightning and thunder require time; the light of the stars requires time; deeds, though done, still require time to be seen and heard. This deed is still more distant from them than most distant stars---*and yet they have done it themselves*.

It has been related further that on the same day the madman forced his way into several churches and there struck up his *requiem aeternam deo*. Led out and called to account, he is said always to have replied nothing but: "What after all are these churches now if they are not the tombs and sepulchers of God?"

Friedrich Nietzsche, *The Gay Science*. Used with permission from Internet Modern History Sourcebook, 1997.

The Coming of the Superman
Friedrich Nietzsche

ZARATHUSTRA'S PROLOGUE.

1

When Zarathustra was thirty years old, he left his home and the lake of his home, and went into the mountains. There he enjoyed his spirit and solitude, and for ten years did not weary of it. But at last his heart changed,—and rising one morning with the rosy dawn, he went before the sun, and spake thus unto it:

Thou great star! What would be thy happiness if thou hadst not those for whom thou shinest!

For ten years hast thou climbed hither unto my cave: thou wouldst have wearied of thy light and of the journey, had it not been for me, mine eagle, and my serpent.

But we awaited thee every morning, took from thee thine overflow and blessed thee for it.

Lo! I am weary of my wisdom, like the bee that hath gathered too much honey; I need hands outstretched to take it.

I would fain bestow and distribute, until the wise have once more become joyous in their folly, and the poor happy in their riches.

Therefore must I descend into the deep: as thou doest in the evening, when thou goest behind the sea, and givest light also to the nether-world, thou exuberant star!

Like thee must I GO DOWN, as men say, to whom I shall descend.

Bless me, then, thou tranquil eye, that canst behold even the greatest happiness without envy!

Bless the cup that is about to overflow, that the water may flow golden out of it, and carry everywhere the reflection of thy bliss!

Lo! This cup is again going to empty itself, and Zarathustra is again going to be a man.

Thus began Zarathustra's down-going.

2

Zarathustra went down the mountain alone, no one meeting him. When he entered the forest, however, there suddenly stood before him an old man, who had left his holy cot to seek roots. And thus spake the old man to Zarathustra:

"No stranger to me is this wanderer: many years ago passed he by. Zarathustra he was called; but he hath altered.

Then thou carriedst thine ashes into the mountains: wilt thou now carry thy fire into the valleys? Fearest thou not the incendiary's doom?

Yea, I recognise Zarathustra. Pure is his eye, and no loathing lurketh about his mouth. Goeth he not along like a dancer?

Altered is Zarathustra; a child hath Zarathustra become; an awakened one is Zarathustra: what wilt thou do in the land of the sleepers?

As in the sea hast thou lived in solitude, and it hath borne thee up. Alas, wilt thou now go ashore? Alas, wilt thou again drag thy body thyself?"

Zarathustra answered: "I love mankind."

"Why," said the saint, "did I go into the forest and the desert? Was it not because I loved men far too well?

Now I love God: men, I do not love. Man is a thing too imperfect for me. Love to man would be fatal to me."

Zarathustra answered: "What spake I of love! I am bringing gifts unto men."

"Give them nothing," said the saint. "Take rather part of their load, and carry it along with them—that will be most agreeable unto them: if only it be agreeable unto thee!

If, however, thou wilt give unto them, give them no more than an alms, and let them also beg for it!"

"No," replied Zarathustra, "I give no alms. I am not poor enough for that."

The saint laughed at Zarathustra, and spake thus: "Then see to it that they accept thy treasures! They are distrustful of anchorites, and do not believe that we come with gifts.

The fall of our footsteps ringeth too hollow through their streets. And just as at night, when they are in bed and hear a man abroad long before sunrise, so they ask themselves concerning us: Where goeth the thief?

Go not to men, but stay in the forest! Go rather to the animals! Why not be like me—a bear amongst bears, a bird amongst birds?"

"And what doeth the saint in the forest?" asked Zarathustra.

The saint answered: "I make hymns and sing them; and in making hymns I laugh and weep and mumble: thus do I praise God.

With singing, weeping, laughing, and mumbling do I praise the God who is my God. But what dost thou bring us as a gift?"

When Zarathustra had heard these words, he bowed to the saint and said: "What should I have to give thee! Let me rather hurry hence lest I take aught away from thee!"—And thus they parted from one another, the old man and

Zarathustra, laughing like schoolboys.

When Zarathustra was alone, however, he said to his heart: "Could it be possible! This old saint in the forest hath not yet heard of it, that GOD IS DEAD!"

3

When Zarathustra arrived at the nearest town which adjoineth the forest, he found many people assembled in the market-place; for it had been announced that a rope-dancer would give a performance. And Zarathustra spake thus unto the people:

I TEACH YOU THE SUPERMAN. Man is something that is to be surpassed. What have ye done to surpass man?

All beings hitherto have created something beyond themselves: and ye want to be the ebb of that great tide, and would rather go back to the beast than surpass man?

What is the ape to man? A laughing-stock, a thing of shame. And just the same shall man be to the Superman: a laughing-stock, a thing of shame.

Ye have made your way from the worm to man, and much within you is still worm. Once were ye apes, and even yet man is more of an ape than any of the apes.

Even the wisest among you is only a disharmony and hybrid of plant and phantom. But do I bid you become phantoms or plants?

Lo, I teach you the Superman!

The Superman is the meaning of the earth. Let your will say: The Superman SHALL BE the meaning of the earth!

I conjure you, my brethren, REMAIN TRUE TO THE EARTH, and believe not those who speak unto you of superearthly hopes! Poisoners are they, whether they know it or not.

Despisers of life are they, decaying ones and poisoned ones themselves, of whom the earth is weary: so away with them!

Once blasphemy against God was the greatest blasphemy; but God died, and therewith also those blasphemers. To blaspheme the earth is now the dreadfulest sin, and to rate the heart of the unknowable higher than the meaning of the earth!

Once the soul looked contemptuously on the body, and then that contempt was the supreme thing:—the soul wished the body meagre, ghastly, and famished. Thus it thought to escape from the body and the earth.

Oh, that soul was itself meagre, ghastly, and famished; and cruelty was the delight of that soul!

But ye, also, my brethren, tell me: What doth your body say about your soul? Is your soul not poverty and pollution and wretched self-complacency?

Verily, a polluted stream is man. One must be a sea, to receive a polluted stream without becoming impure.

Lo, I teach you the Superman: he is that sea; in him can your great contempt be submerged.

What is the greatest thing ye can experience? It is the hour of great contempt. The hour in which even your happiness becometh loathsome unto you, and so also your reason and virtue.

The hour when ye say: "What good is my happiness! It is poverty and pollution and wretched self-complacency. But my happiness should justify existence itself!"

The hour when ye say: "What good is my reason! Doth it long for knowledge as the lion for his food? It is poverty and pollution and wretched self-complacency!"

The hour when ye say: "What good is my virtue! As yet it hath not made me passionate. How weary I am of my good and my bad! It is all poverty and pollution and wretched self-complacency!"

The hour when ye say: "What good is my justice! I do not see that I am fervour and fuel. The just, however, are fervour and fuel!"

The hour when ye say: "What good is my pity! Is not pity the cross on which he is nailed who loveth man? But my pity is not a crucifixion."

Have ye ever spoken thus? Have ye ever cried thus? Ah! would that I had heard you crying thus!

It is not your sin—it is your self-satisfaction that crieth unto heaven; your very sparingness in sin crieth unto heaven!

Where is the lightning to lick you with its tongue? Where is the frenzy with which ye should be inoculated?

Lo, I teach you the Superman: he is that lightning, he is that frenzy!—

When Zarathustra had thus spoken, one of the people called out: "We have now heard enough of the rope-dancer; it is time now for us to see him!" And all the people laughed at Zarathustra. But the rope-dancer, who thought the words applied to him, began his performance.

4

Zarathustra, however, looked at the people and wondered. Then he spake thus:

Man is a rope stretched between the animal and the Superman—a rope over an abyss.

A dangerous crossing, a dangerous wayfaring, a dangerous looking-back, a dangerous trembling and halting.

What is great in man is that he is a bridge and not a goal: what is lovable in man is that he is an OVER-GOING and a DOWN-GOING.

I love those that know not how to live except as down-goers, for they are the over-goers.

I love the great despisers, because they are the great adorers, and arrows of longing for the other shore.

I love those who do not first seek a reason beyond the stars for going down and being sacrifices, but sacrifice themselves to the earth, that the earth of the Superman may hereafter arrive.

I love him who liveth in order to know, and seeketh to know in order that the Superman may hereafter live. Thus seeketh he his own down-going.

I love him who laboureth and inventeth, that he may build the house for the Superman, and prepare for him earth, animal, and plant: for thus seeketh he his own down-going.

I love him who loveth his virtue: for virtue is the will to down-going, and an arrow of longing.

I love him who reserveth no share of spirit for himself, but wanteth to be wholly the spirit of his virtue: thus walketh he as spirit over the bridge.

I love him who maketh his virtue his inclination and destiny: thus, for the sake of his virtue, he is willing to live on, or live no more.

I love him who desireth not too many virtues. One virtue is more of a virtue than two, because it is more of a knot for one's destiny to cling to.

I love him whose soul is lavish, who wanteth no thanks and doth not give back: for he always bestoweth, and desireth not to keep for himself.

I love him who is ashamed when the dice fall in his favour, and who then asketh: "Am I a dishonest player?"—for he is willing to succumb.

I love him who scattereth golden words in advance of his deeds, and always doeth more than he promiseth: for he seeketh his own down-going.

I love him who justifieth the future ones, and redeemeth the past ones: for he is willing to succumb through the present ones.

I love him who chasteneth his God, because he loveth his God: for he must succumb through the wrath of his God.

I love him whose soul is deep even in the wounding, and may succumb through a small matter: thus goeth he willingly over the bridge.

I love him whose soul is so overfull that he forgetteth himself, and all things are in him: thus all things become his down-going.

I love him who is of a free spirit and a free heart: thus is his head only the bowels of his heart; his heart, however, causeth his down-going.

I love all who are like heavy drops falling one by one out of the dark cloud that lowereth over man: they herald the coming of the lightning, and succumb as heralds.

Lo, I am a herald of the lightning, and a heavy drop out of the cloud: the lightning, however, is the SUPERMAN.—

5

When Zarathustra had spoken these words, he again looked at the people, and was silent. "There they stand," said he to his heart; "there they laugh: they understand me not; I am not the mouth for these ears.

Must one first batter their ears, that they may learn to hear with their eyes? Must one clatter like kettledrums and penitential preachers? Or do they only believe the stammerer?

They have something whereof they are proud. What do they call it, that which maketh them proud? Culture, they call it; it distinguisheth them from the goatherds.

They dislike, therefore, to hear of 'contempt' of themselves. So I will appeal to their pride.

I will speak unto them of the most contemptible thing: that, however, is

THE LAST MAN!"

And thus spake Zarathustra unto the people:

It is time for man to fix his goal. It is time for man to plant the germ of his highest hope.

Still is his soil rich enough for it. But that soil will one day be poor and exhausted, and no lofty tree will any longer be able to grow thereon.

Alas! there cometh the time when man will no longer launch the arrow of his longing beyond man—and the string of his bow will have unlearned to whizz!

I tell you: one must still have chaos in one, to give birth to a dancing star. I tell you: ye have still chaos in you.

Alas! There cometh the time when man will no longer give birth to any star. Alas! There cometh the time of the most despicable man, who can no longer despise himself.

Lo! I show you THE LAST MAN.

"What is love? What is creation? What is longing? What is a star?"—so asketh the last man and blinketh.

The earth hath then become small, and on it there hoppeth the last man who maketh everything small. His species is ineradicable like that of the ground-flea; the last man liveth longest.

"We have discovered happiness"—say the last men, and blink thereby.

They have left the regions where it is hard to live; for they need warmth. One still loveth one's neighbour and rubbeth against him; for one needeth warmth.

Turning ill and being distrustful, they consider sinful: they walk warily. He is a fool who still stumbleth over stones or men!

A little poison now and then: that maketh pleasant dreams. And much poison at last for a pleasant death.

One still worketh, for work is a pastime. But one is careful lest the pastime should hurt one.

One no longer becometh poor or rich; both are too burdensome. Who still wanteth to rule? Who still wanteth to obey? Both are too burdensome.

No shepherd, and one herd! Every one wanteth the same; every one is equal: he who hath other sentiments goeth voluntarily into the madhouse.

"Formerly all the world was insane,"—say the subtlest of them, and blink thereby.

They are clever and know all that hath happened: so there is no end to their raillery. People still fall out, but are soon reconciled—otherwise it spoileth their stomachs.

They have their little pleasures for the day, and their little pleasures for the night, but they have a regard for health.

"We have discovered happiness,"—say the last men, and blink thereby.—

And here ended the first discourse of Zarathustra, which is also called "The Prologue": for at this point the shouting and mirth of the multitude interrupted him. "Give us this last man, O Zarathustra,"—they called out—"make us into these last men! Then will we make thee a present of the Superman!" And all the people exulted and smacked their lips. Zarathustra, however, turned sad, and said to his heart:

"They understand me not: I am not the mouth for these ears.

Too long, perhaps, have I lived in the mountains; too much have I hearkened unto the brooks and trees: now do I speak unto them as unto the goatherds.

Calm is my soul, and clear, like the mountains in the morning. But they think me cold, and a mocker with terrible jests.

And now do they look at me and laugh: and while they laugh they hate me too. There is ice in their laughter."

6

Then, however, something happened which made every mouth mute and every eye fixed. In the meantime, of course, the rope-dancer had commenced his performance: he had come out at a little door, and was going along the rope which was stretched between two towers, so that it hung above the market-place and the people. When he was just midway across, the little door opened once more, and a gaudily-dressed fellow like a buffoon sprang out, and went rapidly after the first one. "Go on, halt-foot," cried his frightful voice, "go on, lazy-bones, interloper, sallow-face!—lest I tickle thee with my heel! What dost thou here between the towers? In the tower is the place for thee, thou shouldst be locked up; to one better than thyself thou blockest the way!"—And with every word he came nearer and nearer the first one. When, however, he was but a step behind, there happened the frightful thing which made every mouth mute and every eye fixed—he uttered a yell like a devil, and jumped over the other who was in his way. The latter, however, when he thus saw his rival triumph, lost at the same time his head and his footing on the rope; he threw his pole away, and shot downwards faster than it, like an eddy of arms and legs, into the depth. The market-place and the people were like the sea when the storm cometh on: they all flew apart and in disorder, especially where the body was about to fall.

Zarathustra, however, remained standing, and just beside him fell the body, badly injured and disfigured, but not yet dead. After a while consciousness returned to the shattered man, and he saw Zarathustra kneeling beside him. "What art thou doing there?" said he at last, "I knew long ago that the devil would trip me up. Now he draggeth me to hell: wilt thou prevent him?"

"On mine honour, my friend," answered Zarathustra, "there is nothing of all that whereof thou speakest: there is no devil and no hell. Thy soul will be dead even sooner than thy body: fear, therefore, nothing any more!"

The man looked up distrustfully. "If thou speakest the truth," said he, "I lose nothing when I lose my life. I am not much more than an animal which hath been taught to dance by blows and scanty fare."

"Not at all," said Zarathustra, "thou hast made danger thy calling; therein there is nothing contemptible. Now thou perishest by thy calling: therefore will I bury thee with mine own hands."

When Zarathustra had said this the dying one did not reply further; but he moved his hand as if he sought the hand of Zarathustra in gratitude.

7

Meanwhile the evening came on, and the market-place veiled itself in gloom. Then the people dispersed, for even curiosity and terror become fatigued. Zarathustra, however, still sat beside the dead man on the ground, absorbed in thought: so he forgot the time. But at last it became night, and a cold wind blew upon the lonely one. Then arose Zarathustra and said to his heart:

Verily, a fine catch of fish hath Zarathustra made to-day! It is not a man he hath caught, but a corpse.

Sombre is human life, and as yet without meaning: a buffoon may be fateful to it.

I want to teach men the sense of their existence, which is the Superman, the lightning out of the dark cloud—man.

But still am I far from them, and my sense speaketh not unto their sense. To men I am still something between a fool and a corpse.

Gloomy is the night, gloomy are the ways of Zarathustra. Come, thou cold and stiff companion! I carry thee to the place where I shall bury thee with mine own hands....

THE THREE METAMORPHOSES

Three metamorphoses of the spirit do I designate to you: how the spirit becometh a camel, the camel a lion, and the lion at last a child.

Many heavy things are there for the spirit, the strong load-bearing spirit in which reverence dwelleth: for the heavy and the heaviest longeth its strength.

What is heavy? so asketh the load-bearing spirit; then kneeleth it down like the camel, and wanteth to be well laden.

What is the heaviest thing, ye heroes? asketh the load-bearing spirit, that I may take it upon me and rejoice in my strength.

Is it not this: To humiliate oneself in order to mortify one's pride? To exhibit one's folly in order to mock at one's wisdom?

Or is it this: To desert our cause when it celebrateth its triumph? To ascend high mountains to tempt the tempter?

Or is it this: To feed on the acorns and grass of knowledge, and for the sake of truth to suffer hunger of soul?

Or is it this: To be sick and dismiss comforters, and make friends of the deaf, who never hear thy requests?

Or is it this: To go into foul water when it is the water of truth, and not disclaim cold frogs and hot toads?

Or is it this: To love those who despise us, and give one's hand to the phantom when it is going to frighten us?

All these heaviest things the load-bearing spirit taketh upon itself: and like the camel, which, when laden, hasteneth into the wilderness, so hasteneth the spirit into its wilderness.

But in the loneliest wilderness happeneth the second metamorphosis: here the spirit becometh a lion; freedom will it capture, and lordship in its own wilderness.

Its last Lord it here seeketh: hostile will it be to him, and to its last God; for victory will it struggle with the great dragon.

What is the great dragon which the spirit is no longer inclined to call Lord and God? "Thou-shalt," is the great dragon called. But the spirit of the lion saith, "I will."

"Thou-shalt," lieth in its path, sparkling with gold—a scale-covered beast; and on every scale glittereth golden, "Thou shalt!"

The values of a thousand years glitter on those scales, and thus speaketh the mightiest of all dragons: "All the values of things—glitter on me.

All values have already been created, and all created values—do I represent. Verily, there shall be no 'I will' any more. Thus speaketh the dragon.

My brethren, wherefore is there need of the lion in the spirit? Why sufficeth not the beast of burden, which renounceth and is reverent?

To create new values—that, even the lion cannot yet accomplish: but to create itself freedom for new creating—that can the might of the lion do.

To create itself freedom, and give a holy Nay even unto duty: for that, my brethren, there is need of the lion.

To assume the right to new values—that is the most formidable assumption for a load-bearing and reverent spirit. Verily, unto such a spirit it is preying, and the work of a beast of prey.

As its holiest, it once loved "Thou-shalt": now is it forced to find illusion and arbitrariness even in the holiest things, that it may capture freedom from its love: the lion is needed for this capture.

But tell me, my brethren, what the child can do, which even the lion could not do? Why hath the preying lion still to become a child?

Innocence is the child, and forgetfulness, a new beginning, a game, a self-rolling wheel, a first movement, a holy Yea.

Aye, for the game of creating, my brethren, there is needed a holy Yea unto life: ITS OWN will, willeth now the spirit; HIS OWN world winneth the world's outcast.

Three metamorphoses of the spirit have I designated to you: how the spirit became a camel, the camel a lion, and the lion at last a child.—

Thus spake Zarathustra. And at that time he abode in the town which is called The Pied Cow.

Friedrich Nietzsche. *Thus Spake Zarathustra*. Trans. Thomas Common. Edinbugh: 1909.

God as Projection
Ludwig Feuerbach

WHAT we have hitherto been maintaining generally, even with regard to sensational impressions, of the relation between subject and object, applies especially to the relation between the subject and the religious object.

In the perceptions of the senses consciousness of the object is distinguishable from consciousness of self; but in religion, consciousness of the object and self-consciousness coincide. The object of the senses is out of man, the religious object is within him, and therefore as little forsakes him as his self-consciousness or his conscience; it is the intimate, the closest object. "God," says Augustine, for example, "is nearer, more related to us, and therefore more easily known by us, than sensible, corporeal things." The object of the senses is in itself indifferent—independent of the disposition or of the judgment; but the object of religion is a selected object; the most excellent, the first, the supreme being; it essentially pre-supposes a critical judgment, a discrimination between the divine and the non-divine, between that which is worthy of adoration and that which is not worthy. And here may be applied, without any limitation, the proposition: the object of any subject is nothing else than the subject's own nature taken objectively. Such as are a man's thoughts and dispositions, such is his God; so much worth as a man has, so much and no more has his God. Consciousness of God is self-consciousness, knowledge of God is self-knowledge. By his God thou knowest the man, and by the man his God; the two are identical. Whatever is God to a man, that is his heart and soul; and conversely, God is the manifested inward nature, the expressed self of a man,—religion the solemn unveiling of a man's hidden treasures, the revelation of his intimate thoughts, the open confession of his love-secrets.

But when religion—consciousness of God—is designated as the self-consciousness of man, this is not to be understood as affirming that the religious man is directly aware of this identity; for, on the contrary, ignorance of it is fundamental to the peculiar nature of religion. To preclude this misconception, it is better to say, religion is man's earliest and also indirect form of self-knowledge. Hence, religion everywhere precedes philosophy, as in the history of the race, so also in that of the individual. Man first of all sees his nature as if *out of* himself, before he finds it in himself. His own nature is in the first instance contemplated by him as that of another being. Religion is the childlike condition of humanity; but the child sees his nature—man—out of himself; in childhood a man is an object to himself, under the form of another man. Hence the historical progress of religion consists in this: that what by an earlier religion was regarded as objective, is now recognised as subjective; that is, what was formerly contemplated and worshipped as God is now perceived to be something *human*. What was at first religion becomes at a later period idolatry; man is seen to have adored his own nature. Man has given objectivity to himself, but has not recognised the object as his own nature: a later religion takes this forward step; every advance in religion is therefore a deeper self-knowledge. But every particular religion, while it pronounces its predecessors idolatrous, excepts itself—and necessarily so, otherwise it would no longer be religion—from the fate, the common nature of all religions: it imputes only to other religions what is the fault, if fault it be, of religion in general. Because it has a different object, a different tenour, because it has transcended the ideas of preceding religions, it erroneously supposes itself exalted above the necessary eternal laws which constitute the essence of religion—it fancies its object, its ideas, to be superhuman. But the essence of religion, thus hidden from the religious, is evident to the thinker, by whom religion is viewed objectively, which it cannot be by its votaries. And it is our task to show that the antithesis of divine and human is altogether illusory, that it is nothing else than the antithesis between the human nature in general, and the human individual: that, consequently, the object and contents of the Christian religion are altogether human.

Religion, at least the Christian, is the relation of man to himself, or more correctly to his own nature (*i.e.*, his subjective nature); but a relation to it, viewed as a nature apart from his own. The divine being is nothing else than the human being, or, rather the human nature purified, freed from the limits of the individual man, made objective—*i.e.*, contemplated and revered as another, a distinct being. All the attributes of the divine nature are, therefore, attributes of the human nature.

In relation to the attributes, the predicates, of the Divine Being, this is admitted without hesitation, but by no means in relation to the subject of these predicates. The negation of the subject is held to be irreligion, nay, atheism; though not so the negation of the predicates. But that which has no predicates or qualities, has no effect upon me; that which has no effect upon me, has no existence for me. To deny all the qualities of a being is equivalent to denying the being himself. A being without qualities is one which cannot become an object to the mind; and such a being is virtually non-existent. Where man deprives God of all qualities, God is no longer anything more to him than a negative being. To the truly religious man, God is not a being without qualities, because to him he is a positive, real being. The theory that God cannot be defined, and consequently cannot be known by man, is therefore the offspring of recent times, a product of modern unbelief.

As reason is and can be pronounced finite only where man regards sensual enjoyment, or religious emotion, or aesthetic contemplation, or moral sentiment, as the absolute, the true; so the proposition that God is unknowable or undefinable can only be enunciated and become fixed as a dogma, where this object has no longer any interest for the intellect; where the real, the positive, alone has any hold on man, where the real alone has for him the significance of the essential, of the absolute, divine object, but where at the same time, in contradiction with this purely worldly tendency, there yet exist some old remains of religiousness. On the ground that God is unknowable, man excuses himself to what is yet remaining of his religious conscience for his forgetfulness of God, his absorption in the world: he denies God practically by his conduct,—the world has possession of all his thoughts and inclinations,—but he does not deny him theoretically, he does not attack his existence; he lets that rest. But this existence does not affect or incommode him; it is a merely negative existence, an existence without existence, a self-contradictory existence,—a state of being, which, as to its effects, is not distinguishable from non-being. The denial of determinate, positive predicates concerning the divine nature, is nothing else than a denial of religion, with, however, an appearance of religion in its favour, so that it is not recognised as a denial; it is simply a subtle, disguised atheism. The alleged religious horror of limiting God by positive predicates, is only the irreligious wish to know nothing more of God, to banish God from the mind. Dread of limitation is dread of existence. All real existence, *i.e.*, all existence which is truly such, is qualitative, determinate existence. He who earnestly believes in the Divine existence, is not shocked at the attributing even of gross sensuous qualities to God. He who dreads an existence that may give offence, who shrinks from the grossness of a positive predicate, may as well renounce existence altogether. A God who is injured by determinate qualities has not the courage and the strength to exist. Qualities are the fire, the vital breath, the oxygen, the salt of existence. An existence in general, an existence without qualities, is an insipidity, an absurdity. But there can be no more in God, than is supplied by religion. Only where man loses his taste for religion, and thus religion itself becomes insipid, does the existence of God become an insipid existence—an existence without qualities.

There is, however, a still milder way of denying the Divine predicates than the direct one just described. It is admitted that the predicates of the divine nature are finite, and, more particularly, human qualities, but their rejection is rejected; they are even taken under protection, because it is necessary to man to have a definite conception of God, and since he is man, he can form no other than a human conception of him. In relation to God, it is said, these predicates are certainly without any objective validity; but to me, if he is to exist for me, he cannot appear otherwise than as he does appear to me, namely, as a being with attributes analogous to the human. But this distinction between what God is in himself, and what he is for me, destroys the peace of religion, and is besides in itself an unfounded and untenable distinction. I cannot know whether God is something else in himself or for himself, than he is for me; what he is to me, is to me all that he is. For me, there lies in these predicates under which he exists for me, what he is in himself, his very nature; he is for me what he can alone ever be for me. The religious man finds perfect satisfaction in that which God is in relation to himself; of any other relation he knows nothing, for God is to him what he can alone be to man. In the distinction above stated, man takes a point of view above himself, *i.e.* above his nature, the absolute measure of his being; but this transcendentalism is only an illusion; for I can make the distinction between the object as it is in itself, and the object as it is for me, only where an object can really appear otherwise to me, not where it appears to me such as the absolute measure of my nature determines it to appear—such as it must appear to me. It is true that I may have a merely subjective conception, *i.e.* one which does not arise out of the general constitution of my species; but if my conception is determined by the constitution of my species, the distinction between what an object is in itself, and what it is for me ceases; for this conception is itself an absolute one. The measure of the species is the absolute measure, law, and criterion of man. And, indeed, religion has the conviction that its conceptions, its predicates of God, are such as every man ought to have, and must have, if he would have the true ones—that they are the conceptions necessary to human nature; nay, further, that they are objectively true, representing God as he is. To every religion the gods of *other* religions are only notions concerning God, but its own conception of God is to it God himself, the true God—God such as he is in himself. Religion is satisfied only with a complete Deity, a God without reservation; it will not have a mere phantasm of God; it demands God himself. Religion gives up its own existence when it gives up the nature of God; it is no longer a truth, when it renounces the possession of the true God. Scepticism is the arch-enemy of religion; but the distinction between object and conception—between God as he is in himself, and God as he is for me, is a sceptical distinction, and therefore an irreligious one.

That which is to man the self-existent, the highest being, to which he can conceive nothing higher—that is to him the Divine being. How then should he inquire concerning this being, what He is in himself? If God were an object to the bird, he would be a winged being: the bird knows nothing higher, nothing more blissful, than the winged condition. How ludicrous would it be if this bird pronounced: to me God appears as a bird, but what he is in himself I know not. To the bird the highest nature is the bird-nature; take from him the conception of this, and you take from him the conception of the highest being. How, then, could he ask whether God in himself were winged? To ask whether God is in himself what he is for me, is to ask whether God is God, is to lift oneself above one's God, to rise up against him.

Wherever, therefore, this idea, that the religious predicates are only anthropomorphisms, has taken possession of a man, there has doubt, has unbelief obtained the mastery of faith. And it is only the inconsequence of faint-heartedness and intellectual imbecility which does not proceed from this idea to the formal negation of the predicates, and from thence to the negation of the subject to which they relate. If thou doubtest the objective truth of the predicates, thou must also doubt the objective truth of the subject whose predicates they are. If thy predicates are anthropomorphisms, the subject of them is an anthropomorphism too. If love, goodness, personality, &c., are human attributes, so also is the subject which thou pre-supposest, the existence of God, the belief that there is a God, an anthropomorphism—a presupposition purely human. Whence knowest thou that the belief in a God at all is not a limitation of man's mode of conception? Higher beings—and thou supposest such—are perhaps so blest in themselves, so at unity with themselves, that they are not hung in suspense between themselves and a yet higher being. To know God and not oneself to be God, to know blessedness, and not oneself to enjoy it, is a state of disunity, of unhappiness. Higher beings know nothing of this unhappiness; they have no conception of that which they are not.

Thou believest in love as a divine attribute because thou thyself lovest; thou believest that God is a wise, benevolent being, because thou knowest nothing better in thyself than benevolence and wisdom; and thou believest that God exists, that therefore he is a subject—whatever exists is a subject, whether it be defined as substance, person, essence, or otherwise—because thou thyself existest, art thyself a subject. Thou knowest no higher human good, than to love, than to be good and wise; and even so thou knowest no higher happiness than to exist, to be a subject; for the consciousness of all reality, of all bliss, is for thee bound up in the consciousness of being a subject, of existing. God is an existence, a subject to thee, for the same reason that he is to thee a wise, a blessed, a personal being. The distinction between the divine predicates and the divine subject is only this, that to thee the subject, the existence, does not appear an anthropomorphism, because the conception of it is necessarily involved in thy own existence as a subject, whereas the predicates do appear anthropomorphisms, because their necessity—the necessity that God should be conscious, wise, good, &c.—is not an immediate necessity, identical with the being of man, but is evolved by his self-consciousness, by the activity of his thought. I am a subject, I exist, whether I be wise or unwise, good or bad. To exist is to man the first datum; it constitutes the very idea of the subject; it is presupposed by the predicates. Hence, man relinquishes the predicates, but the existence of God is to him a settled, irrefragable, absolutely certain, objective truth. But, nevertheless, this distinction is merely an apparent one. The necessity of the subject lies only in the necessity of the predicate. Thou art a subject only in so far as thou art a human subject; the certainty and reality of thy existence lie only in the certainty and reality of thy human attributes. What the subject is, lies only in the predicate; the predicate is the *truth* of the subject—the subject only the personified, existing predicate, the predicate conceived as existing. Subject and predicate are distinguished only as existence and essence. The negation of the predicates is therefore the negation of the subject. What remains of the human subject when abstracted from the human attributes? Even in the language of common life the divine predicates—Providence, Omniscience, Omnipotence—are put for the divine subject.

The certainty of the existence of God, of which it has been said that it is as certain, nay, more certain to man than his own existence, depends only on the certainty of the qualities of God—it is in itself no immediate certainty. To the Christian the existence of the Christian God only is a certainty; to the heathen that of the heathen God only. The heathen did not doubt the existence of Jupiter, because he took no offence at the nature of Jupiter, because he could conceive of God under no other qualities, because to him these qualities were a certainty, a divine reality. The reality of the predicate is the sole guarantee of existence.

Whatever man conceives to be true, he immediately conceives to be real (that is, to have an objective existence), because, originally, only the real is true to him—true in opposition to what is merely conceived, dreamed, imagined. The idea of being, of existence, is the original idea of truth; or, originally, man makes truth dependent on existence, subsequently, existence dependent on truth. Now God is the nature of man regarded as absolute truth,—the truth of man; but God, or, what is the same thing, religion, is as various as are the conditions under which man conceives this his nature, regards it as the highest being. These conditions, then, under which man conceives God, are to him the truth, and for that reason they are also the highest existence, or rather they are existence itself; for only the emphatic, the highest existence, is existence, and deserves this name. Therefore, God is an existent, real being, on the very same ground that he is a particular, definite being; for the qualities of God are nothing else than the essential qualities of man himself, and a particular man is what he is, has his existence, his reality, only in his particular conditions. Take away from the Greek the quality of being Greek, and you take away his existence. On this ground, it is true that for a definite positive religion—that is, relatively—the certainty of the existence of God is *immediate*; for just as involuntarily, as necessarily, as the Greek was a Greek, so necessarily were his gods Greek beings, so necessarily were they real, existent beings. Religion is that conception of the nature of the world and of man which is essential to, *i.e.*, identical with, a man's nature. But man does not stand above this his necessary conception; on the contrary, it stands above him; it animates, determines, governs him. The necessity of a proof, of a middle term to unite qualities with existence, the possibility of a doubt, is abolished. Only that which is apart from my own being is capable of being doubted by me. How then can I doubt of God, who is my being? To doubt of God is to doubt of myself. Only when God is thought of abstractly, when his predicates are the result of philosophic abstraction, arises the distinction or separation between subject and predicate, existence and nature—arises the fiction that the existence or the subject is something else than the predicate, something immediate, indubitable, in distinction from the predicate, which is held to be doubtful. But this is only a fiction. A God who has abstract predicates has also an abstract existence. Existence, being, varies with varying qualities.

The identity of the subject and predicate is clearly evidenced by the progressive development of religion, which is identical with the progressive development of human culture. So long as man is in a mere state of nature, so long is his god a mere nature-god—a personification of some natural force. Where man inhabits houses, he also encloses his gods in temples. The temple is only a manifestation of the value which man attaches to beautiful buildings. Temples in honour of religion are in truth temples in honour of architecture. With the emerging of man from a state of savagery and wildness to one of culture, with the distinction between what is fitting for man and what is not fitting, arises simultaneously the distinction between that which is fitting and that which is not fitting for God. God is the idea of majesty, of the highest dignity: the religious sentiment is the sentiment of supreme fitness. The later more cultured artists of Greece were the first to embody in the statues of the gods the ideas of dignity, of spiritual grandeur, of imperturbable repose and serenity. But why were these qualities in their view attributes, predicates of God? Because they were in themselves regarded by the Greeks as divinities. Why did those artists exclude all disgusting and low passions? Because they perceived them to be unbecoming, unworthy, unhuman, and consequently ungodlike. The Homeric gods eat and drink;—that implies: eating and drinking is a divine pleasure. Physical strength is an attribute of the Homeric gods: Zeus is the strongest of the gods. Why? Because physical strength, in and by itself, was regarded as something glorious, divine. To the ancient Germans the highest virtues were those of the warrior; therefore, their supreme god was the god of war, Odin,—war, "the original or oldest law." Not the attribute of the divinity, but the divineness or deity of the attribute, is the first true Divine Being. Thus what theology and philosophy have held to be God, the Absolute, the Infinite, is not God; but that which they have held not to be God, is God: namely, the attribute, the quality, whatever has reality. Hence, he alone is the true atheist to whom the predicates of the Divine Being,—for example, love, wisdom, justice, are nothing; not he to whom merely the subject of these predicates is nothing. And in no wise is the negation of the subject necessarily also a negation of the predicates considered in themselves. These have an intrinsic, independent reality; they force their recognition upon man by their very nature; they are self-evident truths to him; they prove, they attest themselves. It does not follow that goodness, justice, wisdom, are chimaeras, because the existence of God is a chimaera, nor truths because this is a truth. The idea of God is dependent on the idea of justice, of benevolence; a God who is not benevolent, not just, not wise, is no God; but the converse does not hold. The fact is not that a quality is divine because God has it, but that God has it because it is in itself divine: because without it God would be a defective being. Justice, wisdom, in general every quality which constitutes the divinity of God, is determined and known by itself, independently, but the idea of God is determined by the qualities which have thus been previously judged to be worthy of the divine nature; only in the case in which I identify God and justice, in which I think of God immediately as the reality of the idea of justice, is the idea of God self-determined. But if God as a subject is the determined, while the quality, the predicate is the determining, then in truth the rank of the godhead is due not to the subject, but to the predicate.

Not until several, and those contradictory, attributes are united in one being, and this being is conceived as personal—the personality being thus brought into especial prominence—not until then is the origin of religion lost sight of, is it forgotten that what the activity of the reflective power has converted into a predicate distinguishable or separable from the subject, was originally the true subject. Thus the Greeks and Romans deified accidents as substances: virtues, states of mind, passions, as independent beings. Man, especially the religious man, is to himself the measure of all things, of all reality. Whatever strongly impresses a man, whatever produces an unusual effect on his mind, if it be only a peculiar, inexplicable sound or note, he personifies as a divine being. Religion embraces all the objects of the world; everything existing has been an object of religious reverence; in the nature and consciousness of religion there is nothing else than what lies in the nature of man and in his consciousness of himself and of the world. Religion has no material exclusively its own. In Rome even the passions of fear and terror had their temples. The Christians also made mental phenomena into independent beings, their own feelings into qualities of things, the passions which governed them into powers which governed the world, in short, predicates of their own nature, whether recognized as such or not, into independent subjective existences. Devils, cobolds, witches, ghosts, angels, were sacred truths as long as the religious spirit held undivided sway over mankind.

In order to banish from the mind the identity of the divine and human predicates, and the consequent identity of the divine and human nature, recourse is had to the idea that God, as the absolute, real Being, has an infinite fulness of various predicates, of which we here know only a part, and those such as are analogous to our own; while the rest, by virtue of which God must thus have quite a different nature from the human or that which is analogous to the human, we shall only know in the future—that is, after death. But an infinite plenitude or multitude of predicates which are really different, so different that the one does not immediately involve the other, is realized only in an infinite plenitude or multitude of different beings or individuals. Thus the human nature presents an infinite abundance of different predicates, and for that very reason it presents an infinite abundance of different individuals. Each new man is a new predicate, a new phasis of humanity. As many as are the men, so many are the powers, the properties of humanity. It is true that there are the same elements in every individual, but under such various conditions and modifications that they appear new and peculiar. The mystery of the inexhaustible fulness of the divine predicates is therefore nothing else than the mystery of human nature considered as an infinitely varied, infinitely modifiable, but, consequently, phenomenal being. Only in the realm of the senses, only in space and time, does there exist a being of really infinite qualities or predicates. Where there are really different predicates, there are different times. One man is a distinguished musician, a distinguished author, a distinguished physician; but he cannot compose music, write books, and perform cures in the same moment of time. Time, and not the Hegelian dialectic, is the medium of uniting opposites, contradictories, in one and the same subject. But distinguished and detached from the nature of man, and combined with the idea of God, the infinite fulness of various predicates is a conception without reality, a mere phantasy, a conception derived from the sensible world, but without the essential conditions, without the truth of sensible existence, a conception which stands in direct contradiction with the Divine Being considered as a spiritual, *i.e.*, an abstract, simple, single being; for the predicates of God are precisely of this character, that one involves all the others, because there is no real difference between them. If, therefore, in the present predicates I have not the future, in the present God not the future God, then the future God is not the present, but they are two distinct beings. But this distinction is in contradiction with the unity and simplicity of the theological God. Why is a given predicate a predicate of God? Because it is divine in its nature; *i.e.*, because it expresses no limitation, no defect. Why are other predicates applied to Him? Because, however various in themselves, they agree in this, that they all alike express perfection, unlimitedness. Hence I can conceive innumerable predicates of God, because they must all agree with the abstract idea of the Godhead, and must have in common that which constitutes every single predicate a divine attribute. Thus it is in the system of Spinoza. He speaks of an infinite number of attributes of the divine substance, but he specifies none except Thought and Extension. Why? because it is a matter of indifference to know them; nay, because they are in themselves indifferent, superfluous: for with all these innumerable predicates, I yet always mean to say the same thing as when I speak of thought and extension. Why is Thought an attribute of substance? Because, according to Spinoza, it is capable of being conceived by itself, because it expresses something indivisible, perfect, infinite. Why Extension or Matter? For the same reason. Thus, substance can have an indefinite number of predicates, because it is not their specific definition, their difference, but their identity, their equivalence, which makes them attributes of substance. Or rather, substance has innumerable predicates only because (how strange!) it has properly no predicate; that is, no definite, real predicate. The indefinite unity which is the product of thought, completes itself by the indefinite multiplicity which is the product of the imagination. Because the predicate is not *multum*, it is *multa*. In truth, the positive predicates are Thought and Extension. In these two, infinitely more is said than in the nameless innumerable predicates; for they express something definite, in them I have something. But substance is too indifferent, too apathetic, to be *something*; that is, to have qualities and passions; that it may not be something, it is rather nothing.

Now, when it is shown that what the subject is, lies entirely in the attributes of the subject; that is, that the predicate is the true subject; it is also proved that if the divine predicates are attributes of the human nature, the subject of those predicates is also of the human nature. But the divine predicates are partly general, partly personal. The general predicates are the metaphysical, but these serve only as external points of support to religion; they are not the characteristic definitions of religion. It is the personal predicates alone which constitute the essence of religion—in which the Divine Being is the object of religion. Such are, for example, that God is a Person, that he is the moral Law-giver, the Father of mankind, the Holy One, the Just, the Good, the Merciful. It is however at once clear, or it will at least be clear in the sequel, with regard to these and other definitions, that, especially as applied to a personality, they are purely human definitions, and that consequently man in religion—in his relation to God—is in relation to his own nature; for to the religious sentiment these predicates are not mere conceptions, mere images, which man forms of God, to be distinguished from that which God is in himself, but truths, facts, realities. Religion knows nothing of anthropomorphisms; to it they are not anthropomorphisms. It is the very essence of religion, that to it these definitions express the nature of God. They are pronounced to be images only by the understanding, which reflects on religion, and which while defending them yet before its own tribunal denies them. But to the religious sentiment God is a real Father, real Love and Mercy; for to it he is a real, living, personal being, and therefore his attributes are also living and personal. Nay, the definitions which are the most sufficing to the religious sentiment, are precisely those which give the most offence to the understanding, and which in the process of reflection on religion it denies. Religion is essentially emotion; hence, objectively also, emotion is to it necessarily of a divine nature. Even anger appears to it an emotion not unworthy of God, provided only there be a religious motive at the foundation of this anger.

But here it is also essential to observe, and this phenomenon is an extremely remarkable one, characterising the very core of religion, that in proportion as the divine subject is in reality human, the greater is the apparent difference between God and man; that is, the more, by reflection on religion, by theology, is the identity of the divine and human denied, and the human, considered as such, is depreciated.[6] The reason of this is, that as what is positive in the conception of the divine being can only be human, the conception of man, as an object of consciousness can only be negative. To enrich God, man must become poor; that God may be all, man must be nothing. But he desires to be nothing in himself, because what he takes from himself is not lost to him, since it is preserved in God. Man has his being in God; why then should he have it in himself? Where is the necessity of positing the same thing twice, of having it twice? What man withdraws from himself, what he renounces in himself, he only enjoys in an incomparably higher and fuller measure in God.

The monks made a vow of chastity to God; they mortified the sexual passion in themselves, but therefore they had in Heaven, in the Virgin Mary, the image of woman—an image of love. They could the more easily dispense with real woman, in proportion as an ideal woman was an object of love to them. The greater the importance they attached to the denial of sensuality, the greater the importance of the Heavenly Virgin for them: she was to them in the place of Christ, in the stead of God. The more the sensual tendencies are renounced, the more sensual is the God to whom they are sacrificed. For whatever is made an offering to God has an especial value attached to it; in it God is supposed to have especial pleasure. That which is the highest in the estimation of man, is naturally the highest in the estimation of his God—what pleases man, pleases God also. The Hebrews did not offer to Jehovah unclean, ill-conditioned animals; on the contrary, those which they most highly prized, which they themselves ate, were also the food of God (*cibus Dei*, Levit. iii. 2.) Wherever, therefore, the denial of the sensual delights is made a special offering, a sacrifice well-pleasing to God, there the highest value is attached to the senses, and the sensuality which has been renounced is unconsciously restored, in the fact that God takes the place of the material delights which have been renounced. The nun weds herself to God; she has a heavenly bridegroom, the monk a heavenly bride. But the heavenly virgin is only a sensible presentation of a general truth, having relation to the essence of religion.   Man denies as to himself only what he attributes to God. Religion abstracts from man, from the world; but it can only abstract from the limitations, from the phenomena, in short, from the negative, not from the essence, the positive, of the world and humanity: hence, in the very abstraction and negation it must recover that from which it abstracts, or believes itself to abstract. And thus, in reality, whatever religion consciously denies—always supposing that what is denied by it is something essential, true, and consequently incapable of being ultimately denied—it unconsciously restores in God. Thus, in religion man denies his reason; of himself he knows nothing of God, his thoughts are only worldly, earthly; he can only believe what God reveals to him. But on this account the thoughts of God are human, earthly thoughts: like man, He has plans in His mind, he accommodates himself to circumstances and grades of intelligence, like a tutor with his pupils; he calculates closely the effect of his gifts and revelations; he observes man in all his doings; he knows all things, even the most earthly, the commonest, the most trivial. In brief, man in relation to God denies his own knowledge, his own thoughts, that he may place them in God. Man gives up his personality; but in return, God, the Almighty, infinite, unlimited being, is a person; he denies human dignity, the human *ego*; but in return God is to him a selfish, egoistical being, who in all things seeks only Himself, his own honour, his own ends; he represents God as simply seeking the satisfaction of his own selfishness, while yet He frowns on that of every other being; his God is the very luxury of egoism. Religion further denies goodness as a quality of human nature; man is wicked, corrupt, incapable of good; but on the other hand, God is only good—the Good Being. Man's nature demands as an object goodness, personified as God; but is it not hereby declared that goodness is an essential tendency of man? If my heart is wicked, my understanding perverted, how can I perceive and feel the holy to be holy, the good to be good? Could I perceive the beauty of a fine picture, if my mind were aesthetically an absolute piece of perversion? Though I may not be a painter, though I may not have the power of producing what is beautiful myself, I must yet have aesthetic feeling, aesthetic comprehension, since I perceive the beauty that is presented to me externally. Either goodness does not exist at all for man, or, if it does exist, therein is revealed to the individual man the holiness and goodness of human nature. That which is absolutely opposed to my nature, to which I am united by no bond of sympathy, is not even conceivable or perceptible by me. The Holy is in opposition to me only as regards the modifications of my personality, but as regards my fundamental nature it is in unity with me. The Holy is a reproach to my sinfulness; in it I recognise myself as a sinner; but in so doing, while I blame myself, I acknowledge what I am not, but ought to be, and what, for that very reason, I, according to my destination, can be; for an "ought" which has no corresponding capability, does not affect me, is a ludicrous chimaera without any true relation to my mental constitution. But when I acknowledge goodness as my destination, as my law, I acknowledge it, whether consciously or unconsciously, as my own nature. Another nature than my own, one different in quality, cannot touch me. I can perceive sin as sin, only when I perceive it to be a contradiction of myself with myself—that is, of my personality with my fundamental nature. As a contradiction of the absolute, considered as another being, the feeling of sin is inexplicable, unmeaning....

As with the doctrine of the radical corruption of human nature, so is it with the identical doctrine, that man can do nothing good, *i.e.*, in truth, nothing of himself—by his own strength. For the denial of human strength and spontaneous moral activity to be true, the moral activity of God must also be denied; and we must say, with the oriental nihilist or pantheist: the Divine being is absolutely without will or action, indifferent, knowing nothing of the discrimination between evil and good. But he who defines God as an active being, and not only so, but as morally active and morally critical,—as a being who loves, works, and rewards good, punishes, rejects, and condemns evil,—he who thus defines God, only in appearance denies human activity, in fact making it the highest, the most real activity. He who makes God act humanly, declares human activity to be divine; he says: a god who is not active, and not morally or humanly active, is no god; and thus he makes the idea of the Godhead dependent on the idea of activity, that is, of human activity, for a higher he knows not.

Man—this is the mystery of religion—projects his being into objectivity,[9] and then again makes himself an object to this projected image of himself thus converted into a subject; he thinks of himself, is an object to himself, but as the object of an object, of another being than himself. Thus here. Man is an object to God. That man is good or evil is not indifferent to God; no! He has a lively, profound interest in man's being good; he wills that man should be good, happy—for without goodness there is no happiness. Thus the religious man virtually retracts the nothingness of human activity, by making his dispositions and actions an object to God, by making man the end of God—for that which is an object to the mind is an end in action; by making the divine activity a means of human salvation. God acts, that man may be good and happy. Thus man, while he is apparently humiliated to the lowest degree, is in truth exalted to the highest. Thus, in and through God, man has in view himself alone. It is true that man places the aim of his action in God, but God has no other aim of action than the moral and eternal salvation of man: thus man has in fact no other aim than himself. The divine activity is not distinct from the human.

How could the divine activity work on me as its object, nay, work in me, if it were essentially different from me; how could it have a human aim, the aim of ameliorating and blessing man, if it were not itself human? Does not the purpose determine the nature of the act? When man makes his moral improvement an aim to himself, he has divine resolutions, divine projects; but also, when God seeks the salvation of man, He has human ends and a human mode of activity, corresponding to these ends. Thus in God man has only his own activity as an object. But, for the very reason that he regards his own activity as objective, goodness only as an object, he necessarily receives the impulse, the motive, not from himself, but from this object. He contemplates his nature as external to himself, and this nature as goodness; thus it is self-evident, it is mere tautology to say, that the impulse to good comes only from thence where he places the good.

God is the highest subjectivity of man abstracted from himself; hence man can do nothing of himself, all goodness comes from God. The more subjective God is, the more completely does man divest himself of his subjectivity, because God is, *per se*, his relinquished self, the possession of which he however again vindicates to himself. As the action of the arteries drives the blood into the extremities, and the action of the veins brings it back again, as life in general consists in a perpetual systole and diastole; so is it in religion. In the religious systole man propels his own nature from himself, he throws himself outward; in the religious diastole he receives the rejected nature into his heart again. God alone is the being who acts of himself,—this is the force of repulsion in religion; God is the being who acts in me, with me, through me, upon me, for me, is the principle of my salvation, of my good dispositions and actions, consequently my own good principle and nature,—this is the force of attraction in religion.

The course of religious development which has been generally indicated, consists specifically in this, that man abstracts more and more from God, and attributes more and more to himself. This is especially apparent in the belief in revelation. That which to a later age or a cultured people is given by nature or reason, is to an earlier age, or to a yet uncultured people, given by God. Every tendency of man, however natural—even the impulse to cleanliness, was conceived by the Israelites as a positive divine ordinance. From this example we again see that God is lowered, is conceived more entirely on the type of ordinary humanity, in proportion as man detracts from himself. How can the self-humiliation of man go further than when he disclaims the capability of fulfilling spontaneously the requirements of common decency? The Christian religion, on the other hand, distinguished the impulses and passions of man according to their quality, their character; it represented only good emotions, good dispositions, good thoughts, as revelations, operations—that is, as dispositions, feelings, thoughts,—of God; for what God reveals is a quality of God himself: that of which the heart is full, overflows the lips, as is the effect such is the cause, as the revelation, such the being who reveals himself. A God who reveals himself in good dispositions is a God whose essential attribute is only moral perfection. The Christian religion distinguishes inward moral purity from external physical purity; the Israelites identified the two. In relation to the Israelitish religion, the Christian religion is one of criticism and freedom. The Israelite trusted himself to do nothing except what was commanded by God; he was without will even in external things; the authority of religion extended itself even to his food. The Christian religion, on the other hand, in all these external things, made man dependent on himself, *i.e.*, placed in man what the Israelite placed out of himself, in God. Israel is the most complete presentation of positivism in religion. In relation to the Israelite, the Christian is an *esprit fort*, a free-thinker. Thus do things change. What yesterday was still religion, is no longer such to-day; and what to-day is atheism, to-morrow will be religion.

Ludwig Feuerbach. *The Essence of Christianity*. Trans. Marian Evans. London: J. Chapman, 1854.

Religion as the Opiate
of the People
Karl Marx

For Germany, the criticism of religion has been essentially completed, and the criticism of religion is the prerequisite of all criticism.

The profane existence of error is compromised as soon as its heavenly *oratio pro aris et focis* ("speech for the altars and hearths") has been refuted. Man, who has found only the reflection of himself in the fantastic reality of heaven, where he sought a superman, will no longer feel disposed to find the mere appearance of himself, the non-man ("*Unmensch*"), where he seeks and must seek his true reality.

The foundation of irreligious criticism is: Man makes religion, religion does not make man.

Religion is, indeed, the self-consciousness and self-esteem of man who has either not yet won through to himself, or has already lost himself again. But, man is no abstract being squatting outside the world. Man is the world of man—state, society. This state and this society produce religion, which is an inverted consciousness of the world, because they are an inverted world. Religion is the general theory of this world, its encyclopaedic compendium, its logic in popular form, its spiritual *point d'honneur*, it enthusiasm, its moral sanction, its solemn complement, and its universal basis of consolation and justification. It is the fantastic realization of the human essence since the human essence has not acquired any true reality. The struggle against religion is, therefore, indirectly the struggle against that world whose spiritual aroma is religion.

Religious suffering is, at one and the same time, the expression of real suffering and a protest against real suffering. Religion is the sigh of the oppressed creature, the heart of a heartless world, and the soul of soulless conditions. It is the opium of the people.

The abolition of religion as the illusory happiness of the people is the demand for their real happiness. To call on them to give up their illusions about their condition is to call on them to give up a condition that requires illusions.

The criticism of religion is, therefore, in embryo, the criticism of that vale of tears of which religion is the halo.

Criticism has plucked the imaginary flowers on the chain not in order that man shall continue to bear that chain without fantasy or consolation, but so that he shall throw off the chain and pluck the living flower. The criticism of religion disillusions man, so that he will think, act, and fashion his reality like a man who has discarded his illusions and regained his senses, so that he will move around himself as his own true Sun. Religion is only the illusory Sun which revolves around man as long as he does not revolve around himself.

It is, therefore, the task of history, once the other-world of truth has vanished, to establish the truth of this world. It is the immediate task of philosophy, which is in the service of history, to unmask self-estrangement in its unholy forms once the holy form of human self-estrangement has been unmasked.

Thus, the criticism of Heaven turns into the criticism of Earth, the criticism of religion into the criticism of law, and the criticism of theology into the criticism of politics.

Karl Marx. *Introduction to a Contribution to the Critique of Hegel's Philosophy of Right.* Deutsch-Französische Jahrbucher (February, 1844).

Evil and the Existence
of God
Fyodor Dostoyevski

"Well, tell me where to begin, give your orders. The existence of God, eh?"
[Ivan said]

"Begin where you like. You declared yesterday at father's that there was no God." Alyosha looked searchingly at his brother.

"I said that yesterday at dinner on purpose to tease you and I saw your eyes glow. But now I've no objection to discussing with you, and I say so very seriously. I want to be friends with you, Alyosha, for I have no friends and want to try it. Well, only fancy, perhaps I too accept God," laughed Ivan; "that's a surprise for you, isn't it?"

"Yes of course, if you are not joking now."

"Joking? I was told at the elder's yesterday that I was joking. You know, dear boy, there was an old sinner in the eighteenth century who declared that, if there were no God, he would have to be invented. S'il n'existait pas Dieu, il faudrait l'inventer.* And man has actually invented God. And what's strange, what would be marvellous, is not that God should really exist; the marvel is that such an idea, the idea of the necessity of God, could enter the head of such a savage, vicious beast as man. So holy it is, so touching, so wise and so great a credit it does to man. As for me, I've long resolved not to think whether man created God or God man. And I won't go through all the axioms laid down by Russian boys on that subject, all derived from European hypotheses; for what's a hypothesis there is an axiom with the Russian boy, and not only with the boys but with their teachers too, for our Russian professors are often just the same boys themselves. And so I omit all the hypotheses. For what are we aiming at now? I am trying to explain as quickly as possible my essential nature, that is what manner of man I am, what I believe in, and for what I hope, that's it, isn't it? And therefore I tell you that I accept God simply. But you must note this: if God exists and if He really did create the world, then, as we all know, He created it according to the geometry of Euclid and the human mind with the conception of only three dimensions in space. Yet there have been and still are geometricians and philosophers, and even some of the most distinguished, who doubt whether the whole universe, or to speak more widely, the whole of being, was only created in Euclid's geometry; they even dare to dream that two parallel lines, which according to Euclid can never meet on earth, may meet somewhere in infinity. I have come to the conclusion that, since I can't understand even that, I can't expect to understand about God. I acknowledge humbly that I have no faculty for settling such questions, I have a Euclidian earthly mind, and how could I solve problems that are not of this world? And I advise you never to think about it either, my dear Alyosha, especially about God, whether He exists or not. All such questions are utterly inappropriate for a mind created with an idea of only three dimensions. And so I accept God and am glad to, and what's more, I accept His wisdom, His purpose which are utterly beyond our ken; I believe in the underlying order and the meaning of life; I believe in the eternal harmony in which they say we shall one day be blended. I believe in the Word to Which the universe is striving, and Which Itself was 'with God,' and Which Itself is God and so on, and so on, to infinity. There are all sorts of phrases for it. I seem to be on the right path, don't I'? Yet would you believe it, in the final result I don't accept this world of God's, and, although I know it exists, I don't accept it at all. It's not that I don't accept God, you must understand, it's the world created by Him I don't and cannot accept. Let me make it plain. I believe like a child that suffering will be healed and made up for, that all the humiliating absurdity of human contradictions will vanish like a pitiful mirage, like the despicable fabrication of the impotent and infinitely small Euclidian mind of man, that in the world's finale, at the moment of eternal harmony, something so precious will come to pass that it will suffice for all hearts, for the comforting of all resentments, for the atonement of all the crimes of humanity, of all the blood they've shed; that it will make it not only possible to forgive but to justify all that has happened with men- but thought all that may come to pass, I don't accept it. I won't accept it. Even if parallel lines do meet and I see it myself, I shall see it and say that they've met, but still I won't accept it. That's what's at the root of me, Alyosha; that's my creed. I am in earnest in what I say. I began our talk as stupidly as I could on purpose, but I've led up to my confession, for that's all you want. You didn't want to hear about God, but only to know what the brother you love lives by. And so I've told you."

Ivan concluded his long tirade with marked and unexpected feeling.

"And why did you begin 'as stupidly as you could'?" asked Alyosha, looking dreamily at him.

"To begin with, for the sake of being Russian. Russian conversations on such subjects are always carried on inconceivably stupidly. And secondly, the stupider one is, the closer one is to reality. The stupider one is, the clearer one is. Stupidity is brief and artless, while intelligence wriggles and hides itself. Intelligence is a knave, but stupidity is honest and straight forward. I've led the conversation to my despair, and the more stupidly I have presented it, the better for me."

"You will explain why you don't accept the world?" said Alyosha.

"To be sure I will, it's not a secret, that's what I've been leading up to. Dear little brother, I don't want to corrupt you or to turn you from your stronghold, perhaps I want to be healed by you." Ivan smiled suddenly quite like a little gentle child. Alyosha had never seen such a smile on his face before.

Rebellion

"I must make one confession" Ivan began. "I could never understand how one can love one's neighbours. It's just one's neighbours, to my mind, that one can't love, though one might love those at a distance. I once read somewhere of John the Merciful, a saint, that when a hungry, frozen beggar came to him, he took him into his bed, held him in his arms, and began breathing into his mouth, which was putrid and loathsome from some awful disease. I am convinced that he did that from 'self-laceration,' from the self-laceration of falsity, for the sake of the charity imposed by duty, as a penance laid on him. For anyone to love a man, he must be hidden, for as soon as he shows his face, love is gone."

"Father Zossima has talked of that more than once," observed Alyosha; "he, too, said that the face of a man often hinders many people not practised in love, from loving him. But yet there's a great deal of love in mankind, and almost Christ-like love. I know that myself, Ivan."

"Well, I know nothing of it so far, and can't understand it, and the innumerable mass of mankind are with me there. The question is, whether that's due to men's bad qualities or whether it's inherent in their nature. To my thinking, Christ-like love for men is a miracle impossible on earth. He was God. But we are not gods. Suppose I, for instance, suffer intensely. Another can never know how much I suffer, because he is another and not I. And what's more, a man is rarely ready to admit another's suffering (as though it were a distinction). Why won't he admit it, do you think? Because I smell unpleasant, because I have a stupid face, because I once trod on his foot. Besides, there is suffering and suffering; degrading, humiliating suffering such as humbles me--hunger, for instance--my benefactor will perhaps allow me; but when you come to higher suffering--for an idea, for instance--he will very rarely admit that, perhaps because my face strikes him as not at all what he fancies a man should have who suffers for an idea. And so he deprives me instantly of his favour, and not at all from badness of heart. Beggars, especially genteel beggars, ought never to show themselves, but to ask for charity through the newspapers. One can love one's neighbours in the abstract, or even at a distance, but at close quarters it's almost impossible. If it were as on the stage, in the ballet, where if beggars come in, they wear silken rags and tattered lace and beg for alms dancing gracefully, then one might like looking at them. But even then we should not love them. But enough of that. I simply wanted to show you my point of view. I meant to speak of the suffering of mankind generally, but we had better confine ourselves to the sufferings of the children. That reduces the scope of my argument to a tenth of what it would be. Still we'd better keep to the children, though it does weaken my case. But, in the first place, children can be loved even at close quarters, even when they are dirty, even when they are ugly (I fancy, though, children never are ugly). The second reason why I won't speak of grown-up people is that, besides being disgusting and unworthy of love, they have a compensation—they've eaten the apple and know good and evil, and they have become 'like gods.' They go on eating it still. But the children haven't eaten anything, and are so far innocent. Are you fond of children, Alyosha? I know you are, and you will understand why I prefer to speak of them. If they, too, suffer horribly on earth, they must suffer for their fathers' sins, they must be punished for their fathers, who have eaten the apple; but that reasoning is of the other world and is incomprehensible for the heart of man here on earth. The innocent must not suffer for another's sins, and especially such innocents! You may be surprised at me, Alyosha, but I am awfully fond of children, too. And observe, cruel people, the violent, the rapacious, the Karamazovs are sometimes very fond of children. Children while they are quite little—up to seven, for instance—are so remote from grown-up people they are different creatures, as it were, of a different species. I knew a criminal in prison who had, in the course of his career as a burglar, murdered whole families, including several children. But when he was in prison, he had a strange affection for them. He spent all his time at his window, watching the children playing in the prison yard. He trained one little boy to come up to his window and made great friends with him... You don't know why I am telling you all this, Alyosha? My head aches and I am sad."

"You speak with a strange air," observed Alyosha uneasily, "as though you were not quite yourself."

"By the way, a Bulgarian I met lately in Moscow," Ivan went on, seeming not to hear his brother's words, "told me about the crimes committed by Turks and Circassians in all parts of Bulgaria through fear of a general rising of the Slavs. They burn villages, murder, outrage women and children, they nail their prisoners by the ears to the fences, leave them so till morning, and in the morning they hang them—all sorts of things you can't imagine. People talk sometimes of bestial cruelty, but that's a great injustice and insult to the beasts; a beast can never be so cruel as a man, so artistically cruel. The tiger only tears and gnaws, that's all he can do. He would never think of nailing people by the ears, even if he were able to do it. These Turks took a pleasure in torturing children, too; cutting the unborn child from the mothers womb, and tossing babies up in the air and catching them on the points of their bayonets before their mothers' eyes. Doing it before the mothers' eyes was what gave zest to the amusement. Here is another scene that I thought very interesting. Imagine a trembling mother with her baby in her arms, a circle of invading Turks around her. They've planned a diversion: they pet the baby, laugh to make it laugh. They succeed, the baby laughs. At that moment a Turk points a pistol four inches from the baby's face. The baby laughs with glee, holds out its little hands to the pistol, and he pulls the trigger in the baby's face and blows out its brains. Artistic, wasn't it? By the way, Turks are particularly fond of sweet things, they say."

"Brother, what are you driving at?" asked Alyosha.

"I think if the devil doesn't exist, but man has created him, he has created him in his own image and likeness."

"Just as he did God, then?" observed Alyosha.

"'It's wonderful how you can turn words,' as Polonius says in Hamlet," laughed Ivan. "You turn my words against me. Well, I am glad. Yours must be a fine God, if man created Him in his image and likeness. You asked just now what I was driving at. You see, I am fond of collecting certain facts, and, would you believe, I even copy anecdotes of a certain sort from newspapers and books, and I've already got a fine collection. The Turks, of course, have gone into it, but they are foreigners. I have specimens from home that are even better than the Turks. You know we prefer beating—rods and scourges—that's our national institution. Nailing ears is unthinkable for us, for we are, after all, Europeans. But the rod and the scourge we have always with us and they cannot be taken from us. Abroad now they scarcely do any beating. Manners are more humane, or laws have been passed, so that they don't dare to flog men now. But they make up for it in another way just as national as ours. And so national that it would be practically impossible among us, though I believe we are being inoculated with it, since the religious movement began in our aristocracy. I have a charming pamphlet, translated from the French, describing how, quite recently, five years ago, a murderer, Richard, was executed—a young man, I believe, of three and twenty, who repented and was converted to the Christian faith at the very scaffold. This Richard was an illegitimate child who was given as a child of six by his parents to some shepherds on the Swiss mountains. They brought him up to work for them. He grew up like a little wild beast among them. The shepherds taught him nothing, and scarcely fed or clothed him, but sent him out at seven to herd the flock in cold and wet, and no one hesitated or scrupled to treat him so. Quite the contrary, they thought they had every right, for Richard had been given to them as a chattel, and they did not even see the necessity of feeding him. Richard himself describes how in those years, like the Prodigal Son in the Gospel, he longed to eat of the mash given to the pigs, which were fattened for sale. But they wouldn't even give that, and beat him when he stole from the pigs. And that was how he spent all his childhood and his youth, till he grew up and was strong enough to go away and be a thief. The savage began to earn his living as a day labourer in Geneva. He drank what he earned, he lived like a brute, and finished by killing and robbing an old man. He was caught, tried, and condemned to death. They are not sentimentalists there. And in prison he was immediately surrounded by pastors, members of Christian brotherhoods, philanthropic ladies, and the like. They taught him to read and write in prison, and expounded the Gospel to him. They exhorted him, worked upon him, drummed at him incessantly, till at last he solemnly confessed his crime. He was converted. He wrote to the court himself that he was a monster, but that in the end God had vouchsafed him light and shown grace. All Geneva was in excitement about him--all philanthropic and religious Geneva. All the aristocratic and well-bred society of the town rushed to the prison, kissed Richard and embraced him; 'You are our brother, you have found grace.' And Richard does nothing but weep with emotion, 'Yes, I've found grace! All my youth and childhood I was glad of pigs' food, but now even I have found grace. I am dying in the Lord.' 'Yes, Richard, die in the Lord; you have shed blood and must die. Though it's not your fault that you knew not the Lord, when you coveted the pigs' food and were beaten for stealing it (which was very wrong of you, for stealing is forbidden); but you've shed blood and you must die.'And on the last day, Richard, perfectly limp, did nothing but cry and repeat every minute: 'This is my happiest day. I am going to the Lord.' 'Yes,' cry the pastors and the judges and philanthropic ladies. 'This is the happiest day of your life, for you are going to the Lord!' They all walk or drive to the scaffold in procession behind the prison van. At the scaffold they call to Richard: 'Die, brother, die in the Lord, for even thou hast found grace!' And so, covered with his brothers' kisses, Richard is dragged on to the scaffold, and led to the guillotine. And they chopped off his head in brotherly fashion, because he had found grace. Yes, that's characteristic. That pamphlet is translated into Russian by some Russian philanthropists of aristocratic rank and evangelical aspirations, and has been distributed gratis for the enlightenment of the people. The case of Richard is interesting because it's national. Though to us it's absurd to cut off a man's head, because he has become our brother and has found grace, yet we have our own speciality, which is all but worse. Our historical pastime is the direct satisfaction of inflicting pain. There are lines in Nekrassov describing how a peasant lashes a horse on the eyes, 'on its meek eyes,' everyone must have seen it. It's peculiarly Russian. He describes how a feeble little nag has foundered under too heavy a load and cannot move. The peasant beats it, beats it savagely, beats it at last not knowing what he is doing in the intoxication of cruelty, thrashes it mercilessly over and over again. 'However weak you are, you must pull, if you die for it.' The nag strains, and then he begins lashing the poor defenceless creature on its weeping, on its 'meek eyes.' The frantic beast tugs and draws the load, trembling all over, gasping for breath, moving sideways, with a sort of unnatural spasmodic action—it's awful in Nekrassov. But that only a horse, and God has made horses to be beaten. So the Tatars have taught us, and they left us the knout as a remembrance of it. But men, too, can be beaten. A well-educated, cultured gentleman and his wife beat their own child with a birch-rod, a girl of seven. I have an exact account of it. The papa was glad that the birch was covered with twigs. 'It stings more,' said he, and so be began stinging his daughter. I know for a fact there are people who at every blow are worked up to sensuality, to literal sensuality, which increases progressively at every blow they inflict. They beat for a minute, for five minutes, for ten minutes, more often and more savagely. The child screams. At last the child cannot scream, it gasps, 'Daddy daddy!' By some diabolical unseemly chance the case was brought into court. A counsel is engaged. The Russian people have long called a barrister 'a conscience for hire.' The counsel protests in his client's defence. 'It's such a simple thing,' he says, 'an everyday domestic event. A father corrects his child. To our shame be it said, it is brought into court.' The jury, convinced by him, give a favourable verdict. The public roars with delight that the torturer is acquitted. Ah, pity I wasn't there! I would have proposed to raise a subscription in his honour! Charming pictures.

"But I've still better things about children. I've collected a great, great deal about Russian children, Alyosha. There was a little girl of five who was hated by her father and mother, 'most worthy and respectable people, of good education and breeding.' You see, I must repeat again, it is a peculiar characteristic of many people, this love of torturing children, and children only. To all other types of humanity these torturers behave mildly and benevolently, like cultivated and humane Europeans; but they are very fond of tormenting children, even fond of children themselves in that sense. it's just their defencelessness that tempts the tormentor, just the angelic confidence of the child who has no refuge and no appeal, that sets his vile blood on fire. In every man, of course, a demon lies hidden—the demon of rage, the demon of lustful heat at the screams of the tortured victim, the demon of lawlessness let off the chain, the demon of diseases that follow on vice, gout, kidney disease, and so on.

"This poor child of five was subjected to every possible torture by those cultivated parents. They beat her, thrashed her, kicked her for no reason till her body was one bruise. Then, they went to greater refinements of cruelty— shut her up all night in the cold and frost in a privy, and because she didn't ask to be taken up at night (as though a child of five sleeping its angelic, sound sleep could be trained to wake and ask), they smeared her face and filled her mouth with excrement, and it was her mother, her mother did this. And that mother could sleep, hearing the poor child's groans! Can you understand why a little creature, who can't even understand what's done to her, should beat her little aching heart with her tiny fist in the dark and the cold, and weep her meek unresentful tears to dear, kind God to protect her? Do you understand that, friend and brother, you pious and humble novice? Do you understand why this infamy must be and is permitted? Without it, I am told, man could not have existed on earth, for he could not have known good and evil. Why should he know that diabolical good and evil when it costs so much? Why, the whole world of knowledge is not worth that child's prayer to dear, kind God'! I say nothing of the sufferings of grown-up people, they have eaten the apple, damn them, and the devil take them all! But these little ones! I am making you suffer, Alyosha, you are not yourself. I'll leave off if you like."

"Nevermind. I want to suffer too," muttered Alyosha.

"One picture, only one more, because it's so curious, so characteristic, and I have only just read it in some collection of Russian antiquities. I've forgotten the name. I must look it up. It was in the darkest days of serfdom at the beginning of the century, and long live the Liberator of the People! There was in those days a general of aristocratic connections, the owner of great estates, one of those men--somewhat exceptional, I believe, even then--who, retiring from the service into a life of leisure, are convinced that they've earned absolute power over the lives of their subjects. There were such men then. So our general, settled on his property of two thousand souls, lives in pomp, and domineers over his poor neighbours as though they were dependents and buffoons. He has kennels of hundreds of hounds and nearly a hundred dog-boys--all mounted, and in uniform. One day a serf-boy, a little child of eight, threw a stone in play and hurt the paw of the general's favourite hound. 'Why is my favourite dog lame?' He is told that the boy threw a stone that hurt the dog's paw. 'So you did it.' The general looked the child up and down. 'Take him.' He was taken--taken from his mother and kept shut up all night. Early that morning the general comes out on horseback, with the hounds, his dependents, dog-boys, and huntsmen, all mounted around him in full hunting parade. The servants are summoned for their edification, and in front of them all stands the mother of the child. The child is brought from the lock-up. It's a gloomy, cold, foggy, autumn day, a capital day for hunting. The general orders the child to be undressed; the child is stripped naked. He shivers, numb with terror, not daring to cry... 'Make him run,' commands the general. 'Run! run!' shout the dog-boys. The boy runs... 'At him!' yells the general, and he sets the whole pack of hounds on the child. The hounds catch him, and tear him to pieces before his mother's eyes!... I believe the general was afterwards declared incapable of administering his estates. Well—what did he deserve? To be shot? To be shot for the satisfaction of our moral feelings? Speak, Alyosha!

"To be shot," murmured Alyosha, lifting his eyes to Ivan with a pale, twisted smile.

"Bravo!" cried Ivan delighted. "If even you say so... You're a pretty monk! So there is a little devil sitting in your heart, Alyosha Karamazov!"

"What I said was absurd, but-"

"That's just the point, that 'but'!" cried Ivan. "Let me tell you, novice, that the absurd is only too necessary on earth. The world stands on absurdities, and perhaps nothing would have come to pass in it without them. We know what we know!"

"What do you know?"

"I understand nothing," Ivan went on, as though in delirium. "I don't want to understand anything now. I want to stick to the fact. I made up my mind long ago not to understand. If I try to understand anything, I shall be false to the fact, and I have determined to stick to the fact."

"Why are you trying me?" Alyosha cried, with sudden distress. "Will you say what you mean at last?"

"Of course, I will; that's what I've been leading up to. You are dear to me, I don't want to let you go, and I won't give you up to your Zossima."

Ivan for a minute was silent, his face became all at once very sad.

"Listen! I took the case of children only to make my case clearer. Of the other tears of humanity with which the earth is soaked from its crust to its centre, I will say nothing. I have narrowed my subject on purpose. I am a bug, and I recognise in all humility that I cannot understand why the world is arranged as it is. Men are themselves to blame, I suppose; they were given paradise, they wanted freedom, and stole fire from heaven, though they knew they would become unhappy, so there is no need to pity them. With my piti-ful, earthly, Euclidian understanding, all I know is that there is suffering and that there are none guilty; that cause follows effect, simply and directly; that everything flows and finds its level—but that's only Euclidian nonsense, I know that, and I can't consent to live by it! What comfort is it to me that there are none guilty and that cause follows effect simply and directly, and that I know it?--I must have justice, or I will destroy myself. And not justice in some remote infinite time and space, but here on earth, and that I could see myself. I have believed in it. I want to see it, and if I am dead by then, let me rise again, for if it all happens without me, it will be too unfair. Surely I haven't suffered simply that I, my crimes and my sufferings, may manure the soil of the future harmony for somebody else. I want to see with my own eyes the hind lie down with the lion and the victim rise up and embrace his murderer. I want to be there when everyone suddenly understands what it has all been for. All the religions of the world are built on this longing, and I am a believer. But then there are the children, and what am I to do about them? That's a question I can't answer. For the hundredth time I repeat, there are numbers of questions, but I've only taken the children, because in their case what I mean is so unanswerably clear. Listen! If all must suffer to pay for the eternal harmony, what have children to do with it, tell me, please? It's beyond all comprehension why they should suffer, and why they should pay for the harmony. Why should they, too, furnish material to enrich the soil for the harmony of the future? I understand solidarity in sin among men. I understand solidarity in retribution, too; but there can be no such solidarity with children. And if it is really true that they must share responsibility for all their fathers' crimes, such a truth is not of this world and is beyond my comprehension. Some jester will say, perhaps, that the child would have grown up and have sinned, but you see he didn't grow up, he was torn to pieces by the dogs, at eight years old. Oh, Alyosha, I am not blaspheming! I understand, of course, what an upheaval of the universe it will be when everything in heaven and earth blends in one hymn of praise and everything that lives and has lived cries aloud: 'Thou art just, O Lord, for Thy ways are revealed.' When the mother embraces the fiend who threw her child to the dogs, and all three cry aloud with tears, 'Thou art just, O Lord!' then, of course, the crown of knowledge will be reached and all will be made clear. But what pulls me up here is that I can't accept that harmony. And while I am on earth, I make haste to take my own measures. You see, Alyosha, perhaps it really may happen that if I live to that moment, or rise again to see it, I, too, perhaps, may cry aloud with the rest, looking at the mother embracing the child's torturer, 'Thou art just, O Lord!' but I don't want to cry aloud then. While there is still time, I hasten to protect myself, and so I renounce the higher harmony altogether. It's not worth the tears of that one tortured child who beat itself on the breast with its little fist and prayed in its stinking outhouse, with its unexpiated tears to 'dear, kind God'! It's not worth it, because those tears are unatoned for. They must be atoned for, or there can be no harmony. But how? How are you going to atone for them? Is it possible? By their being avenged? But what do I care for avenging them? What do I care for a hell for oppressors? What good can hell do, since those children have already been tortured? And what becomes of harmony, if there is hell? I want to forgive. I want to embrace. I don't want more suffering. And if the sufferings of children go to swell the sum of sufferings which was necessary to pay for truth, then I protest that the truth is not worth such a price. I don't want the mother to embrace the oppressor who threw her son to the dogs! She dare not forgive him! Let her forgive him for herself, if she will, let her forgive the torturer for the immeasurable suffering of her mother's heart. But the sufferings of her tortured child she has no right to forgive; she dare not forgive the torturer, even if the child were to forgive him! And if that is so, if they dare not forgive, what becomes of harmony? Is there in the whole world a being who would have the right to forgive and could forgive? I don't want harmony. From love for humanity I don't want it. I would rather be left with the unavenged suffering. I would rather remain with my unavenged suffering and unsatisfied indignation, even if I were wrong. Besides, too high a price is asked for harmony; it's beyond our means to pay so much to enter on it. And so I hasten to give back my entrance ticket, and if I am an honest man I am bound to give it back as soon as possible. And that I am doing. It's not God that I don't accept, Alyosha, only I most respectfully return him the ticket."

"That's rebellion," murmered Alyosha, looking down.

"Rebellion? I am sorry you call it that," said Ivan earnestly. "One can hardly live in rebellion, and I want to live. Tell me yourself, I challenge your answer. Imagine that you are creating a fabric of human destiny with the object of making men happy in the end, giving them peace and rest at last, but that it was essential and inevitable to torture to death only one tiny creature--that baby beating its breast with its fist, for instance--and to found that edifice on its unavenged tears, would you consent to be the architect on those conditions? Tell me, and tell the truth."

"No, I wouldn't consent," said Alyosha softly.

Fyodor Dostoyevski. *The Brothers Karamazov*. Trans. Constance Garnett. London: Heinemann, 1912.